ISNM

INTERNATIONAL SERIES OF NUMERICAL MATHEMATICS
INTERNATIONALE SCHRIFTENREIHE ZUR NUMERISCHEN MATHEMATIK
SÉRIE INTERNATIONALE D'ANALYSE NUMÉRIQUE

VOL. 37

Numerical Analysis

PROCEEDINGS OF THE COLLOQUIUM ON NUMERICAL ANALYSIS

LAUSANNE, OCTOBER 11–13, 1976

EDITED BY J. DESCLOUX AND J. MARTI

1977
BIRKHÄUSER VERLAG BASEL
UND STUTTGART

CIP-Kurztitelaufnahme der Deutschen Bibliothek

Numerical analysis: proceedings of the Colloquium on Numerical Analysis, Lausanne, October 11 - 13, 1976 / ed. by J. Descloux and J. Marti. - 1. Aufl. - Basel, Stuttgart: Birkhäuser, 1977. - (International series of numerical mathematics; Vol. 37)
ISBN 3-7643-0939-3
NE: Descloux, Jean [Hrsg.]; Colloquium on Numerical Analysis ‹1976, Lausanne›

Numerical analysis is as much an art as a science. Unfortunately there is little opportunity for contact between specialists devoted to the two aspects of this discipline.

We felt that it was appropriate for two Federal Institutes of Technology to organize a Colloquium at which those involved in the theoretical aspects of Numerical Analysis could meet those concerned with its practical applications. The enrolment of seventy participants, including fourteen speakers shows that there was a real need for such a Colloquium on Numerical Analysis.

We wish to thank the Federal Institute of Technology Lausanne for covering the cost of organizing the meeting.

Jean Descloux
EPFL

Jürg Marti
EPFZ

Contents

METHODES NUMERIQUES POUR LES CALCULS D'ECOULEMENTS 2D INSTATIONNAIRES MULTIFLUIDES

par

P.M. LASCAUX
COMMISSARIAT A L'ENERGIE ATOMIQUE
B.P. 27 94190 VILLENEUVE-St-GEORGES - FRANCE

Le présent article a pour but d'exposer et de comparer les méthodes numériques utilisées pour calculer des écoulements bidimensionnels instationnaires de plusieurs matériaux non miscibles. Pour ne pas alourdir l'exposé, nous nous sommes restreints à des écoulements 2D en symétrie plane de matériaux non visqueux, en supposant que le tenseur des contraintes est sphérique. Chacune des restrictions précédentes peut assez facilement être levée. Quelques modifications évidentes sont à faire dans les équations de base pour pouvoir traiter les écoulements 2D axisymétriques. L'introduction d'un tenseur des contraintes général ne pose pas de difficultés numériques. Par contre, les modèles de comportement élastovisco-plastique des matériaux en grande déformation ne sont pas encore entièrement satisfaisants [1] Le traitement de la propagation d'ondes de choc en géométrie 2D par une méthode de pseudo-viscosité n'est pas toujours satisfaisant, mais les méthodes concurrentes de shock fitting, shock capturing ou de caractéristiques sont d'un emploi peu souple pour les écoulements 2D multifluides.

Ici, on fera porter l'attention sur la description des différents systèmes de repères utilisables : variables de Lagrange, d'Euler, intermédiaires, méthodes particulaires, et des schémas numériques correspondants. On ne fera qu'évoquer les questions de stabilité des schémas, en renvoyant à la bibliographie pour une étude plus approfondie. Une classification des méthodes les unes par rapport aux autres peut se faire selon les critères suivants : résolution des interfaces et des surfaces libres, possibilité de calcul d'écoulements tourbillonnaires, complexité de la logique des programmes de calcul correspondants, à laquelle on fera allusion de temps à autre.

.../...

En principe, pour conserver une bonne définition des interfaces, les variables de Lagrange semblent les mieux indiquées. De plus, lorsque l'on emploie les variables de Lagrange, les équations ne contiennnent pas de termes de flux, ce qui est un avantage indéniable. En effet, il n'est pas facile d'avoir des schémas précis pour discrétiser ces termes au voisinage des frontières, surtout lorsque celles-ci sont en mouvement. En conséquence, on utilise en général des schémas d'ordre 1 ou 2, qui pour être stables, renferment implicitement un phénomène de diffusion numérique important (la situation est très différente dans le cas d'écoulements stationnaires, où du fait que le maillage est fixe, on peut utiliser des méthodes numériques d'ordre élevé sans que la logique des programmes de calcul correspondants ne soit trop complexe). Si le mouvement des fluides est trop perturbé (par exemple tourbillonnaire), le calcul devient impossible en variables de Lagrange. On peut envisager des méthodes dans lesquelles le repère varie de façon quelconque, tout en respectant les interfaces, de façon à éviter les distorsions du maillage à l'intérieur de chaque milieu. On peut aussi utiliser les variables d'Euler pour lesquelles le problème du suivi des interfaces ou surfaces libres est difficile à résoudre. Si on veut suivre explicitement une interface, il faut savoir définir son mouvement sur un maillage fixe. On peut aussi traiter l'interface implicitement sans la calculer explicitement : c'est ce qui est fait dans certains codes eulériens "continus" ou "particulaires". De toute façon, il existe toujours des cellules du maillage qui seront couvertes par plusieurs milieux différents : il faudra savoir traiter le cas de ces cellules mixtes. Par ailleurs, il y a certains problèmes à plusieurs milieux qui ne peuvent pas être traités uniquement en variables d'Euler, en particulier les problèmes de couplage de fluides avec des structures minces. Pour ceux-ci, on peut utiliser la méthode couplée Euler-Lagrange.

Le plan de l'article est le suivant :

I Mise en équations du problème
II Comparaison des différents systèmes de repères en 2D
III Discrétisation des équations en variables de Lagrange
IV Discrétisation des termes de flux
V Traitement des termes faisant intervenir la pression dans les cellules mixtes
VI Définition du mouvement des interfaces et surfaces libres
VII Exemples de calcul.

.../...

I - MISE EN EQUATIONS DU PROBLEME

Nous supposerons que le comportement des matériaux est entièrement défini par leurs équations d'états

$$p = f(\rho, e) \tag{1.1}$$

où p, ρ, e sont respectivement la pression, la densité et l'énergie interne par unité de masse. Nous ne considérons donc que le cas où le tenseur des contraintes est isotrope. L'introduction d'un tenseur de contrainte non isotrope dans les équations, ainsi que son approximation numérique n'offre pas de difficultés supplémentaires. Par contre, la modélisation des lois de comportement, dans le cas de grandes déformations, est un problème encore ouvert [1] .

Nous ne prendrons pas en compte, non plus, les phénomènes de diffusion de l'énergie. Ceci reviendrait à introduire des termes supplémentaires dans l'équation de l'énergie.

Un grand nombre d'applications a trait au calcul de la propagation d'ondes de choc. On utilisera la méthode de la pseudo-viscosité [2] . Cela signifie que l'on ajoute au terme de pression un terme artificiel q défini, par exemple, par la formule :

$$q = -\rho\,\sigma\,\mathrm{div}\,\vec{u} \quad \text{où} \quad \sigma = \ell^2 \sup(0, -\mathrm{div}\,\vec{u}) \tag{1.2}$$

$\vec{u}$ étant la vitesse matérielle et ℓ une longueur caractéristique du maillage adopté au cours de la discrétisation des équations. D'autres méthodes plus rigoureuses pour traiter les chocs (méthode du choc-fitting, méthode des caractéristiques) sont difficiles à mettre en oeuvre dans les calculs bidimensionnels.

La mise en équations du problème consiste à écrire les lois de conservation de la masse, la quantité de mouvement et l'énergie.

Cette dernière peut prendre plusieurs formes, selon que l'on fait apparaître l'énergie interne e ou l'énergie totale $E = e + \frac{1}{2}|\vec{u}|^2$ par unité de masse. Pour les calculs d'écoulements à grande vitesse, on préfère utiliser e comme variable indépendante, car si on retient E, on risque de grandes imprécisions sur le calcul de $e = E - \frac{1}{2}|\vec{u}|^2$ (comme différences de deux termes presque égaux) qui se répercutent sur celui de la pression.

L'un des principaux problèmes à résoudre est le choix du système de repérage. Traditionnellement, on utilise soit les coordonnées d'Euler (fixes dans le repère du laboratoire), soit les coordonnées de Lagrange (liées à la matière). En fait, ce ne sont que deux cas particuliers du cas plus général que l'on expose ci-dessous pour une géométrie tridimensionnelle [3] .

.../...

Dans un repère orthonormé fixe $O x_1, x_2, x_3$ les équations de conservation s'écrivent :

(1.3) $$\frac{\partial \rho}{\partial t} + \sum_{j=1}^{3} \frac{\partial}{\partial x_j} (\rho u_j) = 0$$

(1.4) $$\frac{\partial (\rho u_i)}{\partial t} + \sum_{j=1}^{3} \frac{\partial}{\partial x_j} (\rho u_i u_j) + \frac{\partial p}{\partial x_i} = \rho f_i \quad , 1 \leq i \leq 3$$

(1.5) $$\frac{\partial}{\partial t} (\rho e) + \sum_{j=1}^{3} \frac{\partial}{\partial x_j} (\rho e u_j) + p \sum_{j=1}^{3} \frac{\partial u_j}{\partial x_j} = \rho S$$

où les variables ont la signification suivante :

ρ: densité
p: pression (+ pseudo-viscosité éventuellement)
e: énergie interne par unité de masse
u_i: composante de la vitesse $\vec{u}$
f_i: composante de la force extérieure par unité de masse
S: source d'énergie extérieure par unité de masse.

Supposons que le fluide occupe le domaine Ω (o) au temps t = o et Ω (t) au temps $t > 0$, de telle sorte que l'on puisse définir une correspondance biunivoque F entre Ω (o) et Ω (t) dépendant régulièrement de t :

(1.6) $$x_i = F_i (a_1, a_2, a_3, t) \qquad \text{avec} \qquad a_i = F_i (a_1, a_2, a_3, 0)$$

Soit J le jacobien de la transformation $a \to x = F(a,t)$

(1.7) $$J = \frac{D(x_1, x_2, x_3)}{D(a_1, a_2, a_3)} = \frac{D(F_1, F_2, F_3)}{D(a_1, a_2, a_3)}$$

On introduit le vecteur vitesse du repère $\vec{U}$(a,t) de composantes

(1.8) $$U_i = \frac{\partial F_i}{\partial t} .$$

Le repère eulérien correspond au choix de F_i, tel que $U_i = 0$, le repère lagrangien au choix de F_i, tel que $U_i = u_i$.

On va décrire les équations (1.3,4,5) à l'aide des quatre variables indépendantes (a_1, a_2, a_3, t).

Soit $\varphi = \varphi(x, t)$ une fonction donnée, on posera :

(1.9) $$\overline{\varphi} (a, t) = \varphi (F(a, t), t).$$

.../...

D'après la règle des fonctions composées, on peut écrire :

(1.10) $$\frac{\partial \bar{\varphi}}{\partial t}(a,t) = \frac{\partial \varphi}{\partial t}\left(F(a,t),t\right) + \sum_{j=1}^{3} U_j(a,t)\frac{\partial \varphi}{\partial x_j}\left(F(a,t),t\right),$$

(1.11) $$\frac{\partial \bar{\varphi}}{\partial a_i}(a,t) = \sum_{j=1}^{3} \frac{\partial \varphi}{\partial x_j}\left(F(a,t),t\right)\frac{\partial F_j}{\partial a_i}(a,t) \qquad 1 \leq i \leq 3.$$

En résolvant ce système par rapport aux $\frac{\partial \varphi}{\partial x_j}$ on obtient :

(1.12) $$\frac{\partial \varphi}{\partial x_1} = \frac{1}{J}\cdot\frac{D(\bar{\varphi},x_2,x_3)}{D(a_1,a_2,a_3)}, \quad \frac{\partial \varphi}{\partial x_2} = \frac{1}{J}\cdot\frac{D(x_1,\bar{\varphi},x_3)}{D(a_1,a_2,a_3)}, \quad \frac{\partial \varphi}{\partial x_3} = \frac{1}{J}\cdot\frac{D(x_1,x_2,\bar{\varphi})}{D(a_1,a_2,a_3)}.$$

D'autre part, d'après la règle de dérivation d'un déterminant

(1.13) $$\frac{1}{J}\frac{\partial J}{\partial t} = \frac{1}{J}\left\{\frac{D(U_1,x_2,x_3)}{D(a_1,a_2,a_3)} + \frac{D(x_1,U_2,x_3)}{D(a_1,a_2,a_3)} + \frac{D(x_1,x_2,U_3)}{D(a_1,a_2,a_3)}\right\} = \operatorname{div}\vec{U}$$

Les lois de conservation (1 3,4,5) prennent alors la forme suivante dans laquelle $\frac{\partial}{\partial t}$ signifie la dérivation par rapport à la variable t , les a_i étant fixes.

(1.14) $$\frac{\partial}{\partial t}(\rho J) + J\sum_{j=1}^{3}\frac{\partial}{\partial x_j}\left(\rho(u_j - U_j)\right) = 0$$

(1.15) $$\frac{\partial}{\partial t}(\rho u_i J) + J\sum_{j=1}^{3}\frac{\partial}{\partial x_j}\left(\rho u_i(u_j - U_j)\right) + J\frac{\partial p}{\partial x_i} = \rho J f_i \quad 1 \leq i \leq 3$$

(1.16) $$\frac{\partial}{\partial t}(\rho e J) + J\sum_{j=1}^{3}\frac{\partial}{\partial x_j}\left(\rho e(u_j - U_j)\right) + Jp\sum_{i=1}^{3}\frac{\partial u_i}{\partial x_i} = \rho J S$$

sachant que grâce à (1.12) les dérivées par rapport aux x_j peuvent s'exprimer à l'aide des dérivées par rapport aux a_i. A ces équations, il faut ajouter :

(1.17) $$\frac{\partial x_i}{\partial t} = \frac{\partial F_i}{\partial t} = U_i \qquad 1 \leq i \leq 3 .$$

Dans le cas du repère lagrangien ($\vec{u} = \vec{U}$), l'équation (1.16) s'écrit :

(1.18) $$\frac{\partial}{\partial t}(\rho e J) + p\frac{\partial J}{\partial t} = \rho J S .$$

.../...

Les conditions aux limites que nous considérerons seront de deux types :

- sur une partie Γ_1 de la frontière de Ω, on imposera une pression de surface $p = p_s$ donnée ; $\vec{u}$ est alors inconnue ;
- sur l'autre partie Γ_2 de la frontière, on imposera la composante normale de la vitesse u_N = donnée ; la composante tangentielle et la pression de surface sont alors inconnues.

Si l'on considère un domaine contenant deux fluides non miscibles sur l'interface Γ, on doit avoir égalité des pressions de surface et des composantes normales des vitesses $p_s^1 = p_s^2$ et $u_N^1 = u_N^2$.

.../...

II - COMPARAISON DES DIFFERENTS SYSTEMES DE COORDONNEES EN 2D

Pour calculer des écoulements 1D instationnaires de plusieurs milieux, les coordonnées de Lagrange sont d'un usage général, sous réserve que la logique du programme permette de diminuer ou d'augmenter le nombre de mailles, de façon à garder un intervalle d'espace ni trop petit ni trop grand, ce qui n'offre aucune difficulté sur le plan numérique.

La situation est très différente pour les calculs 2D, le choix du système de repérage dépendant énormément des problèmes que l'on veut traiter (fig. 1).

Pour pouvoir, agréablement, suivre les interfaces entre milieux différents ou des surfaces libres, on a intérêt à utiliser les variables de Lagrange. Au temps t = o, on définit un maillage du domaine (en général à l'aide de quadrilatère) qui se déforme au cours du temps, de telle sorte que la vitesse de chaque sommet soit égale à la vitesse de la matière en ce point. Il est évident que si les fluides subissent de grandes distorsions (variations d'angle de vecteurs liés à la matière), l'approximation numérique des gradients sur le maillage distordu sera mauvaise. Sur la figure 2, on a représenté trois exemples de problèmes pour lesquels les variables de Lagrange sont inutilisables si l'on veut poursuivre le calcul des phénomènes suffisamment longtemps.

Si les frontières des fluides restent des courbes ayant des rayons de courbure pas trop faibles, mais que le mouvement du fluide à l'intérieur du domaine ne permet pas l'utilisation des variables de Lagrange, on peut utiliser le processus général d'évolution du maillage. Le maillage évolue avec une vitesse quelconque, de telle sorte que les mailles restent à peu près orthogonales, sous la restriction que les interfaces restent définies par les côtés des mailles. C'est la méthode utilisée dans des programmes récents tels que YAQUI [4] . En général, d'ailleurs, on définit les variations de positions des sommets du maillage par pas de temps pour qu'il en soit ainsi, et on en déduit les lois de vitesse du maillage qui est donc différente de la vitesse matérielle.

Si les fluides ont un mouvement entraînant des distorsions très grandes, y compris au voisinage des frontières, les méthodes précédentes ne sont plus applicables. On peut utiliser les variables d'Euler, mais alors se pose le problème délicat de la poursuite des interfaces ou surfaces libres. Il existe deux types de méthodes selon que l'on suit explicitement l'interface ou non. Dans le premier cas, il faut définir son mouvement et avoir un programme dont la logique permette la prise en compte de toutes les situations où une ligne traverse un réseau de mailles (en général orthogonal). De tels programmes ont été réalisés, par exemple le code HELP [5] traitant le mouvement d'une interface entre deux milieux repérés tous les deux en variables d'Euler, ou le code CEL [5] où un fluide est traité en variables de Lagrange et impose donc le mouvement de l'interface tandis que l'autre est traité en variables d'Euler et agit sur le premier par l'intermédiaire de la définition d'une pression d'interface.

.../...

D'autres méthodes, plus approximatives, ne définissent pas explicitement l'interface, par exemple les méthodes particulaires dans lesquelles chaque fluide est approché par un nuage de particules qui peuvent s'interpénétrer au voisinage de l'interface. La logique de tels programmes de calculs est beaucoup plus simple, mais on tolère implicitement une certaine diffusion purement numérique des matériaux l'un dans l'autre. Des codes tels que PIC [7] ou GAP [8] utilisent ces méthodes particulaires. Il existe également des programmes eulériens capables de traiter une interface entre deux milieux sans la représenter explicitement par une ligne, mais ne faisant pas appel à des méthodes particulaires [24]. De toutes façons, il existe toujours des cellules du maillage qui seront couvertes par plusieurs milieux différents ; il faudra savoir traiter le cas de ces cellules mixtes.

.../...

III - DISCRETISATION DES EQUATIONS EN VARIABLE DE LAGRANGE 2D

Nous parlerons d'abord de la discrétisation spatiale des équations (1.14,15,18), puis de leur discrétisation temporelle. Dans la littérature, on trouve plusieurs méthodes de discrétisation [6] , [9] , [10] , [11] , [12] toutes équivalentes dans le cas de la symétrie plane, légèrement différentes en géométrie axisymétrique. Elles sont toutes basées sur un maillage quadrilatéral pouvant, éventuellement, dégénérer en triangles. Utilisons, par exemple, le formalisme de la méthode des éléments finis dans le cas de la symétrie plane.

Soit Vo, l'espace des fonctions constantes par élément. Les quantités thermodynamiques p, ρ, e sont prises dans cet espace :

$$(3.1) \qquad \begin{bmatrix} p \\ \rho \\ e \end{bmatrix}(x,y) = \sum_Q \begin{bmatrix} p_Q \\ \rho_Q \\ e_Q \end{bmatrix} \chi_Q(x,y).$$

où χ_Q est la fonction caractéristique de l'élément Q.

Soit V_1, l'espace des fonctions définies de façon isoparamétrique bilinéaire [13] . Les coordonnées x,y et les composantes de la vitesse u, v sont choisies dans V_1 et sont donc définies, avec les notations de la figure 3, par :

$$(3.2) \qquad \begin{bmatrix} x \\ y \\ u \\ v \end{bmatrix} = \sum_{i=1}^{4} \begin{bmatrix} x_i \\ y_i \\ u_i \\ v_i \end{bmatrix} \varphi_i(\xi,\eta)$$

où $\varphi_i(\xi,\eta) = \frac{1}{4}(1+\xi_i\xi)(1+\eta_i\eta)$ avec $\xi_i, \eta_i = \pm 1$ de telle sorte que $\varphi_i(\xi_j,\eta_j) = \delta_{ij}$

a,b étant les coordonnées au temps t = o, et x,y celles au temps t > o, l'équation de conservation de la quantité de mouvement prise sous forme faible s'écrit de façon standard :

$$(3.3)\ u \in V_1 \text{ tel que } \frac{d}{dt}\int_{\Omega(o)} \rho J u \varphi \, da\, db - \int_\Omega p \frac{\partial\varphi}{\partial x}\, dx\, dy + \int_{\partial\Omega} p_s \varphi n_x \, dl = \int_\Omega \rho f \varphi \, dx\, dy \quad \forall \varphi \in V_1$$

$$(3.4)\ v \in V_1 \text{ tel que } \frac{d}{dt}\int_{\Omega(o)} \rho J v \varphi \, da\, db - \int_\Omega p \frac{\partial\varphi}{\partial y}\, dx\, dy + \int_{\partial\Omega} p_s \varphi n_y \, dl = \int_\Omega \rho f \varphi \, dx\, dy \quad \forall \varphi \in V_1$$

en supposant, pour l'instant, que la pression de surface est connue sur $\partial\Omega$ (on décrira plus loin le cas où sur une partie de la frontière la vitesse normale u_N est imposée). La matrice de masse a donc pour coefficients :

$$(3.5) \qquad m_{i,j} = \int_{\Omega_o} \rho J \varphi_i \varphi_j \, da\, db = \int_{\Omega_o} \rho_o \varphi_i \varphi_j \, da\, db$$

puisque, en variable de Lagrange $\rho J = \rho_o J_o = \rho_o$, densité au temps t = o.

.../...

On préfère souvent avoir une matrice de masse diagonale que l'on obtient à l'aide de la formule de quadrature suivante :

$$(3.6)\quad \int_{Q_0} f \rho_0 \, da \, db \sim \sum_{i=1}^{4} f(i) \int_{Q_0} \varphi_i \rho_0 \, da \, db$$

En appliquant cette approximation au calcul des $m_{i,j}$, on obtient :

$$(3.7)\quad m_{i,j} = \delta_{i,j} \int_{\Omega_0} \varphi_i \rho_0 \, da \, db = M_i$$

Avec les notations de la figure 4, le schéma obtenu par les équations (3.3,4) et l'approximation matrice de masse diagonale, s'écrit en un point o intérieur :

$$(3.8)\quad M_0 \frac{du_0}{dt} - \sum_{i=1}^{4} \frac{1}{2}(y_i - y_0)(p_i - p_{i-1}) = f_0 = \int_{\Omega} \rho f \varphi_0 \, dx \, dy$$

$$(3.9)\quad M_0 \frac{dv_0}{dt} + \sum_{i=1}^{4} \frac{1}{2}(x_i - x_0)(p_i - p_{i-1}) = g_0 = \int_{\Omega} \rho g \varphi_0 \, dx \, dy$$

où p_i est la pression dans la maille i avec $p_0 \equiv p_4$. Si le point 0 est sur $\partial\Omega$ la formule (3.8) devient :

$$(3.10)\quad M_0 \frac{du_0}{dt} - \frac{1}{2}(y_1 - y_0)(p_{01} - p_4) - \frac{1}{2}(y_3 - y_0)(p_3 - p_{03}) - \frac{1}{2}(y_4 - y_0)(p_4 - p_3) = f_0$$

où p_{01} et p_{03} sont les pressions de surface sur les segments (0,1) et (0,3). On a une formule analogue pour (3.9).

Dans le cas où une partie de la frontière a un mouvement donné et que le fluide glisse dessus, la vitesse normale est donc imposée, mais la vitesse tangentielle et la pression de surface sont inconnues. On introduit un espace V^s, de dimension finie, dans lequel on va chercher la pression de surface, par exemple p^s constant par segment ou linéaire par segment (voir figure 5).

$$(3.11)\quad p^s(\ell) = \sum_j p_j^s \psi_j(\ell)$$

ℓ étant l'abscisse curviligne sur la frontière.

.../...

Introduisons les notations vectorielles suivantes :

(3.12) $U = \{u_i\}, V = \{v_i\}, P = \{P_Q\}, P^s = \{p^s_j\}, F = \{f_i\}, G = \{g_i\}$

et les définitions des matrices M, A, B, C, D :

(3.13) $$\begin{cases} M_{i,j} = \delta_{i,j} M_i, \quad A_{i,Q} = \int_Q \frac{\partial \varphi_i}{\partial x} dx\, dy, \quad B_{i,Q} = \int_Q \frac{\partial \varphi_i}{\partial y} dx\, dy \\ C_{i,j} = \int_{\partial\Omega} \varphi_i \psi_j n_x \, dl, \quad D_{i,j} = \int_{\partial\Omega} \varphi_i \psi_j n_y \, dl \end{cases}$$

Les équations (3.8,9) prennent la forme :

(3.14) $$\begin{aligned} M \frac{dU}{dt} + AP + Cp^s &= F \\ M \frac{dV}{dt} + BP + Dp^s &= G \end{aligned}$$

En plus, le cas échéant, on traduira la condition aux limites $u_N = U_N$ donnée par sa forme faible $\int_{\partial\Omega} (u n_x + v n_y - U_N) \psi \, dl = 0 \; \forall \psi \in V^s$ ce qui s'écrit matriciellement avec $H \{h_j\}$ où $h_j = \int_{\partial\Omega} U_N \psi_j \, dl$

(3.15) $C^T U + D^T V = H$

Dans un but de simplification, si V^s = espace des fonctions linéaires par segment, on peut approcher le calcul des $C_{i,j}$ et $D_{i,j}$ par une formule des trapèzes, auquel cas les matrices C et D sont diagonales.

Remarque 1

On peut traiter par un procédé analogue le glissement entre deux milieux distincts. Du fait que les maillages des deux milieux ne sont plus en coïncidence, il faut introduire une ligne sur laquelle glisseront les sommets des deux milieux en contact. La définition du mouvement de cette ligne n'est pas toujours simple. C'est la raison pour laquelle, dans le passé, on a souvent utilisé des procédures approximatives pour traiter le glissement, qui introduisent une dissymétrie entre les deux milieux, l'un étant supposé guider l'autre [10] . De toute façon, dans un programme de calcul, c'est la partie traitant le glissement de deux milieux l'un sur l'autre qui est la plus complexe sur le plan logique. C'est la raison pour laquelle nous étudions une autre méthode qui devrait être valable lorsque les deux matériaux ont des vitesses matérielles tangentielles pas trop différentes. Dans cette nouvelle méthode, on définit la vitesse des maillages des deux milieux, de façon qu'ils coïncident toujours à l'interface.

.../...

La vitesse normale du maillage est celle de la matière (pour que l'interface reste en coïncidence avec le bord des éléments), la vitesse tangentielle du maillage est différente des vitesses tangentielles matérielles des deux milieux (qui ne sont, d'ailleurs, pas égales). Dans les équations générales (1.14,15,16,17), on n'a plus $\vec{u} = \vec{U}$, l'approximation des termes nouveaux "de flux" qui apparaissent sera traitée au paragraphe suivant.

La discrétisation des équations (1.14) et (1.18) ne pose aucun problème. Dans chaque élément Q, on écrit :

$$(3.16) \quad \frac{d}{dt}\int_Q \rho J \, da\, db = \frac{d}{dt}(\rho_Q \, Vol_Q) = 0$$

où Vol_Q est le volume de l'élément Q, ce qui traduit le fait que la masse de la maille Q $M_Q = \rho_Q Vol_Q$ est constante dans le temps, et

$$(3.17) \quad \frac{d}{dt}(M_Q \, e_Q) + P_Q \frac{d\, Vol_Q}{dt} = M_Q \, S_Q$$

En ce qui concerne la discrétisation temporelle, vu, en général, le caractère fortement non linéaire des écoulements, on ne choisira pas des schémas de haute précision, l'ordre 2 étant suffisant et cohérent avec la discrétisation spatiale exposée ci-dessus. On a le choix entre des schémas explicites ou implicites. Les schémas explicites imposent une condition de stabilité qui limite le pas de temps admissible. Pour des matériaux incompressibles, on doit choisir des schémas implicites, ce qui nécessite la mise au point d'une méthode itérative de résolution [4], [14], [15].

Le schéma explicite usuel est le suivant :

$$(3.18) \quad M\,\frac{U^{n+\frac{1}{2}} - U^{n-\frac{1}{2}}}{\Delta t} + AP^n + C(P^s)^n = F^n$$

$$(3.19) \quad M\,\frac{V^{n+\frac{1}{2}} - V^{n-\frac{1}{2}}}{\Delta t} + BP^n + D(P^s)^n = G^n$$

$$(3.20) \quad C^T U^{n+\frac{1}{2}} + D^T V^{n+\frac{1}{2}} = H^{n+\frac{1}{2}}$$

Si P^s est connu, on obtient explicitement $U^{n+\frac{1}{2}}$ et $V^{n+\frac{1}{2}}$ à l'aide de (3.18) et (3.19). Sinon, on élimine $U^{n+\frac{1}{2}}$ et $V^{n+\frac{1}{2}}$ entre ces trois équations, ce qui conduit à un système linéaire à résoudre pour obtenir $(P^s)^n$ que l'on reporte dans (3.18) et (3.19) pour calculer $U^{n+\frac{1}{2}}$ et $V^{n+\frac{1}{2}}$.

.../...

Connaissant $U^{n+\frac{1}{2}}$ et $V^{n+\frac{1}{2}}$, on calcule X et Y par :

(3.21) $$X^{n+1} = X^{n} + U^{n+\frac{1}{2}} \Delta t \quad \text{et} \quad Y^{n+1} = Y^{n} + V^{n+\frac{1}{2}} \Delta t$$

On peut, alors, calculer le volume des éléments Q au temps t_{n+1}. On obtient, enfin, la pression et l'énergie interne de chaque élément par la résolution couplée, dans chaque élément, de :

(3.22) $$\begin{cases} M_Q(e_Q^{n+1} - e_Q^{n}) + \frac{1}{2}(P_Q^{n+1} + P_Q^{n})(Vol_Q^{n+1} - Vol_Q^{n}) = \Delta t\, M_Q\, S_Q^{n+\frac{1}{2}} \\ P_Q^{n+1} = f\left(\frac{M_Q^{n+1}}{Vol_Q^{n+1}}, e_Q^{n+1}\right) \end{cases}$$

On montre [16] que la condition de stabilité linéarisée d'un tel schéma est la condition de Courant Friedrichs et Lévy.

(3.23) $$\forall Q, \quad \frac{c_Q \Delta t}{\ell_Q} < 1$$

où C_Q est la vitesse du son dans l'élément Q et ℓ_Q une "épaisseur", rapport de la surface sur la "longueur" L_Q, cette dernière étant définie par une pondération des longueurs des diagonales de l'élément.

Remarque 2

Dans le cas où l'on introduit un terme de pseudo-viscosité, on conserve un schéma explicite en ajoutant à P^n l'expression :

(3.24) $$q^n = \begin{cases} \ell^2 \rho^n \left[\frac{\rho^n - \rho^{n-1}}{\Delta t} \cdot \frac{2}{\rho^n + \rho^{n-1}}\right]^2 & \text{si } \rho^n > \rho^{n-1} \\ 0 & \text{si } \rho^n < \rho^{n-1} \end{cases}$$

puisqu'en variable de Lagrange div $\vec{u} = \frac{-1}{\rho}\frac{\partial \rho}{\partial t}$.

Cela conduit à une condition de stabilité supplémentaire du type $\frac{\rho^n - \rho^{n-1}}{\rho^n + \rho^{n-1}} < C^{te}$ qui est en réalité une limite sur le pas de temps admissible, d'autant plus que, simultanément, (3.23) devient $\frac{c_Q \Delta t}{\ell_Q} < C^{te} < 1$.

Un schéma implicite s'obtient en remplaçant P^n par $\frac{1}{4}[p^{n+1} + 2p^n + p^{n-1}]$ ou, plus simplement $\frac{1}{2}(p^{n+1} + p^n)$ dans les équations (3.18,19). On montre dans [16] la convergence, pour le problème linéarisé, d'une méthode itérative analogue à celle de [4] .

.../...

Remarque 3

Il est bien connu que ces méthodes lagrangiennes développent un type d'instabilité "en sablier". Diverses techniques de suppression de ces instabilités ont été proposées. On trouvera dans [16] une liste de références ayant trait à ces techniques dont nous ne parlerons pas ici.

.../...

IV - DISCRETISATION DES TERMES DE FLUX

Dans les équations (1.14,15,16), nous voyons que si on n'utilise pas les coordonnées de Lagrange, donc si $\vec{u} \neq \vec{U}$, il existe des termes du type :

$$(4.1) \quad J \sum_{j=1}^{3} \frac{\partial}{\partial x_j} (\rho \varphi (u_j - U_j))$$

où $\varphi = 1, u_i$ ou e qu'il faut approcher.

Pour ne pas alourdir la présentation, nous ne détaillerons, ci-dessous, que l'approximation de l'équation de conservation de la masse (1.14). Le traitement des autres équations est très semblable.

Nous allons présenter un schéma de discrétisation, d'abord dans le cas le plus simple ; c'est-à-dire lorsque l'on utilise les variables d'Euler ($\vec{U}$ = o) sur un maillage orthogonal parallèle aux axes, pour un élément intérieur au domaine. Ensuite, nous considérerons le cas plus complexe des éléments coupés par une surface libre. Puis on introduira la modélisation numérique de ces termes de flux par des méthodes particulaires utilisées lorsque le suivi d'une interface serait trop difficile. On montrera, également, comment on peut discrétiser ces termes de flux sur un maillage quadrilatéral quelconque. Finalement, on traitera le cas où un élément est traversé par une interface. Pour les détails techniques, nous renvoyons à [5] , [6] , [7] , [15] .

A - Variable d'Euler, maille intérieure

Puisque la vitesse du repère est nulle J = 1, si on intègre (1.14) sur une maille Q de frontière ∂Q, on obtient :

$$(4.2) \quad \frac{d}{dt} \int_Q \rho \, dx \, dy + \int_Q \mathrm{div}(\rho \vec{u}) \, dx \, dy = \frac{d}{dt} \int_Q \rho \, dx \, dy + \int_{\partial Q} \rho \vec{u} \cdot \vec{n} \, ds = 0$$

Connaissant $\vec{u}$ aux 4 sommets et sachant que $\vec{u}$ varie linéairement sur chaque côté, l'évaluation de l'intégrale sur ∂Q est immédiate dès que l'on a défini la valeur de ρ sur ∂Q. Ici se pose un problème puisque l'on a choisi ρ constant par élément, et donc non défini sur ∂Q. Un choix "naturel" semble être de définir la valeur de ρ sur chaque côté comme moyenne des valeurs de ρ dans les mailles adjacentes. En fait, la discrétisation spatiale est liée à la discrétisation temporelle par la nécessité d'obtenir un schéma stable. Là, intervient de façon fondamentale, le caractère explicite ou implicite (en temps) du schéma. Les schémas implicites nécessitant la résolution de système d'équations sont généralement coûteux en géométrie 2D, on préférera des schémas explicites qui, malheureusement, ne sont pas toujours stables.

.../...

On peut s'en rendre compte facilement sur l'équivalent 1D de l'équation de transport (dans le cas où la vitesse est constante).

$$(4.3) \quad \frac{\partial \rho}{\partial t} + u \frac{\partial \rho}{\partial x} = 0 .$$

Si ρ_i^n désigne l'approximation de ρ (i Δ x, n Δt), le schéma explicite centré

$$(4.4) \quad \frac{1}{\Delta t}\left(\rho_i^{n+1} - \rho_i^n\right) + \frac{u}{\Delta x}\left[\frac{\rho_{i+1}^n + \rho_i^n}{2} - \frac{\rho_i^n + \rho_{i-1}^n}{2}\right] = 0$$

est instable ; voir [17] .

La solution la plus simple pour obtenir un schéma stable est le schéma décentré partiellement ou totalement (donor cell) :

$$(4.5) \quad \frac{1}{\Delta t}\left(\rho_i^{n+1} - \rho_i^n\right) + \frac{u}{\Delta x}\left[\frac{(1-\alpha)\rho_{i+1}^n + (1+\alpha)\rho_i^n}{2} - \frac{(1+\alpha)\rho_i^n + (1-\alpha)\rho_{i-1}^n}{2}\right] = 0$$

avec $\alpha \in [-1, +1]$ $\quad sign(\alpha) = sign(u)$ qui est stable sous la condition

$$(4.6) \quad |u| \frac{\Delta t}{\Delta x} \leq |\alpha|$$

D'autres solutions plus raffinées existent : schémas de Lax Wendroff [18] , de Kasahara [19] , de Roberts et Weiss [20] , de Boris et Book [21] , mais leur emploi pour les mailles en contact avec des frontières quelconques est parfois délicat. Ce traitement des termes de transport par un schéma du type décentré est le point faible de la discrétisation des équations de l'hydrodynamique en variable non lagrangienne. Il est connu que ce schéma est très dissipatif (il lisse les chocs, par exemple). Sa seule raison pour être utilisé est sa simplicité, ce qui est fondamental au voisinage de frontières quelconques, surtout lorsqu'elles sont en mouvement. A notre connaissance, pour traiter des problèmes multi-milieux instationnaires avec des interfaces mobiles, aucun autre schéma n'a été utilisé dans un programme de calcul industriel.

.../...

Finalement, dans le cas 2D, et avec des notations évidentes (i,j pour les centres des éléments, et i + 1/2, j + 1/2 pour les côtés), on utilise le schéma suivant pour discrétiser (1.14), par exemple dans le cas totalement décentré ($|\alpha| = 1$) :

$$(4.7)\quad \frac{1}{\Delta t}\left(\rho^{n+1}_{i,j} - \rho^{n}_{i,j}\right)\Delta x\,\Delta y + \Delta y\left[u_{i+\frac12,j}\,\rho_{i+\frac12,j} - u_{i-\frac12,j}\,\rho_{i-\frac12,j}\right] +$$

$$+ \Delta x\left[v_{i,j+\frac12}\,\rho_{i,j+\frac12} - v_{i,j-\frac12}\,\rho_{i,j-\frac12}\right] = 0$$

où $u_{i+\frac12,j} = \frac12\left(u_{i+\frac12,j+\frac12} + u_{i+\frac12,j-\frac12}\right)$ et $\rho_{i+\frac12,j} = \begin{cases}\rho_{i,j} & u_{i+\frac12,j} > 0\\ \rho_{i+1,j} & u_{i+\frac12,j} < 0,\end{cases}$

les autres valeurs de ρ et u étant définies de façon analogue.

Le traitement des termes de transport dans les autres équations de conservation est absolument identique.

B - Maille au voisinage d'une surface libre

On prendra les notations de la figure 6. On définit la valeur de ρ dans la cellule d'intégration qui est $\tilde{Q} = Q \cap \Omega$. Sur la frontière de $\tilde{Q}$ on a $\vec{U} = 0$ sur BC, CD, DE et $(\vec{U}-\vec{u},\vec{n}) = 0$ sur EA et AB. On remarque qu'en réalité la transformation $\Omega(0) \rightarrow \Omega(t)$ n'est pas régulière, ce qui se traduit par l'apparition ou la disparition de mailles contenues dans Ω (t) au cours du temps, et complique sérieusement la logique des programmes de calculs. Néanmoins, on obtiendra une approximation de l'équation de conservation de la masse en l'intégrant sur $\tilde{Q}$.

$$(4.8)\quad \int_{\tilde{Q}^{n+1}} \rho J\, da\, db - \int_{\tilde{Q}^{n}} \rho J\, da\, db + \Delta t\int_{\partial\tilde{Q}} \rho(\vec{u}-\vec{U},\vec{n})\, dS = 0$$

avec

$$(4.9)\quad \int_{\tilde{Q}^{n}} \rho J\, da\, db = \rho^{n}_{Q}\ \mathrm{Vol}\,\tilde{Q}^{n}.$$

Quant à l'intégrale sur $\partial\tilde{Q}$, elle est nulle sur $\partial\tilde{Q} \cap \partial\Omega$ et s'évalue sur les côtés fixes de la même façon que ci-dessus par un schéma décentré.

C - Méthodes particulaires : cas d'un seul fluide

On reviendra au paragraphe suivant sur le traitement des termes faisant intervenir la pression dans les équations (1.14,15,16), en particulier dans les mailles contenant plusieurs matériaux.

.../...

Nous voulons montrer ici par quel modèle numérique on approche les termes de transport dans ces équations.

On suppose que le fluide est représenté par des particules ayant une masse donnée invariante au cours du temps, placées à l'instant t = o sur un maillage orthogonal fixe. Connaissant la distribution de vitesse du fluide au temps t_n sur ce maillage, on déplace les particules, à chaque pas de temps, de la quantité $\vec{u}_P \; \Delta t$, où $\vec{u}_P$ est la vitesse du fluide au point P où se trouve la particule ($\vec{u}_P$ est obtenu par interpolation bilinéaire, à partir des vitesses définies aux noeuds du maillage). On ajoute alors les masses de chaque particule dans une cellule donnée pour avoir la masse totale contenue dans cette cellule, puis on divise par le volume (constant dans le temps!) de la cellule pour obtenir la densité au temps t_{n+1}. C'est la méthode utilisée dans le programme PIC [7] . On conçoit aisément que la précision obtenue dépend du nombre de particules disponibles par mailles. Avec les ordinateurs actuels les plus puissants, on peut disposer de plusieurs dizaines de particules par mailles. Une telle méthode ne donne, en général, que des résultats assez "qualitatifs". Son principal avantage est sa simplicité, en particulier en ce qu'elle ne nécessite pas la définition explicite des frontières (interfaces ou surfaces libres). Néanmoins, on voit immédiatement certains vices de cette méthode. Par exemple, si on ne dispose que d'un petit nombre de particules par maille, il peut se faire - pour des pas de temps petits - qu'aucune particule ne rentre ni ne sorte d'une maille donnée, laissant la densité inchangée, même si $\vec{u} \neq o$, d'où l'idée d'une méthode plus élaborée comme la méthode GAP.

On considère qu'une particule de masse m située en P, au lieu de contribuer uniquement à la masse de la cellule qui la contient, contribue aux masses des quatre cellules voisines, proportionnellement au volume de l'intersection de chaque cellule avec une cellule centrée en P. La masse d'une maille Q devient : (voir figure 7)

$$(4.10) \quad M_Q = \sum_P m_P \frac{Vol\,(S_P \cap Q)}{Vol\,(Q)}$$

la sommation étant étendue à toutes les particules. De cette façon, on obtient une représentation beaucoup plus lisse de la densité, et on évite les fluctuations caractéristiques de la méthode PIC dues à la "quantification" de la masse.

Le traitement des termes de transport dans les équations de conservation de la quantité de mouvement ou de l'énergie se fait de façon identique.

.../...

D - Méthodes "continues" sur un maillage quelconque

Le traitement de l'équation de conservation de la masse (1.14) sur un maillage quadrilatéral quelconque est simple, puisqu'on se limite aux approximations où ρ est constant par maille. Par intégration de (1.14) sur l'élément Q, on obtient encore :

$$(4.11) \quad \frac{d}{dt}\int_Q \rho J \, da \, db + \int_{\partial Q} \rho(\vec{u}-\vec{U},\vec{n}) \, d\ell = 0$$

Avec les notations de la figure 8, on obtient le schéma suivant :

$$(4.12) \quad \frac{1}{\Delta t}\left[\rho_Q^{n+1} \mathrm{Vol}_Q^{n+1} - \rho_Q^n \mathrm{Vol}_Q^n\right] + \sum_{\ell=1}^{4} \rho_{\ell+\frac{1}{2}} \left(\frac{\vec{u}_\ell - \vec{U}_\ell + \vec{u}_{\ell+1} - \vec{U}_{\ell+1}}{2}, \vec{n}_{\ell+\frac{1}{2}}\right) L_{\ell+\frac{1}{2}} = 0$$

où $L_{\ell+\frac{1}{2}}$ est la longueur du côté $(\ell, \ell+1)$, les indices devant être pris modulo **4** dans la formule (4.12).

On retrouve, évidemment, la nécessité de définir $\rho_{\ell+\frac{1}{2}}$ sur ∂Q par exemple par une méthode (partiellement) décentrée. En général, on utilise une méthode explicite, donc tous les termes de la sommation dans (4.12) sont pris au temps t_n.

La discrétisation des termes de flux dans l'équation de l'énergie est identique. Par contre, celle des termes de flux dans l'équation de la quantité de mouvement est différente, puisque les vitesses sont évaluées aux sommets des éléments. On peut partir de la formulation faible :

$$(4.13) \quad \frac{d}{dt}\int_{\Omega(0)} \rho J u_i \varphi \, da \, db - \int_{\Omega(t)} \rho u_i (\vec{u}-\vec{U}, \mathrm{grad}_x \varphi) \, dx \, dy = 0 \quad \forall \varphi \in V_1 .$$

Reprenant les notations de la figure 4, on voit que si on prend dans cette équation $\varphi = \varphi_0$ fonction de base associée au point o, on obtiendra une équation liant les composants de la vitesse en 9 points. Par contre, si on utilise la formule de quadrature (3.6), seules les vitesses des points (0,1,2,3,4) interviendront dans (4.13).

E - Cas des mailles mixtes

Revenons sur le traitement des termes de flux dans les mailles mixtes, c'est-à-dire les mailles contenant deux ou plusieurs matériaux différents.

.../...

Lorsque l'on utilise un système de coordonnées variables (non eulériennes), on s'arrange pour que les interfaces Γ entre deux milieux restent sur les côtés des mailles, en imposant sur Γ égalité des vitesses normales du fluide et des coordonnées. De cette façon, on évite les mailles mixtes. Par contre, si on utilise les coordonnées d'Euler pour traiter des problèmes multi-milieux, il existera nécessairement des mailles mixtes. La discrétisation des termes de flux est analogue à celle décrite en B ou C.

Pour l'équation de conservation de la masse, dans une méthode particulaire, on procède par déplacement des particules comme en B, sauf qu'il faut comptabiliser séparément les particules de chaque espèce.

Dans une méthode "continue", on calcule les flux sur chaque côté, de la façon suivante, avec les notations de la figure 9. Le côté commun aux mailles A et B étant coupé par l'interface Γ, on calcule des flux de masse de matériaux 1 et 2, en prenant les densités et surfaces respectives.

$$(4.14)\quad \begin{cases} \Delta_{m_1} = \rho_1 S_1 u \Delta t & \rho_1 = (1+\alpha)\rho_1^A + (1-\alpha)\rho_1^B \\ \Delta_{m_2} = \rho_2 S_2 u \Delta t & \rho_2 = (1+\alpha)\rho_2^A + (1-\alpha)\rho_2^B \end{cases}$$

On retranche les quantités Δm_i aux masses de la cellule donneuse pour les ajouter aux masses de la cellule receveuse. Au cours du déplacement de l'interface, une cellule (par exemple A) devra se vider d'un matériau (par exemple 2). Il arrivera nécessairement un instant où, pendant le pas de temps, on aura $m_2^A < \Delta m_2$, et si on ne prend pas de précaution, on créera des masses négatives. Là encore, on entrevoit tous les tests dont il faut s'entourer dans l'écriture d'un programme industriel.

Pour l'équation de l'énergie, on procède de la façon suivante : Dans une méthode particulaire, une cellule mixte est définie par l'ensemble des (M_i, e_i) masse et énergie interne par unité de masse du matériau i avec $M_i = \sum_P m_{i,p}$ où $m_{i,p}$ est la masse de la particule P du matériau i. Dans la phase de transport, on attribue à chaque particule l'énergie $m_{i,p}\, e_i$, et après avoir déplacé les particules, on comptabilise l'énergie de chaque matériau dans chaque cellule. Dans une méthode "continue" on définit des flux d'énergie de chaque matériau par pas de temps :

$$(4.15)\quad \begin{cases} \Delta e_1 = \rho_1 e_1 S_1 u \Delta t & \rho_1 e_1 = (1+\alpha)\rho_1^A e_1^A + (1-\alpha)\rho_1^B e_1^B \\ \Delta e_2 = \rho_2 e_2 S_2 u \Delta t & \rho_2 e_2 = (1+\alpha)\rho_2^A e_2^A + (1-\alpha)\rho_2^B e_2^B \end{cases}$$

et on procède comme pour les flux de masse, en ajoutant à une cellule ce qu'on retranche à l'autre.

.../...

Pour l'équation de la quantité de mouvement, et puisqu'on suppose que les différents matériaux ont la même vitesse, on ne distingue pas les matériaux pour le calcul des flux de quantité de mouvement.

Dans [15] les auteurs recommandent de toujours utiliser un schéma aux différences, même à l'intérieur d'un code particulaire.

.../...

V - TRAITEMENT DES TERMES FAISANT INTERVENIR LA PRESSION DANS LES CELLULES MIXTES

Dans les équations générales (1.14,15,16), il apparaît deux sortes de termes : les termes de transport du type J div ($\rho\varphi(\vec{u} - \vec{U})$) et les termes faisant intervenir la pression. Plaçons-nous dans le cadre où l'on applique une méthode de découpage des opérateurs : le premier opérateur est celui du transport, le deuxième, celui faisant intervenir les termes de pression.

L'intégration des équations pendant un pas de temps Δt sera découpée en deux phases, la première phase prenant en compte les termes de transport, la deuxième les termes de pression. Désignons avec des $\sim$ les valeurs de $e, p, \vec{u}$ après la phase de transport. Il faut donc intégrer les équations :

(5.1) $\frac{\partial}{\partial t}(\rho J) = 0$

(5.2) $\frac{\partial}{\partial t}(\rho u J) + J \, \mathrm{grad}\, p = \rho J f$

(5.3) $\frac{\partial}{\partial t}(\rho e J) + Jp \, \mathrm{div}\, \vec{u} = \rho J S$

Dans le cas d'une cellule constituée d'un seul matériau, il n'y a aucun problème de discrétisation. (5.1), intégrée sur un élément Q se traduit par :

(5.4) $M \int_Q \rho J \, da \, db = \text{constante}$

(5.2) se traduit par les équations (3.18,19), qui au point o sur la figure 4 s'écrivent :

(5.5) $M_o \dfrac{\vec{u}_o^{n+\frac{1}{2}} - \tilde{\vec{u}}_o}{\Delta t} + (\nabla\tilde{P})_o = M_o \vec{F}_o$

l'opérateur ∇P étant défini par les équations (3.8,9).

L'équation (5.3) intégrée sur chaque élément Q, entraîne :

(5.6) $\frac{1}{\Delta t} M(e^{n+1} - \tilde{e}) + \frac{1}{2}(p^{n+1} + \tilde{p}) \left[\int_{\partial Q} \vec{u}\cdot\vec{n}\, dl\cdot\right]^{n+\frac{1}{2}} = M S^{n+\frac{1}{2}}$

qui est couplée à l'équation d'état du fluide :

(5.7) $p^{n+1} = f(\rho^{n+1}, e^{n+1})$ avec $\rho^{n+1} = M / Vol^{n+1}$

.../...

Dans le cas de cellule mixte, l'équation (5.2) sera intégrée sans distinction de matériaux (on suppose que la vitesse des différents matériaux est la même) ; encore faut-il connaître la pression qui règne dans une maille mixte. En général, on utilise le modèle physico-numérique simple suivant [5] , [7] , [15] . A la fin de la phase de transport, on connaît dans les cellules mixtes les masses M_i et les énergies internes par unité de masse e_i de chaque matériau. On détermine la pression p et les volumes partiels V_i occupés par chaque matériau en résolvant :

(5.8) $\sum_{i=1}^{I} V_i$ = Volume de la cellule

(5.9) $p = f_i\left(\frac{M_i}{V_i}, e_i\right) \quad 1 \leq i \leq I$

Si les équations d'état f_i sont complexes, la résolution d'un tel système par une méthode itérative peut être longue. Aussi, des procédures simplifiées ont-elles été mises au point dans [7] . L'équation (5.1) traduit le fait que la masse de chaque matériau contenue dans une cellule est invariante. L'équation (5.3), intégrée sur toute la cellule, donne la variation d'énergie interne de l'ensemble de la matière contenue dans la cellule. Mais cette variation doit être répartie entre les différents matériaux. Différents modèles physico-numériques ont été présentés dans la littérature :

Dans le code HELP [5] , on part du principe que la pression et la vitesse sont les mêmes pour les différents matériaux dans une même maille. Si on intègre (5.3) sur chacun des domaines occupés par les différents matériaux, on déduit que la variation d'énergie interne d'un matériau est proportionnelle au volume qu'il occupe, soit :

(5.10) $\frac{1}{\Delta t} M_i \left(e_i^{n+1} - \tilde{e}_i\right) + K_i \, \Delta e = M_i \, S_i$

(5.11) où $K_i = V_i$ / Volume de la maille

(5.12) $\Delta e = \tilde{p} \int_Q \tilde{u} \cdot \vec{n} \, dl$

On remarque que le terme de pression dans Δe n'est pas centré en temps, pour éviter les itérations (au détriment de la précision).

Dans le code PIC [7] , on envisage d'autres façons de définir K_i, par exemple $K_i = \frac{1}{I}$ ou $K_i = \frac{M_i}{\Sigma M_i}$, ...

Dans le code GILA [15] , on utilise une technique implicite, basée sur une variation des volumes partiels occupés par les différents matériaux, de façon à maintenir l'égalité des pressions dans chaque matériau.

.../...

VI - DEFINITION DU MOUVEMENT DES INTERFACES ET SURFACES LIBRES

A - Les interfaces coïncident en permanence avec les côtés des mailles

C'est en particulier le cas, si on utilise les coordonnées de Lagrange, mais on peut se placer plus généralement dans un cas où le repère possède une vitesse différente de celle de la matière, pourvu que sur les interfaces la vitesse normale du repère soit égale à la vitesse normale de la matière.

Lorsque l'on admet qu'il n'y a pas de glissement entre les deux matériaux, les équations du mouvement pour les points d'une interface sont les mêmes que pour les points intérieurs. Il n'y a donc aucune difficulté supplémentaire pour traiter le mouvement d'une interface.

Lorsque l'on autorise les matériaux à glisser l'un sur l'autre, la logique des programmes de calculs devient plus complexe. Si les maillages peuvent, néanmoins, rester en coïncidence (figure 10), grâce à la définition d'une vitesse du repère différente des vitesses de la matière (ce qui, en pratique, n'est utilisable que dans les cas où le glissement est faible, c'est-à-dire les composantes tangentielles des vitesses des deux matériaux, peu différentes l'une de l'autre), la logique du programme de calcul ne sera pas très compliquée [22] . On procède, comme indiqué au paragraphe 3, par l'introduction d'une pression d'interface définie de telle sorte que les vitesses normales des deux matériaux soient identiques. Comme les maillages coïncident, on peut utiliser une formule des trapèzes pour évaluer les intégrales sur l'interface Γ, auquel cas on obtient les valeurs de cette pression d'interface P_S, explicitement, sans résolution de système.

Lorsque l'on ne peut pas définir une vitesse du repère dans les deux matériaux, de telle sorte que les maillages, de part et d'autre de l'interface, restent en coïncidence, la logique du programme de calcul devient plus complexe. Le calcul des vitesses et pression d'interface peut se faire comme c'est suggéré au paragraphe 3, mais le déplacement du maillage n'est fait, la plupart du temps, que de façon approximative [23] (par exemple en imposant à un milieu de guider l'autre). Cela dépend du degré de généralité dans les situations géométriques que l'on veut être capable de traiter. Par exemple, on conçoit que la situation de la figure 11 ne soit pas simple à implémenter dans un programme de calcul. De plus, il existe des cas où les interfaces entre milieux n'existent pas au temps $t = o$, mais se créent à $t > o$, par fermeture de vide entre deux milieux (figure 12). La logique d'un programme de calcul auquel on impose de pouvoir traiter ce genre de situation est évidemment assez complexe, puisqu'il faudra diagnostiquer les instants où les sommets du maillage d'un matériau arrivent en contact avec la surface de l'autre matériau. Il peut aussi se produire la situation inverse, où deux matériaux, initialement en contact, se décollent.

.../...

B - Les interfaces ne coïncident pas avec les côtés des mailles

Il s'agit, en général, du cas où les milieux sont traités en variables d'Euler, donc sont définis sur un maillage fixe sur lequel une ligne représentant l'interface doit évoluer. Plusieurs méthodes ont été envisagées :

B1 - Méthodes particulaires [7] , [8]

Ces méthodes résolvent le problème en le niant ! En effet, l'interface n'est jamais définie explicitement et on peut simplement la reconstituer "à l'oeil nu" sur un dessin, à partir de la position des particules de différents matériaux (figure 1). Ce sont des méthodes simples qui peuvent ne donner que des résultats qualitatifs. Notons qu'il existe des versions "continues" de PIC pour le calcul du mouvement de deux fluides, c'est-à-dire des codes eulériens incluant la possibilité logique de cellules mixtes, mais n'utilisant pas de particules. L'interface n'est pas représentée par une ligne dont on suivrait le mouvement. Néanmoins, pour le calcul des termes de flux entre deux cellules mixtes, on définit par une procédure approximative (tenant compte des proportions des mélanges des deux cellules) les portions de surface traversées par chaque fluide [24] .

B2 - Code HELP [5]

La ligne représentant l'interface est définie par un certain nombre de points dont la vitesse est simplement calculée par interpolation bilinéaire, à partir des valeurs des vitesses aux noeuds du maillage (figure 1). On admet qu'il n'y a pas de glissement entre les deux matériaux, de sorte que la vitesse matérielle soit définie de façon unique à l'interface. La logique d'un tel programme de calcul n'est pas simple, car il faut prendre en compte toutes les situations possibles d'intersection de l'interface avec les côtés des mailles. De plus, il faut éviter de calculer des quantités (densité, pression...) dans des portions de cellule trop petites. Le programme doit donc comporter des techniques spéciales de répartition de la masse et de l'énergie contenue dans une portion de cellule de volume trop faible dans les cellules voisines [6] .

Dans le cas du traitement d'une surface libre, on ne peut plus définir les vitesses des sommets par interpolation, puisque le fluide n'est situé que d'un seul côté de la surface. On pourrait utiliser des procédures d'extrapolation, mais l'expérience prouve qu'elles sont imprécises et sujettes au développement d'instabilités. Une autre façon de procéder consiste à calculer la composante normale de la vitesse des sommets de la surface libre, en intégrant l'équation de la quantité de mouvement sur un domaine entourant chaque sommet et contenu dans le fluide [25] (voir figure 13).

.../...

C - Méthode couplée Euler-Lagrange

Dans cette méthode, l'un des matériaux est traité en variables d'Euler, l'autre en variables de Lagrange (voir figure 1). L'interface Γ coïncide avec le bord des mailles du matériau traité en variables de Lagrange et coupe arbitrairement les mailles de celui traité en variable d'Euler. De plus, on autorise les matériaux à glisser l'un sur l'autre, puisque l'on n'impose pas une continuité de la vitesse à l'interface, mais que l'on définit une pression sur l'interface qui sert à calculer la vitesse dans chaque matériau.

Plus précisément, connaissant au temps t_n la pression P_s^n sur l'interface Γ^n, on peut calculer dans le milieu traité en variables de Lagrange la vitesse $\vec{u}^{\,n+\frac{1}{2}}$, puis la position de l'interface Γ^{n+1}, et enfin les densité, pression et énergies internes au temps t_{n+1}, en utilisant les équations du paragraphe 3. Dans le milieu traité en variables d'Euler, on peut calculer d'une part les termes de flux par une méthode analogue à celle du paragraphe IV B (connaissant la géométrie et les valeurs de ρ, e et $\vec{u}$ au temps t_n), puisqu'il n'y a pas de flux à travers l'interface, d'autre part les termes faisant intervenir la pression, puisque l'on connaît la pression dans les mailles eulériennes et la pression sur l'interface. De cette façon, on connaît les valeurs des vitesse et quantités thermodynamiques au temps t_{n+1} dans le milieu traité en variables d'Euler.

La définition de la pression d'interface sur Γ est importante pour la précision du calcul. On définira une valeur sur chaque segment obtenu comme intersection de Γ et des mailles eulériennes Q. Une méthode rudimentaire consiste à prendre sur ces segments la valeur de la pression de la maille eulérienne Q elle-même. Une méthode plus raffinée consiste à faire une interpolation entre cette dernière et la pression régnant dans la maille lagrangienne adjacente aux segments.

.../...

VII - EXEMPLE : IMPACT D'UN PROJECTILE SUR UNE CIBLE

On présente un calcul classique fait avec plusieurs méthodes. Il s'agit de l'impact d'un cylindre d'acier de 9cm de hauteur et 3cm de rayon, animé d'une vitesse initiale de 3.000 m/s sur un cylindre d'aluminium de 9cm de hauteur et 15cm de rayon.

La difficulté principale tient au traitement de l'interface entre les deux matériaux. On ne connait évidemment pas bien les hypothèses physiques qu'il faut adopter, en particulier à propos du glissement éventuel des matériaux l'un sur l'autre.

On présente plusieurs calculs faits en variables de Lagrange et un autre fait à l'aide d'un code particulaire de type PIC (figures 17 et 18).

Le calcul lagrangien a été fait dans les deux cas suivants : en supposant que les deux matériaux glissent l'un sur l'autre et en supposant qu'ils ne glissent pas (figure 16).

Dans le cas où l'on suppose que les matériaux glissent l'un sur l'autre, on a choisi de déplacer l'interface, dans un cas en suivant les noeuds du projectile en acier (figure 14) et dans l'autre en suivant les noeuds de la cible en aluminium (figure 15). Cela signifie qu'à chaque pas de temps on calcule le déplacement de tous les noeuds frontières des deux matériaux. On conserve exactement ceux du matériau "guide" qui définissent donc l'interface, et on repositionne ceux de l'autre matériau sur cette interface (par projection orthogonale, par exemple).

On a utilisé des mailles de 0,6cm de côté qui restent fixes dans le calcul particulaire et qui se déforment dans le calcul lagrangien.

Les figures 14, 15 et 16 représentent l'état du maillage à différents temps dans les trois cas de calculs passés en variables de Lagrange.

Sur la figure 14, le matériau "guide" est le projectile en acier. Cela explique que l'on voit certains noeuds de ce matériau pénétrer dans la cible de façon arbitraire. Le calcul a été arrêté au temps $t = 18$ µs car le pas de temps donné par la condition de stabilité est devenu trop petit à cause de l'existence de mailles qui sont devenues très allongées et très fines, mais de toute façon la validité des calculs est à mettre en doute.

Sur la figure 15,le matériau "guide" est la cible. Dans ce cas on évite la pénétration de noeud du projectile dans la cible. On peut poursuivre le calcul pour des temps aux environs de $t = 30$ µs où on l'arrête là encore car le pas de temps est très petit.

Sur la figure 16, on voit les résultats dans le cas où l'on suppose que les matériaux ne glissent pas l'un sur l'autre.

Il est évident que les variables de Lagrange sont mal adaptées pour traiter ce genre de problème à cause de l'interface qui prend une forme avec des courbures importantes. C'est la raison pour laquelle une méthode "à grille variable", où le mouvement des seuls points intérieurs peut être différent du mouvement lagrangien, n'apporte pas une amélioration importante.

Par contre, une méthode utilisant les variables d'Euler doit permettre de poursuivre le calcul plus longtemps, à condition que l'interface ne crée pas d'ennuis. C'est pourquoi nous avons choisi d'effectuer un calcul avec une méthode particulaire du type PIC.

Au temps initial on a disposé 36 particules par maille dans le projectile et seulement 16 particules par maille dans la cible. Du fait que les mailles ne se déforment pas on peut utiliser un pas de temps plus grand que dans une méthode lagrangienne.

Sur les figures 17 et 18, on voit les résultats de ce calcul. La figure 17 donne la position des particules à différents temps ; la figure 18 représente les vecteurs vitesse du fluide dans les mailles. Les contours sont tracés à l'aide de particules qui suivent le mouvement mais n'interviennent pas explicitement dans le calcul. Les résultats globaux sont semblables à ceux obtenus en variable de Lagrange, mais on note des différences au niveau de l'interface et des surfaces libres. On remarque que les cylindres ont tendance à se dilater plus que sur le calcul lagrangien. Par ailleurs on voit apparaître des oscillations sur les contours. Cela est dû au traitement peu satisfaisant des surfaces libres par les méthodes particulaires.

Les résultats présentés ici sont le fruit du travail de plusieurs ingénieurs du C.E.A., en particulier Messieurs DESGRAZ et ROUSSEL que je remercie vivement.

DIFFERENTS SYSTEMES de REPERAGE POUR LES CALCULS d'ECOULEMENTS 2D MULTI-MILIEUX

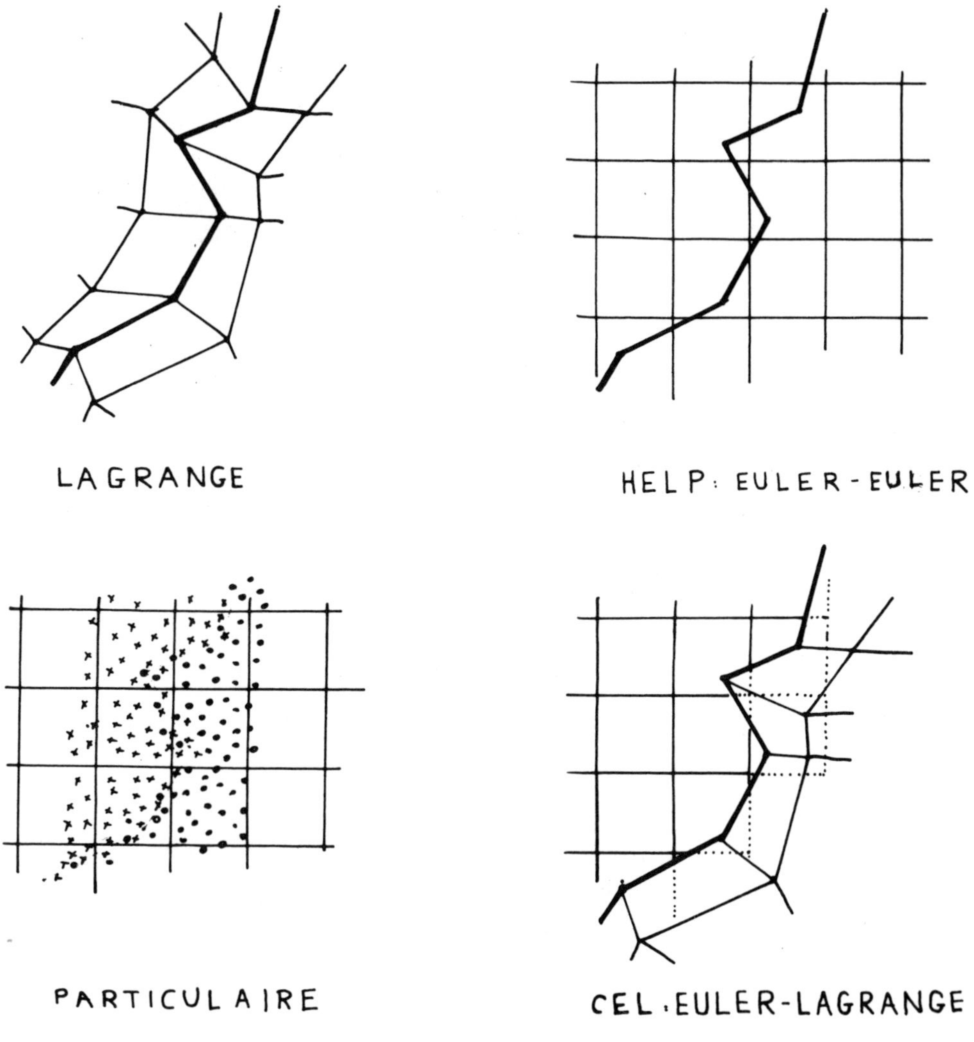

Figure 1

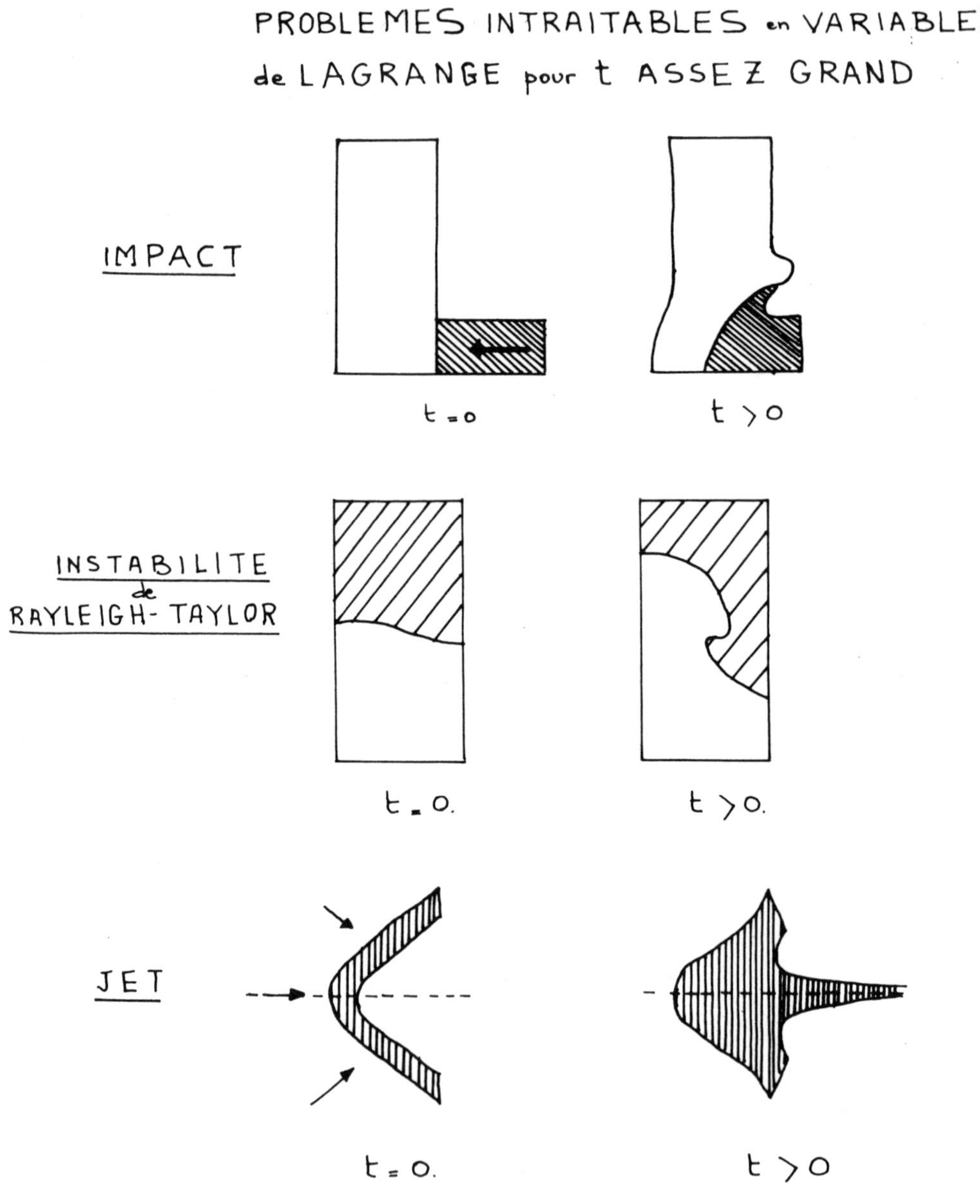
PROBLEMES INTRAITABLES en VARIABLE
de LAGRANGE pour t ASSEZ GRAND
IMPACT
t = o
t > o
INSTABILITE
de
RAYLEIGH-TAYLOR
t = o.
t > o.
JET
t = o.
t > o

Figure 2

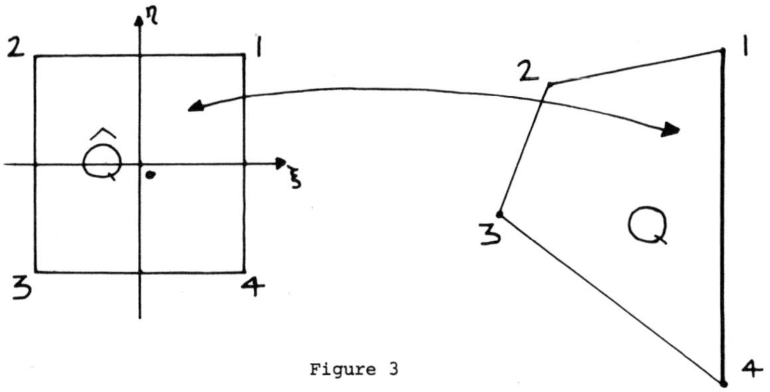

Figure 3

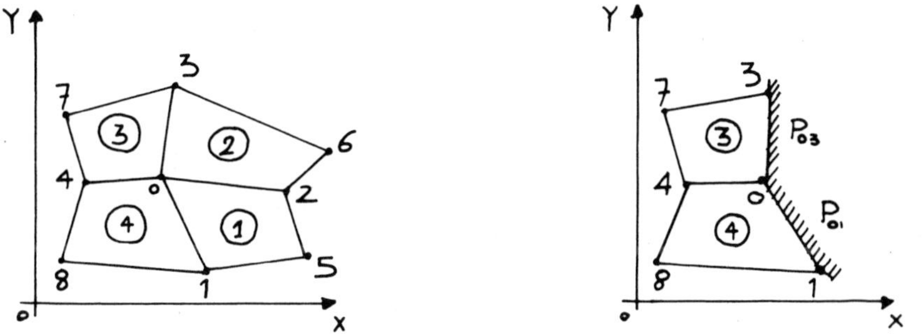

Figure 4

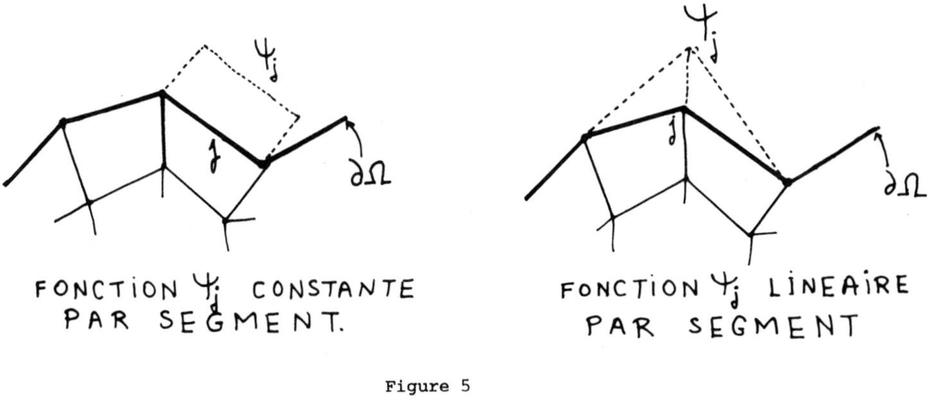

Figure 5

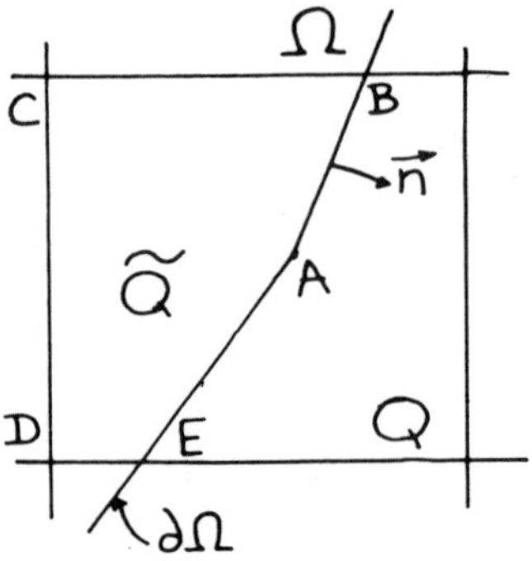

Figure 6

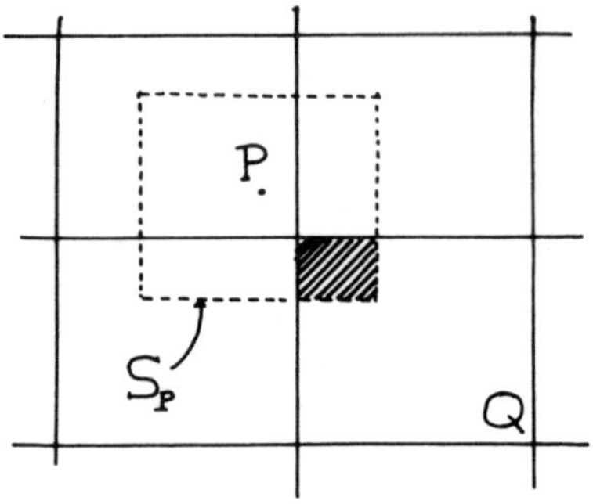

Figure 7

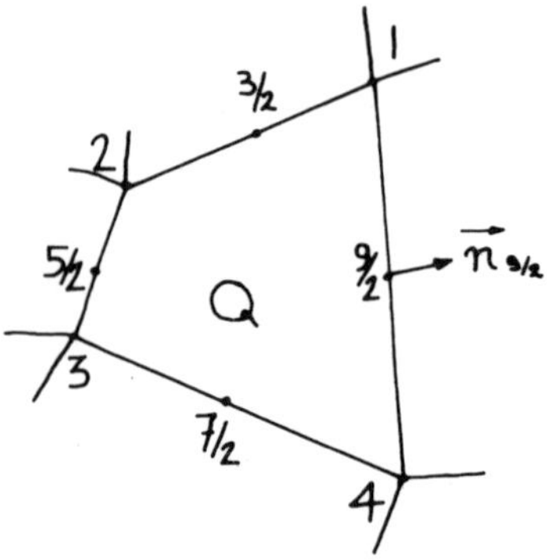

Figure 8

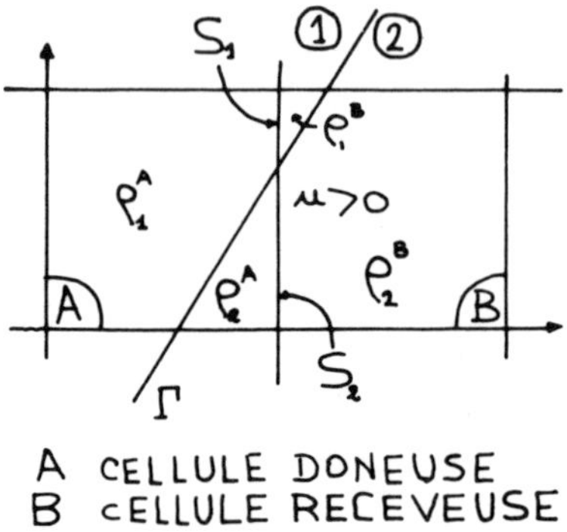

Figure 9

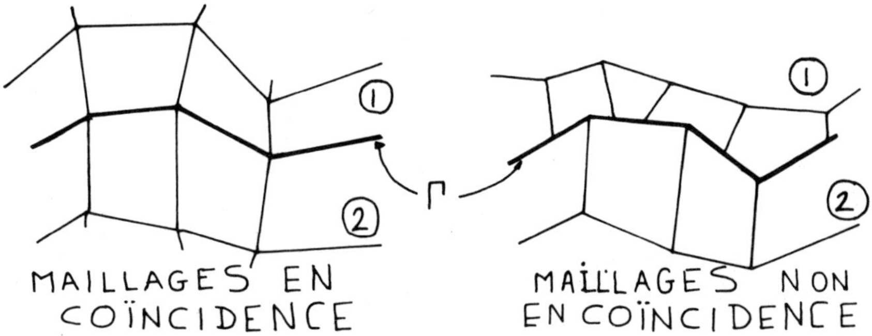

Figure 10

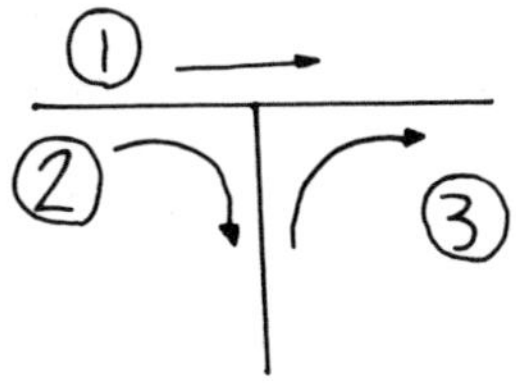

Figure 11

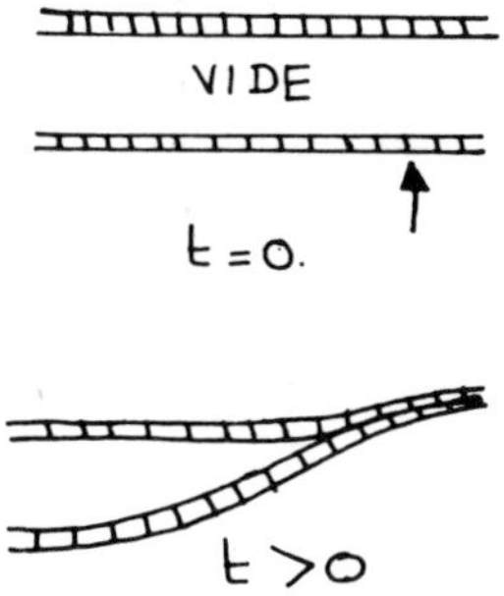

Figure 12

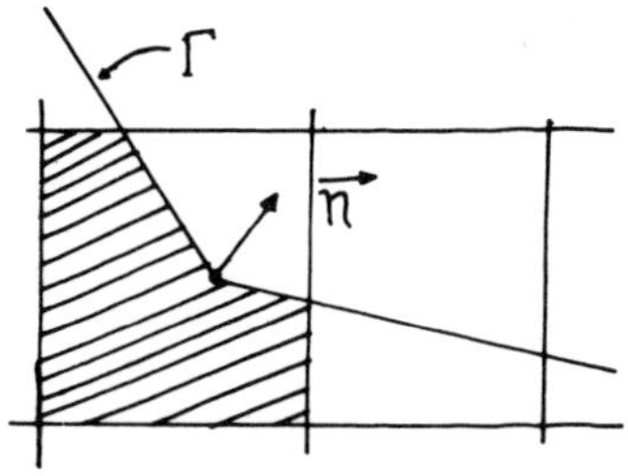

Figure 13

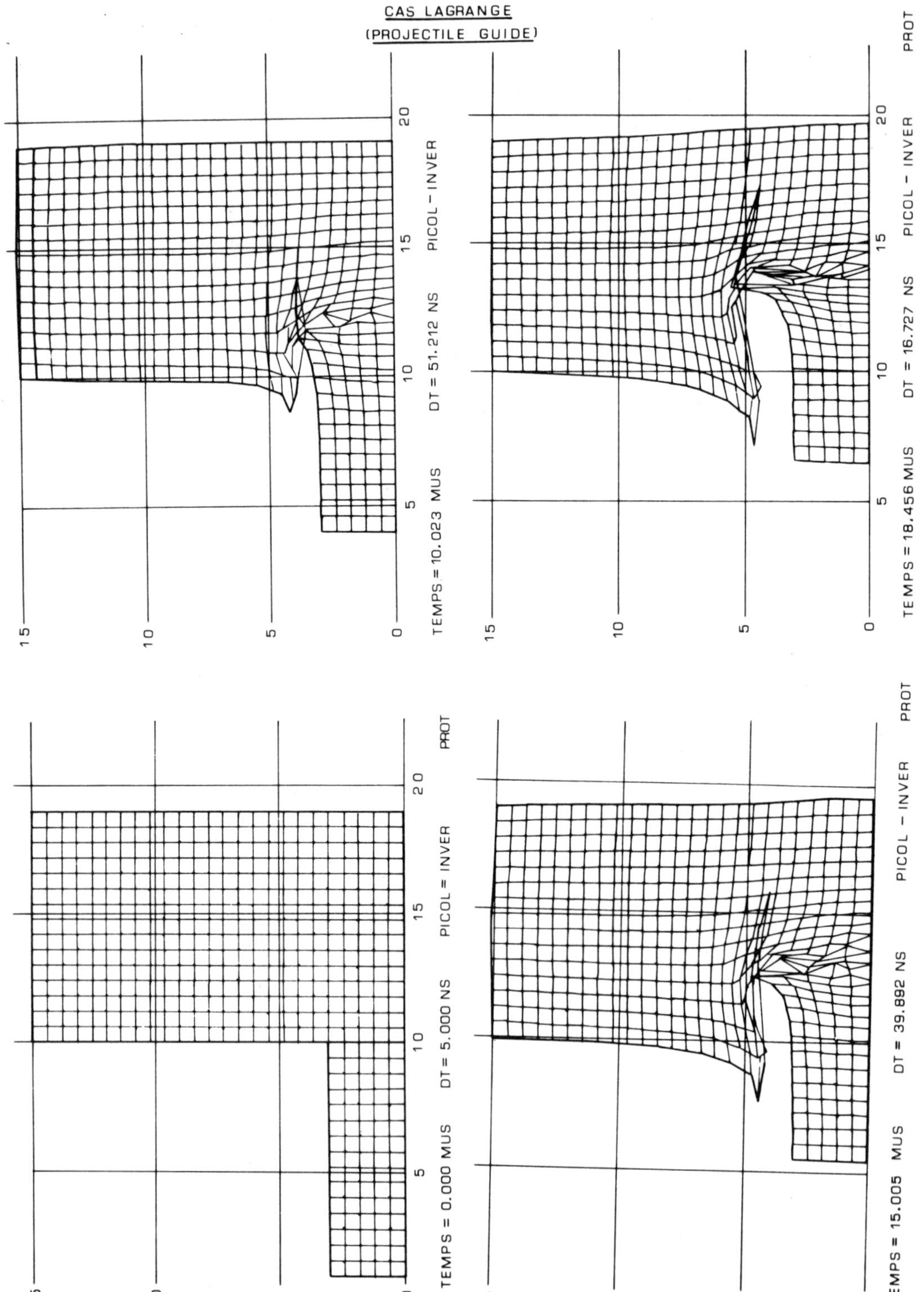
CAS LAGRANGE
(PROJECTILE GUIDE)
TEMPS = 0.000 MUS
DT = 5.000 NS
PICOL = INVER
PROT
TEMPS = 10.023 MUS
DT = 51.212 NS
PICOL - INVER
TEMPS = 15.005 MUS
DT = 39.892 NS
PICOL - INVER
PROT
TEMPS = 18.456 MUS
DT = 16.727 NS
PICOL - INVER
PROT

Figure 14

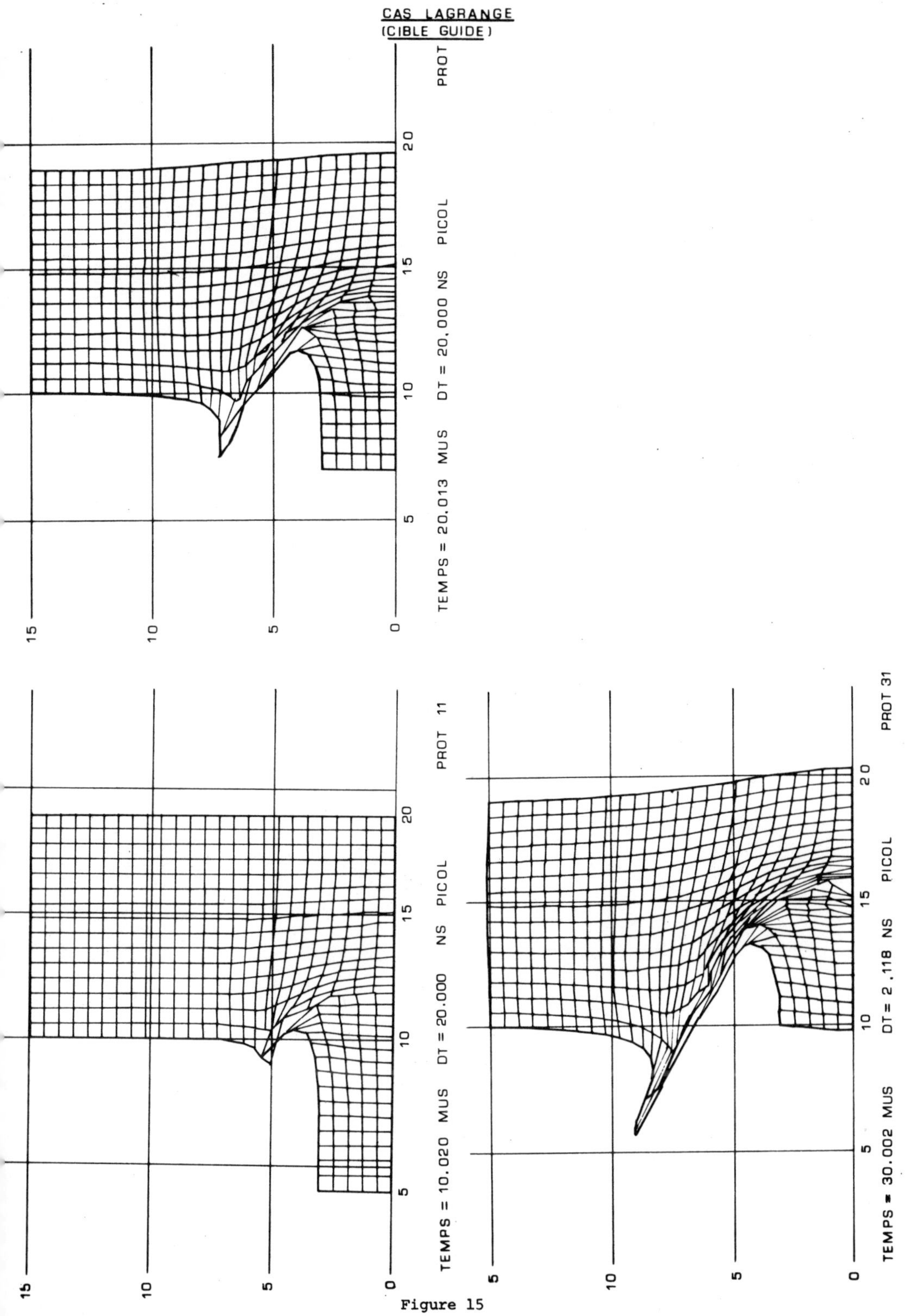
CAS LAGRANGE
(CIBLE GUIDE)
TEMPS = 20.013 MUS DT = 20.000 NS PICOL PROT
TEMPS = 10.020 MUS DT = 20.000 NS PICOL PROT 11
TEMPS = 30.002 MUS DT = 2.118 NS PICOL PROT 31

Figure 15

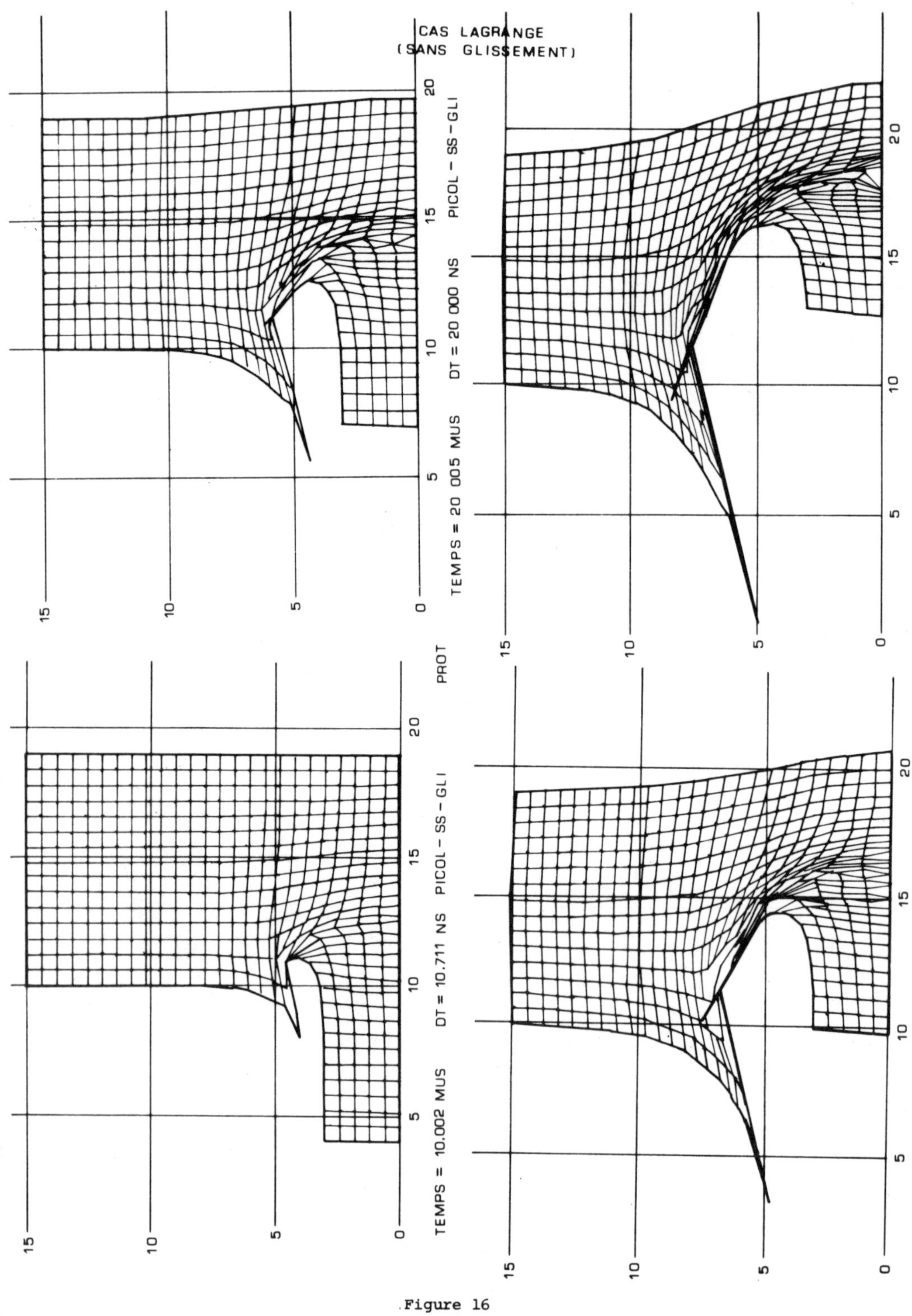

CAS LAGRANGE
(SANS GLISSEMENT)
TEMPS = 10.002 MUS DT = 10.711 NS PICOL - SS - GLI PROT
TEMPS = 20 005 MUS DT = 20 000 NS PICOL - SS - GLI
TEMPS = 30.004 MUS DT = 12.722 NS PICOLI - SS - GLI PROT 31
TEMPS = 40.002 MUS DT = 6.499 NS PICOL - SS - GIL PROT41

Figure 16

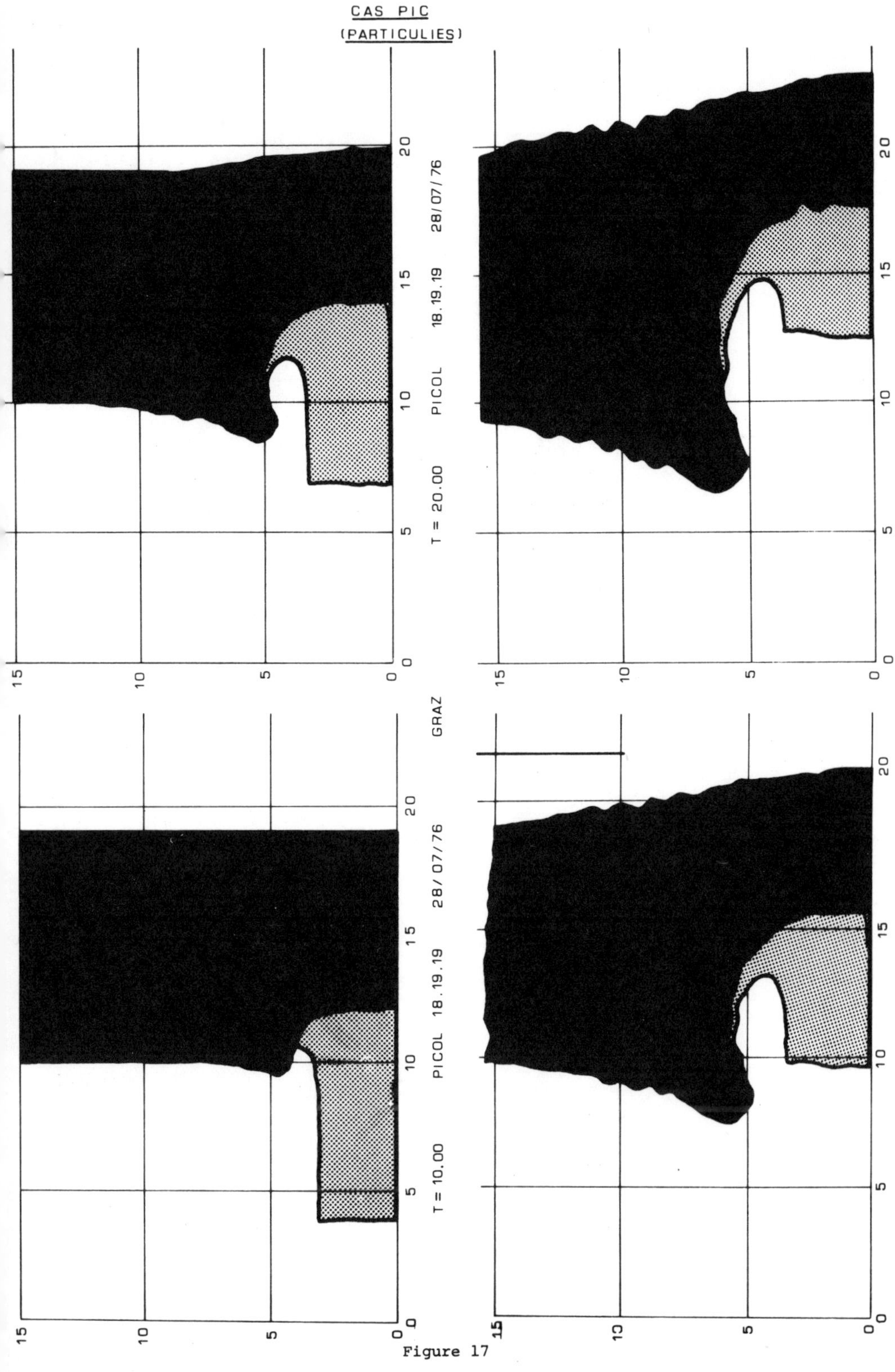
CAS PIC
(PARTICULIES)
T = 10.00 PICOL 18.19.19 28/07/76 GRAZ
T = 20.00 PICOL 18.19.19 28/07/76
T = 30.00 PICOL 18.19.19 28/07/76 GRAZ
T = 40.00 PICOL 18.19.19 28/07/76

Figure 17

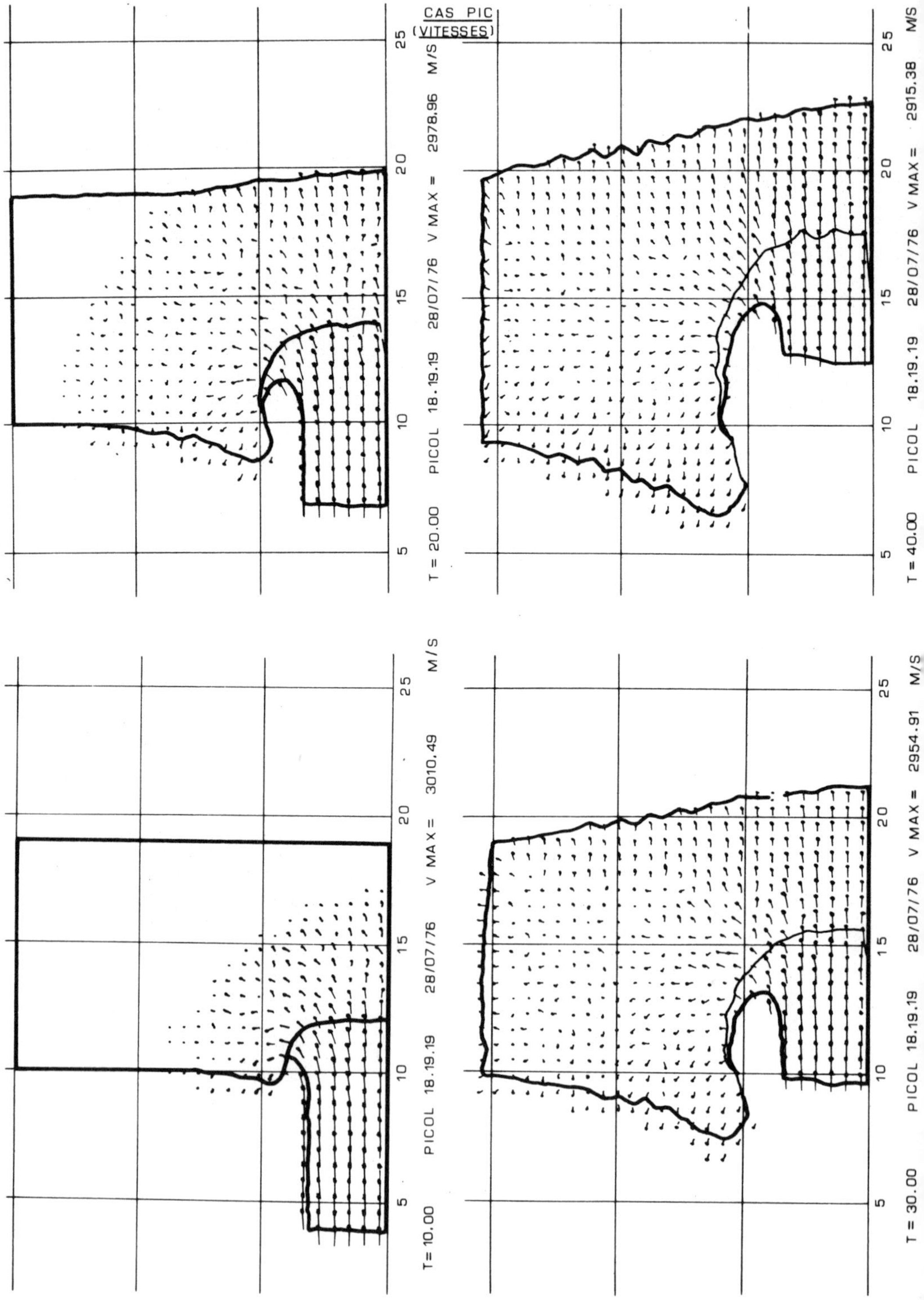
CAS PIC
(VITESSES)
T = 20.00 PICOL 18.19.19 28/07/76 V MAX = 2978.96 M/S
T = 40.00 PICOL 18.19.19 28/07/76 V MAX = 2915.38 M/S
T= 10.00 PICOL 18.19.19 28/07/76 V MAX= 3010.49 M/S
T = 30.00 PICOL 18.19.19 28/07/76 V MAX = 2954.91 M/S
5
10
15
20
25

Figure 18

BIBLIOGRAPHIE

[1] - T. BELYTSCHKO - "Non Linear Analysis Descriptions and Numerical Stability" to appear in Computer Programs in Shock and Vibration.

[2] - R.D. RICHTMYER and K.W. MORTON - "Differences methods for initial value problems" - Interscience publishers (1967).

[3] - P.A. RAVIART - communication privée.

[4] - A.A. AMSDEN and C.W. HIRT - "YAQUI an arbitrary lagrangian eulerian computer program for fluid flow at all speeds" - Los Alamos Scientific Laboratory - report LA 5100 (1973).

[5] - L.J. HAGEMAN and J.M. WALSH - "An eulerian code for transient compressible elastoplastic flow in 2D" - BRL contract report n° 39 3SR-350.

[6] - W.F. NOH - "CEL a time dependant two space dimensional coupled Eulerian Lagrangian code" in Method in Computational Physics - Vol. 3 (1964) Academic Press.

[7] - A.A. AMSDEN - "The particle in cell method for the calculation of the dynamics of compressible fluids" - Los Alamos Scientific Laboratory - report LA 3466 (1966).

[8] - B.M. MARDER - "GAP - A PIC - type fluid code" - Math. of Comput. Vol. 29 n° 130 (april 1975) pp. 434-446.

[9] - W.B. GOAD - "WAT a numerical method for 2D unsteady fluid flow" - Los Alamos Scientific Laboratory - report LAMS 2365 (1960).

[10] - M.L. WILKINS - "Calculation of elastic plastic flow" in Method in Computational Physics - Vol. 3 (1964) Academic Press.

[11] - A. JOUANICOU - "Discrétisation spatiale de l'équation de conservation de la quantité de mouvement dans un solide élastique" - CEA publication interne.

[12] - S.L. HANCOCK - "Finite difference equations for PISCES 2 DELK" - TCAM 76-2 - Physics International Compagny.

[13] - P. CIARLET and P.A. RAVIART - "Interpolation theory over curved elements with application to the finite element method" - Comp. Math. Appl. Mech. Eng. - vol. 1 (1972) pp 217-249.

[14] - C.W. HIRT, J.L. COOK and T.D. BUTLER - "A Lagrangian method for calculating the dynamics of an incompressible fluid with free surface" - J. Comput. Physics - Vol. 5 (1970) pp 103-124.

......

[15] - F.H. HARLOW and A.A. AMSDEN - "Multi fluid flow calculation at all mach numbers" - J. Compt. Physics - Vol. 16 (1974) pp 1-19.

[16] - J.C. DESGRAZ et P.M. LASCAUX - "Stabilité de la discrétisation des équations de l'hydrodynamique lagrangienne 2D" - Colloque IRIA à Versailles (décembre 1975) - à paraitre dans Lecture Notes in Computer Sciences - Springer Verlag.

[17] - P.M. LASCAUX - "Numerical methods for time dependent equations - applications to fluid flow problems" - TIFR Lectures on mathematics and physics n° 52 (Bombay).

[18] - P.D. LAX and B. WENDROFF - "System of conservation laws" - Comm. Pure Appl. Math. - Vol. 13 (1969) pp 217-237.

[19] - A. KASAHARA - "On certain finite difference methods fluid dynamics" - U.S. Monthly Weather Review - Vol. 93 (1965) pp 27-31.

[20] - K.V. ROBERTS and W.O. WEISS - "Convective differences schemes" - Math. of Comput. - Vol. 20 (1966) pp 272-229.

[21] - J.P. BORIS and D.L. BOOK - "Flux corrected transport III minimal error FCT algorithms" - J. Comput. Physics - Vol. 20 (1976) pp 397-431.

[22] - P. CORNILLE - "Méthodes d'hydrodynamique à grille variable" - CEA publication interne.

[23] - J.C. BONIFACIO - "Etude d'une nouvelle formulation du glissement" - CEA publication interne.

[24] - M. RICH - "A method for Eulerian fluid dynamics" - Los Alamos Scientific Laboratory - report LAMS 2826 (1963).

[25] - H. BOUCHON, P. CALLEJA et J.C. DESGRAZ - "Application de la méthode de Noh à l'intégration des équations de l'hydrodynamique 2D"- CEA publication interne.

ON PROJECTION METHODS FOR THE PLATE PROBLEM

Joachim A. Nitsche

The model of the clamped plate is considered in order to illustrate the finite element method.

0. Introduction

The aim of this paper is to discuss from the mathematical viewpoint some typical features of what is called 'finite element method'. We will restrict ourselves to the plate problem: Let $\Omega \subseteq R^2$ be a bounded domain with boundary $\partial\Omega$ (for simplicity we assume $\partial\Omega$ sufficiently smooth). The deflection $u(x,y)$ of an elastic clamped plate covering Ω under the load $f(x,y)$ is the solution of the boundary value problem

$$(1) \qquad \begin{aligned} \Delta^2 u &= f \quad \text{in} \quad \Omega \ , \\ u = u_n &= 0 \quad \text{on} \quad \partial\Omega \ . \end{aligned}$$

Here Δ^2 is the biharmonic operator and u_n denotes the normal derivative.

If (1.1) is multiplied by a function v satisfying the same boundary conditions (1.2) and integrated over Ω then partial integration gives

$$(2) \qquad (\Delta u, \Delta v) = (f, v)$$

with $(.,.)$ being the inner L_2-product

$$(3) \qquad (v,w) = \iint_\Omega vw \, dx \, dy \quad .$$

Because of the identity

$$(4) \qquad \iint_\Omega \{u_{xx} v_{yy} + u_{yy} v_{xx} - 2 u_{xy} v_{xy}\} \, dx \, dy = 0$$

for any two functions u,v satisfying (1.2) relation (2) is equivalent to

$$(5) \qquad a(u,v) = (f,v)$$

with

$$(6) \qquad a(u,v) := \iint_\Omega \{u_{xx} v_{xx} + 2u_{xy} v_{xy} + u_{yy} v_{yy}\} \, dx \, dy \quad .$$

The 'variational equation' (2) resp. (5) is the starting point for the finite element method : Let S_h be a proper approximating space fulfilling the boundary conditions (1.2). An approximation $u_h \in S_h$ on the solution of (1) is defined by

$$(7) \qquad a(u_h, \chi) = (f, \chi) \qquad \text{for} \quad \chi \in S_h \quad .$$

This is the classical Ritz-method. In practical applications two types of difficulties arise:

1) for general domains the construction of approximation spaces fulfilling the boundary conditions will be hard,

ii) the defining relation (7) affords - at least in a weak sense - the existence of second derivatives of the elements in S_h which will be cumbersome.

In Section 1 we will give the precise formulation of equation (5) combined with some notational remarks and the definition of finite-element-spaces. Section 2 is devoted to the Ritz-method and Sections 3 to 5 give certain generalizations.

1. Notations, Finite Elements

In the following $H_k = W_2^k(\Omega)$ denotes the Sobolev-space of functions having generalized, square-integrable derivatives up to order k (see AGMON [1]) and $\|\cdot\|_k$ the corresponding norm. $\overset{\circ}{H}_k$ is the closure of the C^∞-functions with compact support in Ω under this norm.

In addition we will use the abbreviations

$$\text{(8)}\qquad \begin{aligned} < v,w > &= \oint_{\partial\Omega} vw \, ds \quad , \\ |v| &= < v,v >^{1/2} \quad . \end{aligned}$$

The precise definition of a 'weak' solution u of the boundary value problem (1) is:

i) u is an element of $\overset{\circ}{H}_2$,
ii) (5) holds for all $v \in \overset{\circ}{H}_2$.

Finite elements to be used as approximation spaces S_h are constructed in the following way: Let Γ_h be a subdivision of Ω into generalized triangles Δ - respective squares which will be considered in Section 4 - i.e. Δ is a triangle if $\Delta \cap \partial\Omega$ consists of at most one point and otherwise one side may be curved. Throughout the paper we will restrict ourselves to $\varkappa$-regular triangulations: for any $\Delta \in \Gamma_h$ there are two circles with radii $\varkappa^{-1}h$ and

κh contained in Δ resp. containing Δ . In this way the parameter h is a measure of the width of Γ_h .

The 'finite-element'-space S_h consists of all functions whose restriction to any $\Delta \in \Gamma_h$ is a polynomial of a - fixed - degree less than t . Moreover, continuity up to an order $s-1$ may be imposed: Then we say that S_h is of class (s.t) . The typical approximation properties of these finite elements are (see AZIZ-BABUŠKA [3], pp.83-110):

Let $v \in H_k$ $(k \leq t)$ be given. Then there exists an element $\chi \in S_h$ according to

$$\|v-\chi\|_l \leq c\; h^{k-l} \|v\|_k \tag{9}$$

for $l = 0,1,\dots, \text{Min}\,(s,k)$.

Correspondingly the functions of S_h satisfy Bernstein-type inequalities:

For $l \leq s-1$ and $\chi \in S_h$ inverse relations

$$\|\chi\|_{l+1} \leq c\; h^{-1}\; \|\chi\|_l \tag{10}$$

hold true.

Here c depends on the regularity parameter κ and the degree t .

Here and in the following c denotes a numerical constant which may be different at different places.

In order to have $S_h \subseteq H_1$ only continuity, i.e. $s = 1$, is needed. The construction of S_h is then quite simple and t may be any integer ≥ 2 . For $S_h \subseteq H_2$ continuity of the first derivatives $(s = 2)$ is needed. As was shown by BRAMBLE-ZLAMAL the choice $t \geq 6$ is possible (for the case $t = 5$ see SCOTT [14].

If the boundary $\partial\Omega$ is not a polygon the functions of

S_h will not vanish on $\partial\Omega$ resp. have a zero-normal derivative unless they are identical zero in a strip along $\partial\Omega$ of width proportional to h. In this case the subspace $\overset{\circ}{S}_h = S_h \cap \overset{\circ}{H}_2$ would not fulfill the wanted approximation properties (9). As was shown by CIARLET-RAVIART [7] and ZLAMAL [15] this can be overcome by 'isoparametric' modifications in the curved triangles, we will not give the details here.

2. The Ritz-Method

In this section let S_h denote the quintic Bramble-Zlamal elements with isoparametric modifications such that $S_h \subseteq \overset{\circ}{H}_2$ and (9), (10) holds with $s = 2$, $t = 6$. Let further u_h be defined by (7). Since the exact solution satisfies the same relation we get the defining equation

$$(11) \qquad a(e,\chi) = 0 \qquad \text{for} \quad \chi \in S_h$$

for the error

$$(12) \qquad e = e_h = u - u_h \quad .$$

With an appropriate approximation $U_h \in S_h$ on u we use the splitting

$$(13) \qquad \begin{aligned} e &= \varepsilon - \Phi \,, \\ \varepsilon &= u - U_h \,, \quad \Phi = u_h - U_h \quad . \end{aligned}$$

Obviously we have $\Phi \in S_h$ and therefore we get from (11) with $\chi = \Phi$

$$(14) \qquad a(\Phi,\Phi) = a(\Phi,\varepsilon) \quad .$$

In $\overset{\circ}{H}_2$ the quadratic form $a(v,v)$ is positive definite and equivalent to the square of the 2-norm, i.e. (with a constant $c > 0$)

(15) $c^{-1}\|v\|_2^2 \le a(v,v) \le c\|v\|_2^2$ for $v \in \overset{\circ}{H}_2$.

Because of $a(\Phi,\varepsilon) \le a(\Phi,\Phi)^{1/2}\, a(\varepsilon,\varepsilon)^{1/2}$ we come from (14) with (15) to

(16) $$\|\Phi\|_2 \le c\|\varepsilon\|_2 \quad .$$

Using the fact that $U_h \in S_h$ is arbitrary and $\|e\|_2 \le \|\varepsilon\|_2 + \|\Phi\|_2$ (16) leads to

(17) $$\|e\|_2 \le c \inf_{\chi\in S_h} \|u-\chi\|_2 \quad .$$

For $u \in H_k$ $(2 \le k \le 6)$ this gives the qualitative error estimate

(18) $$\|e\|_2 \le c\, h^{k-2}\|u\|_k \quad .$$

By the now standard duality argument (see AUBIN [2] , NITSCHE [9]) in the L_2-norm the improved convergence-order

(19) $$\|e\|_0 \le c\, h^k\|u\|_k$$

can be shown. If moreover the k-th derivatives are in $L_p(1 \le p \le \infty)$ then the error in L_p has the same behavior

(20) $$\|e\|_{L_p} \le c\, h^k\|u\|_{W_p^k} \quad .$$

This can be proved by means of the method of weighted norms as was done in detail for the second order case and the L_2-projection in NITSCHE [11], [12].

3. Boundary-Modifications

In this section we still will consider the quintic Bramble-Zlamal elements but without isoparametric modifications. In two dimensions a quintic polynomial has 21 degrees of freedom. If the values of the function and the derivatives up to order 2 are prescribed in the knots of the triangulation then in each triangle 18 parameters are fixed. The remaining are given by the normal derivatives in the midpoints of the edges. This choice guarantees continuity of the first derivatives and so $S_h \subseteq H_2$. Now we impose in the knots on the boundary the conditions (the index 's' denotes tangential derivation)

(21) $$\chi = \chi_s = \chi_{ss} = \chi_n = 0$$

and in the midpoints on the boundary

(22) $$\chi_n = 0 \quad .$$

Let $\overset{\circ}{S}_h$ be the restricted subspace of S_h . For curved elements then χ will not vanish on $\partial\Omega$ but has 'nearly zero' boundary values. It turns out that for any $\chi \in \overset{\circ}{S}_h$

(23) $$\begin{aligned} |\chi| &\leq c\ h^{5/2}\|\chi\|_2 \quad , \\ |\chi_n| &\leq c\ h^{3/2}\|\chi\|_2 \quad . \end{aligned}$$

A possible approximation on u is now given by the same relation (7) as in Section 2 but now with the space $\overset{\circ}{S}_h$.

The approximation is unique since the form $a(.,.)$ is positive definite not only in $\overset{\circ}{H}_2$ but also in $\overset{\circ}{S}_h$. The convergence-properties of this method are not as good as of the method of Section 2. In order to understand this let us for simplicity replace the form $a(v.w)$ by the - in $\overset{\circ}{H}_2$ equivalent - form $(\Delta v, \Delta w)$. Partial integration gives for the right hand side of (7)

(24) $$\begin{aligned} (f,\chi) &= (\Delta^2 u, \chi) \\ &= (\Delta u, \Delta\chi) + \langle \Delta u_n, \chi\rangle - \langle \Delta u, \chi_n\rangle \quad . \end{aligned}$$

If therefore u_h is defined by

$$(\Delta u_h, \Delta\chi) = (f,\chi) \qquad \text{for} \quad \chi \in \overset{\circ}{S}_h$$

then the error $e = u - u_h$ solves

(25) $$(\Delta e, \Delta\chi) = \langle\Delta u, \chi_n\rangle - \langle\Delta u_n, \chi\rangle \quad .$$

While the defining relation (11) of the first method is homogenuous in e we have now inhomogenuous terms in (25), such methods are called 'nonconforming'. The corresponding error in the 2-norm admits the estimate - compare with (18) -

(26) $$\|e\|_2 \le c\ h^m \|u\|_k$$

with

(27) $$m = \text{Min}\ (k-2,\ 3/2) \quad .$$

Also in the L_2-norm only a reduced convergence order is valid.

By adding appropriate boundary terms it is possible to improve the convergence rate of the method. Let us define the bilinear form

(26) $$\begin{aligned}\tilde{a}(v.w) = (\Delta v, \Delta w) + \langle\Delta v_n, w\rangle + \langle v, \Delta w_n\rangle - \\ - \langle\Delta v, w_n\rangle - \langle v_n, \Delta w\rangle \quad ,\end{aligned}$$

and the approximation $u_h \in \overset{\circ}{S}_h$ by

(27) $$\tilde{a}(u_h, \chi) = (f,\chi) \qquad \text{for} \quad \chi \in \overset{\circ}{S}_h \quad .$$

The error of this method obeys similar to (11)

(28) $$\tilde{a}(e.\chi) = 0 \qquad \text{for} \quad \chi \in \overset{\circ}{S}_h$$

and the estimates (18), (20) hold.

4. Reduced Regularity

As mentioned in the introduction and illustrated in Section 1 the construction of subspaces $S_h \subseteq H_2$ gives rise to difficulties. We will restrict ourselves here to one example of a space S_h not contained in H_2 but still suitable for the plate problem, and refer for more details to CIARLET [6]. Let for simplicity Ω be the unit square and Γ_h be a subdivision into squares of side length h . The elements to be discussed here - see CIARLET [6] - consist of those functions whose restriction to any sub-square is a linear-combination of a cubic polynomial and the two terms x^3y and xy^3 . In addition continuity up to the order 2 in the meshpoints is assumed. The so defined space S_h is in H_1 but not in H_2. The form $a(.,.)$ has to be extended in order to use (7). The simplest way is to take

$$(29)\quad a'(r,w) = \sum_{\square\in\Gamma_h} \iint_{\square} \{v_{xx}w_{xx} + 2v_{xy}w_{xy} + v_{yy}w_{yy}\}\, dx\, dy\ .$$

As it turns out the continuity of the second derivatives in the gridpoints of the functions in S_h are strong enough such that the form $a'(.,.)$ is positive definite in S_h . Referring to NITSCHE [10] for the details in the L_2-norm the error can be estimated by

$$(30)\qquad \|e\|_0 \leq c\ h^3 \|u\|_4 \quad .$$

5. Hybrid Methods

The method discussed here is due to CIARLET-RAVIART [8] , see also BREZZI [5] and SCHOLZ [13].

By introducing $v = -\Delta u$ as a new function the fourth order problem (1) can be written as a system of two second order equations

$$(31)\qquad \begin{aligned} -\Delta u &= v \\ -\Delta v &= f \\ u = u_n &= 0 \end{aligned} \qquad \begin{aligned} &\text{in } \Omega \\ &\text{on } \partial\Omega \quad . \end{aligned}$$

Now we multiply (31.1) with an arbitrary function $w \in H_1$ and integrate over Ω . Since $u_n = 0$ partial integration gives

$$(32)\qquad D(u,w) = (v,w)$$

with $D(.,.)$ being the Dirichlet integral

$$(33)\quad D(u,w) = \iint_{\Omega} \{u_x w_x + u_y w_y\}\, dx\, dy \quad .$$

The corresponding relation

$$(34)\qquad D(v,z) = (f,z)$$

comes from (31.2) but now only for $z \in \overset{\circ}{H}_1$ since v does not fulfill any boundary condition. (32), (34) lead to:

The pair $(u, v = -\Delta u)$ with u being the solution of (1) satisfies $u \in \overset{\circ}{H}_1$, $v \in H_1$ and

$$(35)\qquad \begin{aligned} D(u,w) &= (v,w) \quad \text{for } w \in H_1 \quad , \\ D(v,z) &= (f,z) \quad \text{for } z \in \overset{\circ}{H}_1 \quad . \end{aligned}$$

It is easy to see that $(u,v) \in \overset{\circ}{H}_1 \times H_1$ is uniquely defined by (35). It is sufficient to show that $u = v = 0$ is the only solution in case $f = 0$. From (35.2) we would then get with $z = u$

$$(36)\qquad D(u,v) = 0$$

and then from (35.1) with $w = v$

(37) $$\|v\|^2 = 0 \quad ,$$

i.e. v vanishes. Now the choice $w = u$ gives

(38) $$D(u,u) = 0$$

and since the square root of the Dirichlet integral is a norm in $\overset{\circ}{H}_1$ we get also $u = 0$.

The idea of a hybrid method is now to choose two subspaces $S_h \subset H_1$ and $\overset{\circ}{S}_h \subset \overset{\circ}{H}_1$ and to define an approximation $(u_h, v_h) \in \overset{\circ}{S}_h \times S_h$ on the pair $(u, v = -\Delta u)$ by means of the relations.

(39) $$\begin{aligned} D(u_h,\chi) &= (v_h,\chi) \qquad \text{for} \quad \chi \in S_h \quad , \\ D(v_h,\varphi) &= (f,\varphi) \qquad \text{for} \quad \varphi \in \overset{\circ}{S}_h \quad . \end{aligned}$$

Under reasonable conditions on $\overset{\circ}{S}_h$ and S_h - f.i. $\overset{\circ}{S}_h \subseteq S_h$ - the pair (u_h, v_h) is unique.

The advantage of this method is that the subspaces S_h, $\overset{\circ}{S}_h$ must be only in H_1 resp. $\overset{\circ}{H}_1$ and not any longer in $\overset{\circ}{H}_2$. As a typical example for the behavior of the error let us take for S_h cubic finite elements and for $\overset{\circ}{S}_h$ the corresponding isoparametric modification in order to have $\overset{\circ}{S}_h \subseteq \overset{\circ}{H}_1$. Then asymptotic error estimates

(40) $$\begin{aligned} \|u-u_h\| &\leq c\ h^4 \|u\|_4 \\ \|v-v_h\| &\leq c\ h^2 \|u\|_4 \end{aligned}$$

hold.

For completeness we mention that also here corresponding L_p-estimates are available. Similarily the idea of nearly-zero boundary values and the modification as discussed in Section 3 can be applied also for this method.

Literature

[1] AGMON, S.: Lectures on elliptic boundary value problems, Toronto-New York-London: D. van Nostrand Comp., Inc., 1965

[2] AUBIN, J.P.: Approximation des espaces de distributions et des operateurs differentiels. Bull. Soc. Math. France Mem. 12, 1-139 (1967)

[3] AZIZ, A.K., BABUSKA, I.: The mathematical foundations of the finite element method with applications to partial differential equations. Academic Press 1972

[4] BRAMBLE, J.H., ZLAMAL, M.: Triangular elements in the finite element method. Math. of Comp. 24, 809-820 (1970)

[5] BREZZI, F.: On the existence, uniqueness and approximation of saddle-point problems arising from Lagrangian multipliers. R.A.I.R.O. R-2, 129-151 (1974)

[6] CIARLET, P.G.: Conforming and nonconforming finite element methods for solving the plate problem. In: Conf. Numerical Sol. Differential Equations. Ed. G.A. Watson. Univ. Dundee, July 3-6, 1973. Berlin-Heidelberg-New York: Springer-Verlag, 21-31, 1974

[7] CIARLET, P.G., RAVIART, P.A.: Interpolation theory over curved elements with applications to finite element methods. Comp. Methods in Appl. Mech. and Eng. 1, 217-249, (1972)

[8] CIARLET, P.G., RAVIART, P.A.: A mixed finite element method for the biharmonic equation. In: In: Mathematical Aspects of Finite Elements in Partial Differential Equations. Ed. C. de Boor. Proc. Symp. Math. Res. Center, Univ. Wisconsin, April 1-3, 1974. New York-San Francisco-London: Academic Press, 125-145 (1974)

[9] NITSCHE, J.A.:Ein Kriterium für die Quasi-Optimalität des Ritzschen Verfahrens. Num. Math. 11, 346-348 (1968)

[10] NITSCHE, J.A.: Convergence of nonconforming methods. Proceedings of a Symposium on Mathematical Aspects of Finite Elements in Partial Differential Equations, Madison, Wisc., April 1974, Academic Press, Inc., 15-53 (1974)

[11] NITSCHE, J.A.: L_∞-Convergence of Finite Element Approximation.
2nd Conference on Finite Elements, Rennes 1975

[12] NITSCHE, J.A.: Über L_∞-Abschätzungen von Projektionen auf finite Elemente.
Bonner Mathematische Schriften Nr.89, Tagungsband des Sonderforschungsbereiches 72, 13-30 (1976)

[13] SCHOLZ, R.: Approximation von Sattelpunkten mit finiten Elementen.
Bonner Mathematische Schriften Nr.89, Tagungsband des Sonderforschungsbereiches 72, 53-66 (1976)

[14] SCOTT, R.: C^1 continuity via constraints for 4th order problems.
Proceedings of a Symposium on Mathematical Aspects of Finite Elements in Partial Differential Equations, Madison, Wisc., April 1974,
Academic Press, Inc., 171-193 (1974)

[15] ZLAMAL, M.: Curved element in the finite element method.
SIAM J. Numer. Anal., Part I: 10, 229-240 (1973),
SIAM J. Numer. Anal., Part II: 11, 347-362 (1974).

Joachim A. Nitsche
Institut für Angewandte Mathematik
Albert-Ludwigs-Universität
Hermann-Herder-Str.10
7800 Freiburg
Federal Republic of Germany

MULTIEXPONENTIAL FITTING METHODS

H.Niessner

Brown Boveri & Co.Ltd
Baden

Abstract:

Some methods for multiexponential fitting or approximation by sums of exponentials are shortly discussed, together with an adaptation of two of them to a practical problem related to positive sums of exponentials.

1.) Formulation of the problem

For the design of electrical components it is often necessary to forecast the rise in temperature due to electrical losses in resistances at critical points. These losses may vary with time. In many cases electrical analogues are used consisting of several RC networks in series (see fig.1)

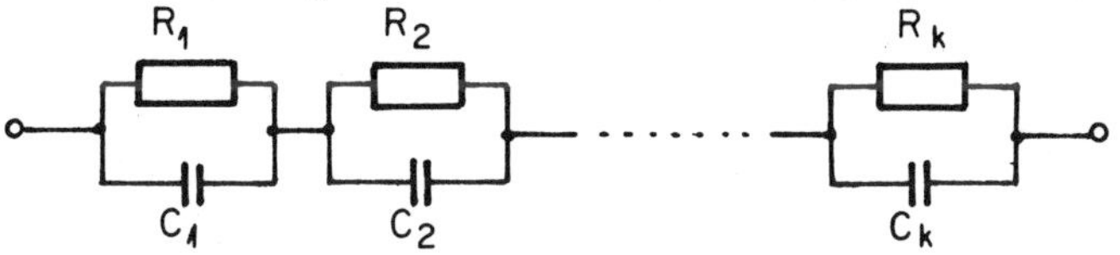

Fig. 1

Resistances R_ν and capacitances C_ν are determined from heating curves, describing the development of temperature Z(t) with time t after switching on a constant electrical current equivalent to a thermal current of unit intensity.

Switching on in fig.1 at t=0 a constant current of unit intensity leads to a voltage at time t of

$$f_k(t) = \sum_{\nu=1}^{k} R_\nu (1 - e^{-t/\tau_\nu}) \qquad (1.1)$$

where

$$\tau_\nu = R_\nu C_\nu \qquad (1.2)$$

is the time constant of RC network ν. Obviously for R_ν and C_ν only positive values are considered.

The problem is to determine resistances and time constants

$$R_1, \tau_1, R_2, \tau_2, \ldots, R_k, \tau_k \qquad (1.3)$$

with a number k of terms as small as possible, so that the difference $f_k(t) - Z(t)$ remains satisfactorily small for arbitrary $t \geq 0$. Thereby the constraints

$$R_\nu > 0 \quad \text{and} \quad \tau_\nu > 0 \qquad (\nu = 1,2,..,k) \quad (1.4)$$

must be observed. Usually the heating curve is defined by a certain number of experimentally determined points.

If $Z(\infty)$ is known, one can reduce the problem to fitting a "positive" sum of exponentials (positive because the coefficients R_ν of the exponential terms are positive)

$$\bar{f}_k(t)=\sum_{\nu=1}^{k} R_\nu e^{-t/\tau_\nu} \qquad (R_\nu>0) \tag{1.5}$$

to the function

$$\bar{Z}(t)=Z(\infty)-Z(t) \tag{1.6}$$

The general form of a sum of exponentials is

$$E(\vec{c},\vec{\lambda};t)=\sum_{\nu=1}^{l}\sum_{\mu=0}^{k_\nu-1} c_{\nu\mu} t^{\mu} e^{\lambda_\nu t} \tag{1.7}$$

where $c_{\nu\mu}$ are called the coefficients and λ_ν the exponents or "frequencies". Frequently coefficients and exponents are supposed to be real.

The next sections are devoted to the discussion of some methods of fitting sums of exponentials to prescribed data points or functions. Since determination of the coefficients for known exponents leads to the well known problem of fitting linear forms, the more difficult problem of adjusting the exponents will be emphasized. The problem of analyzing heating curves will be returned to in the last two sections.

2.) Collocation on equidistant points

A method already mentioned by De Prony (1) is discussed in Lanczos' book (2). Using 2k equidistant points with a spacing as large as possible, the coefficients of a linear difference equation are calculated. From the k roots of its characteristic polynomial the exponents can be determined. For theoretical reasons the method may be used for general sums of exponentials. In practical computations, however, it suffers from considerable numerical difficulties, particularly in case of data with experimental errors.

Obviously, sums of exponentials with real exponents are not well defined by equidistant points. They are better defined by points which are close together for small values of t and widespread for large values of t. This is the case, for instance, with points which are equidistant with respect to log t.

An elegant solution with the aid of the qd-algorithm is given by Rutishauser (3)(decomposition of the z-transform into partial fractions). He also uses equidistant points.

3.) The method of Gardner et al.

Sums of exponentials with real negative exponents of the form

$$f(t)=\sum_{\nu=1}^{n} c_\nu e^{-\lambda_\nu t} \qquad (\lambda_\nu>0) \tag{3.1}$$

can be represented as Laplace transform

$$f(t)=\int_0^\infty e^{-\lambda t} g(\lambda)\,d\lambda \tag{3.2}$$

of a "function"

$$g(\lambda)=\sum_{\nu=1}^{n} c_\nu \delta(\lambda-\lambda_\nu) \tag{3.3}$$

which is a sum of delta functions. Thus a plot of $g(\lambda)$ corresponding to an experimentally determined function f(t) is expected to contain several peaks. Location and area assigned to a peak indicate exponent and coefficient of an exponential term. Gardner et al. (4) compute $g(\lambda)$ by Fourier transform techniques.

One could think of a method where the Laplace transform of the experimentally determined function is approximated by a rational function with a polynomial of degree n in the nominator and a polynomial of degree (n-1) in the denominator. The roots of the nominator polynomial are estimates of the exponents.

4.)Chebyshev approximations

Detailed theoretical investigations on exponential approximation have been carried out by Rice (5) and Braess (6)(see also Werner (8)). For the Chebyshev approximation in a closed interval[a,b] Braess comes to the following results((6)p313 and p318):

a)For every function continous in [a,b] there is at least one best approximation among the set of general sums of exponentials of maximal degree n

$$\left.\begin{array}{l} E_k(\vec{\alpha},\vec{\lambda};t)=\sum_{\nu=1}^{\ell}\sum_{\mu=0}^{k_\nu-1}\alpha_{\nu\mu}t^{\mu}e^{\lambda_\nu t} \\ (k\leq n,\quad \alpha_{\nu\mu}=\text{real},\quad \alpha_{\nu k_\nu-1}\neq 0\ ) \end{array}\right\}\quad(4.1)$$

where

$$k=\sum_{\nu=1}^{\ell}k_\nu \qquad (4.2)$$

is called the degree of $E_k(\vec{\alpha},\vec{\lambda};t)$.

b)If there is a best approximation among the set of "simple" sums of exponentials of maximal degree n

$$\left.\begin{array}{l} E_k^{\circ}(\vec{\alpha},\vec{\lambda};t)=\sum_{\nu=1}^{k}\alpha_\nu e^{\lambda_\nu t} \\ (k\leq n,\quad \alpha_\nu=\text{real}\neq 0\ ) \end{array}\right\}\quad(4.3)$$

it is at the same time the only best approximation among the set of general exponential sums of equal maximal degree.

c)For every function continuous in [a,b] there is one and only one best approximation by positive sums of exponentials of maximal degree n

$$\left.\begin{array}{l} E_k^{+}(\vec{\alpha},\vec{\lambda};t)=\sum_{\nu=1}^{k}\alpha_\nu e^{\lambda_\nu t} \\ (k\leq n,\quad \alpha_\nu>0) \end{array}\right\}\quad(4.4)$$

When this approximation E^{+}_{n*} is of full degree n, then
- it is also the best approximation available from the set of simple as well as general exponential sums of degree n,
- even the best approximation $E^{+}_{(n-1)*}$ among the set of positive sums of exponentials with maximal degree n-1 is of full degree and
- between two successive exponents of E^{+}_{n*} there is one exponent of $E^{+}_{(n-1)*}$ ("separation property" of the exponents).

Braess (7) proposed that a sequence of best Chebyshev approximations be calculated with the aid of a Remes-type algorithm (linearization at the extreme points of the error curve) as previously indicated by Rice (5). Starting values for the exponents are determined from increasingly ordered values $\lambda_1^{(n)}, \lambda_2^{(n)}, \ldots, \lambda_\ell^{(m)}$ received for the previous approximation as follows ((7)p270):

$$\lambda_{\nu,start}^{(m+1)} = \begin{cases} \lambda_1^{(m)} - \dfrac{3}{b-a} & \text{if } \nu = 1 \\ \dfrac{1}{2}\left(\lambda_\nu^{(m)} + \lambda_{\nu-1}^{(m)}\right) & \text{if } 2 \le \nu \le \ell \\ \lambda_\ell^{(m)} + \dfrac{3}{b-a} & \text{if } \nu = \ell+1 \end{cases} \tag{4.5}$$

Braess((6)p310 and p320) has pointed out that, in contrast to Chebyshev-approximation, more than one best L_p-approximation may exist to one given function even when restricted to positive sums of exponentials. In case of discrete approximations exponents must be bound to a finite interval, otherwise best approximations may not exist((6)p319).

5.) The peeling method

A manual procedure widely used for adjusting simple sums of exponentials is the so called "peeling" method:
- the experimental data $x(t)$ are plotted in a scale logarithmic for x and linear for t,
- a straight line is fitted through as many successive points as are possible including the furthest right point, the slope of this line representing the exponent and the intercept the logarithm of the corresponding coefficient.
- The exponential term thus determined is subtracted from the data and the procedure is repeated, disregarding the points already used.

Mancini and Pilo (9) describe an adaptation of this method to the digital computer:

a) The exponential sum containing k terms and a constant is fitted to the l last successive points.
b) If the resulting χ^2-value is smaller than some predetermined value, an additional point is added (l:=l+1) and

the procedure continued from (a) unless all points have already been used, in which case it is stopped.

c) If the value is not smaller and there is a sufficient degree of freedom, an additional exponential term is added (k:=k+1). The initial estimates of the previous step are used as starting values together with

$$\alpha_k = 0 \quad \text{and} \quad \lambda_k = 3\lambda_{k-1}$$

The starting values are refined by applying the fitting routine with fixed exponents $\lambda_1, \lambda_2, .., \lambda_{k-1}$ and the procedure is restarted from (a).

The whole procedure is initialized with k=1, $l \geq 3$ and zero for the constant as well as the coefficient and exponent of the first exponential term. The fitting routine is based on the Gauss algorithm for overdetermined systems of nonlinear equations. To save computer time it could have been interrupted as soon as an acceptable χ^2-value had been gained.

6.) Least-square fit by function minimization

Of course the problem of multiexponential fitting might be formulated as a search for those coefficients and those exponents which give minimum least squares. Lemaitre and Malengé (10) proposed that a search be made for this minimum alternately in the space of coefficients by solving normal equations for fixed exponents and in the space of exponents by function minimization methods, starting from an initial guess of the exponents. In this way a sequence of fits with increasing number of exponentials is calculated, using a statistical test (χ^2 or F) as stopping criterion.

Lemaitre and Malengé claim that the computing time of their method is proportional to 10^n. This may be due to a moderate minimization algorithm. Furthermore it is our experience that, for a wide variety of practical problems with negative real exponents, an ordinary minimization algorithm works more economically if the parameters searched for are $\log(-\lambda_\nu)$ instead of λ_ν.

7.) Jain's Method

For approximating a real function x(t) square integrable from 0 to ∞ by a sum of exponentials, Jain(11) proposes the following procedure:

- by repeated integration calculate the set of (n+1) functions defined for $t \geq 0$

$$\left.\begin{aligned} x_0(t) &= x(t) \\ x_{\nu+1}(t) &= \int_{\infty}^{t} x_\nu(t')\,dt' \quad (\nu = 0, 1, .., n-1) \end{aligned}\right\} \quad (7.1)$$

- compute the elements

$$G_{\nu\mu} = \int_0^\infty x_\nu(t)\, x_\mu(t)\, dt \qquad (7.2)$$

of the (n+1)×(n+1) matrix G and
- determine the exponents λ_ν as the roots of the polynomial equation

$$\sum_{\nu=0}^{n} \sqrt{\det_{\nu\nu}(G)}\; \lambda^{n-\nu} = 0 \qquad (7.3)$$

where $\det_{\nu\mu}(G)$ is the determinant of the matrix obtained by neglecting row ν and column μ of G.

If x(t) can not be exactly represented by a sum of exponentials of degree n, the determinant of G does not vanish and $\det_{\nu\nu}(G)$ can be calculated from

$$\det_{\nu\nu}(G) = (G^{-1})_{\nu\nu} \times \det(G) \qquad (7.4)$$

The method is applicable even for complex exponents, which occur then in conjugate pairs. If the function to be approximated is given pointwise, intermediate values must be defined by some interpolation procedure possibly after changing from variable t to log t and after smoothing the data. This is also valied for the next method to be discussed.

8.) The integral equation method

Any sum of exponentials $E_n(t)$ of degree n can be considered as the solution of an ordinary differential equation with constant coefficients of order n

$$\frac{d^n}{dt^n} E_n(t) + \sum_{\nu=0}^{n-1} a_\nu \frac{d^\nu}{dt^\nu} E_n(t) = 0 \qquad (8.1)$$

By n repetitions of integration over t one gets an integral relation of the following type

$$E_n(t) + \sum_{\nu=0}^{n-1} \Big\{ a_\nu \underbrace{\int_0^t \cdots \int_0^t}_{(n-\nu)\times} E_n(t)\, dt \ldots dt + b_\nu t^\nu \Big\} = 0 \qquad (8.2)$$

This relation will generally not hold exactely, if we replace the, as yet unknown, sum of exponentials $E_n(t)$ by the function $x(t)$ to be approximated, let us say in the interval [0,T].

We define

$$\varepsilon(t) = x(t) + \sum_{\nu=0}^{n-1} \Big\{ a_\nu \underbrace{\int_0^t \cdots \int_0^t}_{(n-\nu)\times} x(t)\, dt \ldots dt + b_\nu t^\nu \Big\} \tag{8.3}$$

and determine the coefficients a_ν and b_ν by requiring

$$\int_0^T \{\varepsilon(t)\}^2 dt \longrightarrow \min \tag{8.4}$$

As the a_ν are calculated, the exponents of the approximating sum of exponentials can be found as the roots of the characteristic equation

$$\lambda^n + \sum_{\nu=0}^{n-1} a_\nu \lambda^\nu = 0 \tag{8.5}$$

of the corresponding differential equation.

Such a procedure has been proposed by Squire(12) and by Diamessis (13). According to Squire (12) the method is good when applied to precise data, but loses accuracy when the data are affected by small random errors. Perhaps smoothing the data and using more data points could help in such cases.

If the repeated integration over t had been performed from ∞ to t, as in Jain's method, the coefficients b_ν representing initial conditions would have vanished for x(t) square integrable in $[0,\infty)$ and the a_ν could have been calculated from the normal equations

$$\sum_{\nu=0}^{n-1} a_\nu G_{n-\nu,\, n-\mu} = - G_{0,\, n-\mu} \qquad (\mu = 0,1,\ldots,n-1) \tag{8.6}$$

assuming $T=\infty$ and using definition (7.2) for G. This seems to be a computationally less involved alternative to Jain's method, since no determinants need to be calculated.

Moore (14) essentially determines a_ν and b_ν from (8.3) by collocation.

Sometimes the direct use of the differential equations has been proposed for establishing linear equations for a_ν (Froberg, see (14), and Bellman, see(12) p146: "differential quadrature"). But as is pointed out, the error in numerical computation of the derivatives involved affects the accuracy of the method considerably.

9.) The method of LAL and MOORE

Lal and Moore (15) start from the observation that for ordinary sums of exponentials of degree n

$$E_n^0(t) = \sum_{\nu=1}^{n} c_\nu e^{\lambda_\nu t} \tag{9.1}$$

the following relation holds

$$\left(\frac{d}{dt}-\lambda_\mu\right)E_n^\circ(t)=\sum_{\nu=1}^{n}(\lambda_\nu-\lambda_\mu)c_\nu e^{\lambda_\nu t} \quad (\mu=1,2,..,n) \tag{9.2}$$

Thus the exponents should be adjusted so that the function x(t) to be approximated satisfies a similar relation.

$$\left(\frac{d}{dt}-\lambda_\mu\right)x(t)=\sum_{\nu\neq\mu} C_\nu^{(\mu)} e^{\lambda_\nu t}+\varepsilon(t) \tag{9.3}$$

with $\varepsilon(t)$ small. Integration from t_o to t leads to

$$x(t)-x(t_o)-\lambda_\mu\int_{t_o}^{t}x(t')dt'=\sum_{\nu\neq\mu}\frac{C_\nu^{(\mu)}}{\lambda_\nu}e^{\lambda_\nu t}+\tilde{\varepsilon}(t) \tag{9.4}$$

Lal and Moore determine the n^2 unknowns $\lambda_\mu, C_\nu^{(\mu)}$ $(\nu\neq\mu)$ by collocation for n different values of t. The resulting n^2 equations are solved iteratively; in doing so it is noted that all n equations belonging to a fixed value of μ are linear in λ_μ and $C_\nu^{(\mu)}$.

10.) Simulation of a manual procedure for analyzing heating curves

As discussed in section 1 the model function for transient thermal resistance Z(t) has the form

$$f_k(t)=\sum_{\nu=1}^{k}R_\nu\left(1-e^{-t/\tau_\nu}\right) \tag{10.1}$$

with $R_\nu > 0$ and $\tau_\nu > 0$. It starts at t=0 with zero and approaches some asymptotic value for $t\to\infty$. If the asymptotic value is known, the model function can be transformed into a positive sum of exponentials. Unfortunately the methods dealt with so far do not allow a direct restriction to positive coefficients, except the peeling and the minimization method. A modified version of each of them will be presented in this and the next section.

For analyzing heating curves some engineers apply the following procedure, similar to the peeling method:

-Starting from t=0 a function of the form

$$\Delta f_k(t)=R_k\left(1-e^{-t/\tau_k}\right) \tag{10.2}$$

is fitted to the data curve Z=Z(t) over a range extending to large values of t as far as possible.

-The function $\Delta f_k(t)$ is subtracted from the data curve (see fig.2) and the procedure repeated until all data can be fitted.

Fig. 2

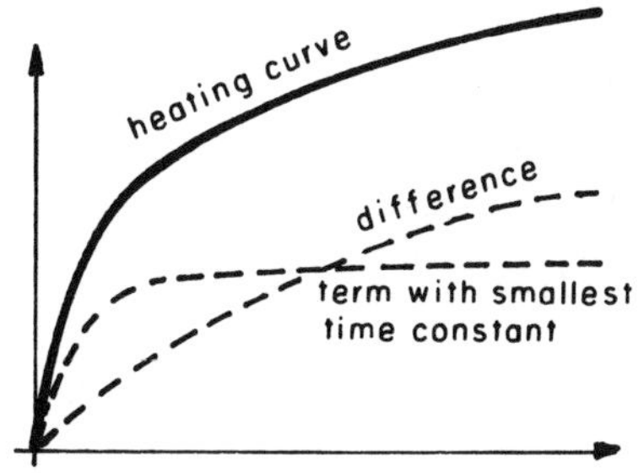

Assuming Z(t) to be defined by m points

$$Z_j = Z(t_j) \qquad (j = 1, 2, \ldots, m) \qquad (10.3)$$

corresponding to consecutive values of t, the method has been simulated on a digital computer as follows:

a) Set k=1, l=4 and initial values

$$R_k = Z_{l-2} \qquad \tau_k = t_{l-2} \qquad (10.4)$$

b) To the first l points fit a function of the form (10.1) by adjusting $R_v > 0$, $\tau_v > 0$ $(v = 1, 2, \ldots, k)$ so that the sum of the squared errors per "degree of freedom"

$$\varepsilon_k^2 = \frac{1}{l-2k} \sum_{j=1}^{m} \{ f_k(t_j) - Z_j \}^2 \qquad (10.5)$$

is not greater than a prescribed value ε^2 or reaches its minimum value.

c) Repeat step (b) with one more point (l:=l+1) if any of the following conditions are fulfilled

-if the curve $f_k(t)$ exceeded the heating curve by more than ε_k (see fig.2; the condition that the time constants exceed a certain limit could be used as an equivalent criterion)

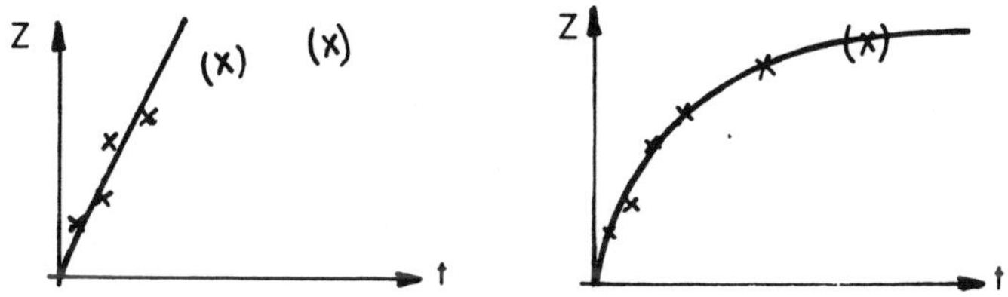

Fig.3. One more point causes the fitted function not to exceed the data points.

-as long as the sum ε_k^2 of the squared errors per degree of freedom (= ~per point) is not greater than ε^2 (this condition might be replaced by a χ^2 test)

-if the sum of the squared errors does not grow by more than ε^2 by adding that point (might be replaced by an F test)

d) If in this manner not all m points can be used for the fit (l<m), add a further term (k:=k+1) and use four more points (l:=l+4) if possible. Set rough initial estimates for the new term

$$R_k := Z_{l-2} \quad \text{and} \quad \tau_k := t_{l-2} \tag{10.6}$$

e) Adjust the new term to the first l points of the difference curve

$$\Delta Z^{(k)}(t) = Z(t) - f_{k-1}(t) \tag{10.7}$$

augmented by ε_{k-1} in order to make the curve "more positive" (otherwise it is sometimes hardly fitted by a term with positive resistance and reasonable time constant).

f) Repeat step (e) with one more point (l:=l+1) under similar conditions as in step (c). If none of them is satisfied go to (b).

The procedure stops with an overall minimization if all points have been used for the fit or if the maximum number of terms has been reached.

The constraints

$$R_\nu > 0 \quad \text{and} \quad \tau_\nu > 0 \tag{10.8}$$

are handled by transforming the unknown parameters R_ν and τ_ν to

$$A_{2\nu-1} = \log R_\nu \quad \text{and} \quad A_{2\nu} = \log \tau_\nu \tag{10.9}$$

Minimizing ε_k^2 is carried out by the method of Fletcher-Powell with modified linear search (no derivatives are required for the linear search). As an option least -2^Nth-power fits can be used instead of least square fits (N= integer ≥ 1).

Special features of the method which are thought to be essential for its effectiveness and which could be included in an implementation of the original peeling method like the one of Mancini Pilo (9) are:

-the criterion for stopping the minimization algorithm (see step (b))
-increasing the number of points used as far as possible during the phase of adjustment of a new term (this is cheaper than a simultaneous fit of all terms)
-the use of the transformed parameters $\log \tau_\nu$ instead of τ_ν and
-by using four more points (one could reasonably increase this number to 7), when adding a new term. Thus the number of parameters is automatically smaller than the number of degrees of freedom.

Example: m=27, ε=3% of 5.95

j	t	Z	j	t	Z	j	t	Z
1	1	0.1	11	30	2.14	21	700	5.29
2	1.4	0.18	12	40	2.36	22	1000	5.54
3	2	0.3	13	50	2.54	23	1300	5.74
4	3	0.54	14	60	2.69	24	1600	5.84
5	4	0.72	15	70	2.79	25	2000	5.91
6	6	0.98	16	100	3.12	26	2300	5.95
7	8	1.18	17	150	3.49	27	2500	5.95
8	10	1.36	18	200	3.84			
9	14	1.58	19	400	4.70			
10	20	1.84	20	500	4.96			

Progress of the computation:

Fig. 4

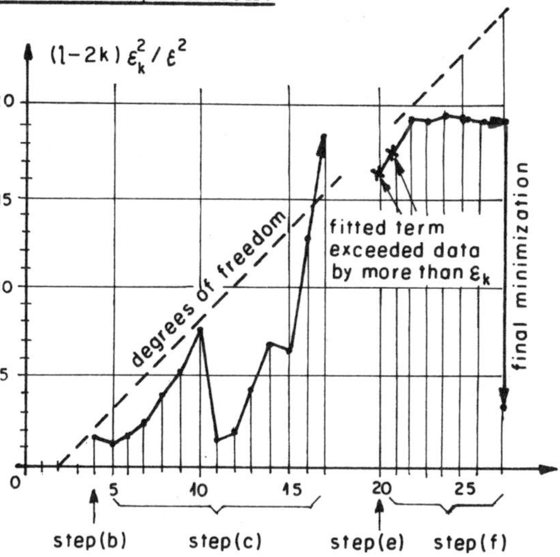

Result: R_1=0.0208 R_2=0.0380
τ_1= 11.6 τ_2=345.

CPU time on IBM 370/168 = 0.69sec (~sFr 2.-)

11.) The minimization method applied to the analysis of heating curves

The decomposition of the heating curve into a sum (10.1) of k terms may be formulated as a nonlinear optimization problem with the 2k independent variables

$$R_1, \tau_1, R_2, \tau_2, \ldots, R_k, \tau_k \tag{11.1}$$

the objective function

$$\sum_{j=1}^{m}\{f_k(t_j)-Z_j\}^2 \longrightarrow min \qquad (11.2)$$

and the constraints

$$R_\nu > 0 \quad and \quad \tau_\nu > 0 \quad (\nu=1,2,..,k) \qquad (11.3)$$

which vanish by changing the independent variables to

$$A_{2\nu-1} = \log R_\nu \quad and \quad A_{2\nu} = \log \tau_\nu \qquad (11.4)$$

Usually k is not known in advance, so a sequence of optimization problems stopped by some error test must be solved. The following is a proposal for this:

a) Set k:=1 and initial values

$$R_1 := Z_m \quad and \quad \tau_1 := t_m/2 \qquad (11.5)$$

b) Fit (10.1) with k terms to all m points by solving the aforementioned optimization problem starting from initial values.

c) If the mean error is greater than a prescribed value ε (this criterion may be replaced by a χ^2or F test) set k:=k+1 and initial values (thinking of the separation property of the exponents in case of Chebyshev-approximation by positive sums of exponentials)

$$R_\nu := \begin{cases} R_1/2 & if \ \nu=1 \\ (R_\nu+R_{\nu-1})/2 & if \ 1<\nu<k \\ R_{k-1}/2 & if \ \nu=k \end{cases} \qquad (11.6)$$

$$\tau_\nu := \begin{cases} \tau_1/2 & if \ \nu=1 \\ \sqrt{\tau_\nu \tau_{\nu-1}} & if \ 1<\nu<k \\ 2\tau_{k-1} & if \ \nu=k \end{cases} \qquad (11.7)$$

Go to (b).

d) Stop if the mean error is smaller than ε.

For the example of the preceding section this procedure, using the same minimization algorithm, leads to the following results:

Time constants:

k	$\tau_1, \tau_2, \ldots, \tau_k$				
1	90.3				
2	11.6	345			
3	9.68	148	586		
4	8.13	29.6	217	731	
5	8.13	29.3	212	610	945

Resistances:

k	$R_1, R_2, \ldots, R_k$				
1	5.43				
2	2.08	3.80			
3	1.80	1.86	2.30		
4	1.43	0.64	2.28	1.67	
5	1.43	0.64	2.18	1.20	0.57

Errors in percent of max $\{Z_j\}$:

k	in the mean	maximum
1	9.256	16.8
2	1.198	2.2
3	0.726	1.6
4	0.718	1.7
5	0.759*	1.7

CPU-time on IBM 370/168(in sec):

k	for one opt. prbl.	cumulative
1	0.10	0.10
2	0.35	0.45
3	1.18	1.63
4	4.52	6.15
5	9.64	15.79

If stopped at k=2 the CPU-time would have been smaller than with the method of the preceding section,which indicates that minimization is not worse than peeling.We very roughly estimate the CPU-time required for any of the two methods to be proportional to $m*n^3$ with $n=\max\{k\}$ and the constant of proportionality of the order of 10msec for peeling and 5msec for minimization, both on IBM 370/168.

REFERENCES:

(1) R.De Prony "Essai experimental et analytique" J.Ec.Polytech.Paris 1 (1795) pp 24-76(ref.from(9)p14).
(2) C.Lanczos "Applied Analysis" Pitman 1957,pp272-280.
(3) H.Rutishauser "Der Quotienten-Differenzen-Algorithmus" Mitt.Inst.angew.Math.Nr.8,ETH Zürich 1957,pp43-48.

* best solution obviously not found

(4) D.G.Gardener,J.C.Gardener,G.Laush,W.W.Meinke "Method for analysis of multicomponent exponential decay curves" J.Chem.Phys.31 (1959) pp 978-986.
(5) J.R.Rice "Chebyshev Approximation by Exponentials" SIAM J.Appl.Meth.10(1962) pp 149-161.
(6) D.Braess "Approximation mit Exponentialsummen" Computing 2 (1967) pp 309-321.
(7) D.Braess "Die Konstruktion der Tschebyscheff-Approximierenden bei der Anpassung mit Exponentialsummen" J.Approx. Theory 3 (1970) pp 261-173.
(8) H.Werner "Tschebyscheff-Approximation with Sums of Exponentials" from A.Talbot (ed.) "Approximation Theory" Academic Press 1970, pp 109-136.
(9) P.Mancini, A.A.Pilo "A computer program for multiexponential fitting by the peeling method" Computers and Biomedical Research 3 (1970) pp1-14.
(10) A.Lemaitre,J.-P.Malengé "An efficient method for multiexponential fitting with a computer" Computers and Biomedical Research 4 (1971)pp 555-560.
(11) V.K.Jain "Decoupled method for approximation of signals by exponentials" IEEE Trans.on System Science and Cybernetics,July 1970, pp 244-246.
(12) W.Squire "A simple integral method for system identification" Mathematical Biosciences 10 (1971) pp 145-148.
(13) J.E.Diamessis "Least-Square-Exponential Approximation" Electronics Letters 8, Nr 18, September 1972,pp 454-455.
(14) E.Moore "Exponential fitting using integral equations" Int.J.Num.Meth.Eng.8 (1974) pp 271-276.
(15) M.Lal, E.Moore "An iterative technique for fitting exponentials" I.J.Num.Meth.Eng.10 (1976) pp 979-990.

DATA FITS WITH EXPONENTIAL FUNCTIONS

D.J. Randazzo
Wissenschaftliches Rechenzentrum
CIBA-GEIGY AG, 4002 Basel

I. Introduction

The problem of calculating data fits with exponential functions has been one of great interest in recent years. In the fields of pharmacokinetics and chemistry a number of frequently employed mathematical models (JACQUEZ [1972]; RESCIGNO and SEGRE [1966]; WEI and PRATER [1962]) are described by differential equations whose solutions are composed of sums of exponential functions. These functions often depend on important model parameters and when one attempts to interpret the experimental results using the model, these parameters must be fit to the data using some suitable fitting procedure.

The classical fitting procedure and the one most often used for this purpose is the least-squares fit. The theory behind this method may be found in many textbooks (for example; cf. DRAPER and SMITH [1966]) and need not be discussed here. It suffices to say that in the course of such a calculation one always derives a system of equations for the unknown parameters, the normal equations, and the parameters representing the best fit are a solution of these. These equations for exponential functions are nonlinear and extremely complicated, so that one must usually resort to iterative methods in any attempt to solve them. This case thus differs from the one for intrinsically linear type systems, which may be solved for unique values of the fit parameters using the well known techniques of matrix algebra. Anyone attempting to solve these equations for exponential functions is faced with a problem with two aspects. First how does one solve the normal equations at all. Second these equations may, and very often do, have more than one solution. Unless the one corresponding to the absolute minimum is found, however, the solution, although least-squares in its neighborhood, will not be a maximum likelihood solution and thus it must lack the corresponding statistical properties which make this solution so desirable (see CRAMER [1946]).

In spite of the great amount of research which has been done on the topic, the number of different nonlinear fitting algorithms available for this type of problem is surprisingly limited. Virtually all of the present ones do not deal with the nonlinearized normal equations as such. They usually first procede to the residual sum which one is trying to minimize and then first linearize this in the neighborhood of a set of initial parameter estimates. A set of optimal corrections to these is then computed using standard linear least-square techniques; this further reduces the residual sum of squares. The complete process is now repeated continuously and if the initial parameter estimates were chosen sufficiently close to a minimum, this procedure will converge after a finite number of iterations to this minimum. A modified version of this technique has been given by HARTLEY [1961], and MARQUARDT [1963] has combined this method with a "steepest descent" method. A major problem with all such iteration procedures concerns the choice of suitable starting values for the initial iteration step. This point is crucial and a bad set of starting values can result in convergence to a local minimum or to a point which is neither a local- nor an absolute minimum. For exponential functions this problem is usually handled by a "peeling" process discussed by FOSS [1969] in which the individual exponential terms are peeled off one at a time from a semilogarithmic plot of the data. In addition to this a second major problem with iteration procedures arises when one has a multiple solution parameter space in which more than one set of parameters satsifies the normal equations. These procedures offer no additional information as to the number and type of possible solutions and the parameter space under consideration is usually so complicated that no predictions concerning its structure can be made. The only alternative when the existence of multiple solutions is suspected is to try a number of different starting values for the iteration.

Recently RANDAZZO [1976] has described a calculating procedure in which he takes a radically new approach to the problem. In this all of the linear parameters and one nonlinear parameter may be expressed as a function of a second nonlinear parameter; thus the fitting problem is recuced to one with a single degree of freedom (as compared to four or more with the usual iteration techniques). This procedure, however, suffers from the disadvantage that it is not a general method which is applicable to least-squares problems with all types of functions. It was expressly conceived with the problem for exponential functions in mind and in this it appears to do away with the disadvantages of the existing iteration procedures which were previously mentioned. It is the purpose of the present article to review the salient points of RANDAZZO's method for the two exponential calculation and to briefly indicate the problems encountered in attempting to apply it to fits with three or more exponentials.

II. Mathematical Description of the Procedure

One has a set of N data point pairs (t_i, y_i), $i = 1, \ldots, N$, where $N \geq 4$. The t_i represent values of the independent variable t and y_i the corresponding values of the dependent variable y. The assumed functional model between y and t is:

$$y = \sum_{i=1}^{2} a_i e^{k_i t} \tag{1}$$

With this model the residual sum for the given data pairs becomes:

$$\Delta = \sum_{j=1}^{N} (y_j - \sum_{i=1}^{2} a_i e^{k_i t_j})^2 \tag{2}$$

One must now choose the a_i, k_i, $i = 1, 2$ parameters in such a way that the residual sum Δ is minimized. One does this by taking the derivative of Δ with respect to each of the four parameters and setting it equal to zero. This procedure yields the system of normal equations shown in Eqs. (3a - 3d):

$$\sum_{i=1}^{N} y_i \rho_1^{t_i} = \sum_{j=1}^{2} \sum_{i=1}^{N} a_j (\rho_1 \rho_j)^{t_i} \tag{3a}$$

$$\sum_{i=1}^{N} y_i \rho_2^{t_i} = \sum_{j=1}^{2} \sum_{i=1}^{N} a_j (\rho_j \rho_2)^{t_i} \tag{3b}$$

$$\sum_{i=1}^{N} t_i y_i \rho_1^{t_i} = \sum_{j=1}^{2} \sum_{i=1}^{N} a_j t_i (\rho_1 \rho_j)^{t_i} \tag{3c}$$

$$\sum_{i=1}^{N} t_i y_i \rho_2^{t_i} = \sum_{j=1}^{2} \sum_{i=1}^{N} a_j t_i (\rho_j \rho_2)^{t_i} \tag{3d}$$

The substitution $\rho_i = e^{k_i}$, $i = 1, 2$ has been made in these equations. The optimum set of parameters being sought is a solution of these and thus we now turn our attention to their solution. For the presentation here the discussion will be restricted only to those cases which have solutions in which k_1 and k_2 are negative. These are the ones which are by far most frequently encountered in practice and they are the only ones which are usually significant when one is working with a chemical or biological model. For these cases one thus has the following restriction on the k_i parameters, $-\infty < k_1, k_2 \leq 0$, and the equivalent condition in the ρ_1, ρ_2 space is $0 < \rho_1, \rho_2 \leq 1$.

The method for solving Eqs. (3a - 3d) starts out by considering any three of these. For the sake of clarity Eqs. (3a - 3c) are chosen and (3d) is not considered for the present. Due to the fortuitous circumstance that a_1 and a_2 are linear parameters in all these equations, one may solve (3a) and (3b) for these in terms of the remaining ρ_1, ρ_2 parameters and then use these results in (3c). The resulting equation, when expressed in terms of powers of ρ_1, becomes:

$$F(\rho_1,\rho_2) = \frac{\sum_{i,j=1}^{N} a_{ij} \rho_1^{2t_i+t_j} + \sum_{i,j,k=1}^{N} b_{ijk} \rho_1^{t_i+t_j+t_k}}{\sum_{i=1}^{N} \rho_1^{2t_i} \sum_{j=1}^{N} \rho_2^{2t_j} - \left(\sum_{i=1}^{N} (\rho_1\rho_2)^{t_i}\right)^2} = 0 \tag{4}$$

where

$$a_{ij} = (t_j y_j - t_j y_i) \sum_{k=1}^{N} \rho_2^{2t_k}$$

$$b_{ijk} = (y_i t_j - y_i t_i) \rho_2^{(t_j + t_k)}$$

The values of ρ_1, ρ_2 are not determined uniquely in Eq. (4) and there exist an infinite number of (ρ_1, ρ_2) pairs which satisfy $F(\rho_1, \rho_2) = 0$. When, however, the ρ_2 parameter is assigned a specific value, the a_{ij} and b_{ijk} parameters become uniquely determined and Eq. (4) becomes a polynomial equation in the single unknown ρ_1. This may in principle be solved for ρ_1 and once this is known the corresponding values of a_1, a_2, and the residual sum Δ defined in (2) may also be determined. The solution of Eq. (4) will be discussed presently. For the present it is assumed that it can be solved so that one may proceed with the description of the method.

We now consider the entire region of solution of ρ_2 $(0 < \rho_2 \leq 1)$. This region is subdivided into a number of equidistant values and for each of these Eq. (4) is solved for ρ_1 and the corresponding a_1, a_2, and Δ values. When the calculation is completed one has a set of Δ values corresponding to the respective ρ_2 values and furthermore, the Δ are direct functions of ρ_2 only, i.e., there is only one degree of freedom in this reduced system. One must now imagine the (ρ_2, Δ) pairs plotted on a diagram whose abscissa is ρ_2 and whose ordinate is Δ. The curve so described (hereafter referred to as a "residual curve") shows the variation of Δ as ρ_2 sweeps through its entire domain of solution and as we simultaneously satisfy the first three normal equations (3a - 3c). Those points at which the slope of the residual curve is zero deserve special consideration. At these points one has:

$$\frac{d\Delta}{d\rho_2} = 0 \tag{5}$$

In order to understand the significance of these points, one must calculate the derivative of Δ with respect to ρ_2. Since a_1, a_2, and ρ_1

are now all functions of ρ_2 on such a curve one has:

$$\frac{d\Delta}{d\rho_2} = \frac{\partial\Delta}{\partial a_1}\frac{da_1}{d\rho_1} + \frac{\partial\Delta}{\partial a_2}\frac{da_2}{d\rho_2} + \frac{\partial\Delta}{\partial\rho_1}\frac{d\rho_1}{d\rho_2} + \frac{\partial\Delta}{\partial\rho_2} \tag{6}$$

The Eqs. (3a), (3b), and (3c) are automatically satisfied at every point on this curve and thus one has always:

$$\frac{\partial\Delta}{\partial a_1} = \frac{\partial\Delta}{\partial a_2} = \frac{\partial\Delta}{\partial\rho_1} = 0$$

The derivative in (6) thus reduces to:

$$\frac{d\Delta}{d\rho_2} = \frac{\partial\Delta}{\partial\rho_2} = \frac{1}{\rho_2}\frac{\partial\Delta}{\partial k_2} \tag{7}$$

and since $\rho_2 \neq 0$, one concludes that at the points of zero slope the condition $\frac{\partial\Delta}{\partial\rho_2} = 0$ is also satisfied. Thus in addition to every point on the residual curve representing a solution to the first three equations in (3), the points of zero slope offer a simultaneous solution of the fourth normal equation as well. These points are thus solutions of the normal equations of our system and therefore represent either a local minimum or maximum, or a global minimum. The least-squares problem, as viewed using the concept of a residual curve, has become quite easy to visualize. One calculates such a curve and then moves along it until a point of zero slope is attained; at this point an exact solution of the normal equations exists. In addition to this, once a solution has been obtained, one may continue on along the curve in order to detect any additional solutions that may exist. In principle, and providing one scans far enough along the curve, all possible solutions to the normal equations may be obtained in this manner.

III. Numerical Aspects

The type of calculation just described may be carried out with a minimum of difficulty on a computer and a program which utilizes the preceding ideas is presently in operation. In it ρ_2 is allowed to vary between 0 and 1.00 in 0.01 steps. The $\Delta\rho_2 = 0.01$ step appears to be sufficiently fine to describe the residual curve and to detect all variations in its structure and up to the present no data has been found for which this is not the case.

Certainly the only difficult aspect of the calculation is the solution of Eq. (4) for ρ_1 once a specific ρ_2 value has been assigned. Since the coefficients a_{ij} and b_{ijk} in (4) are continuous functions of ρ_2, one may rigorously prove that the ρ_1 values which satisfy (4) vary continuously as ρ_2 varies continuously. This implies a continuity of the residual curve everywhere and this fact is used in seeking a solution. Since the curve is continuous one knows that a solution must exist between any two ρ_1 values for which $F(\rho_1,\rho_2)$ has opposite signs. The procedure presently used is basically a combination of search procedure and Newton-Raphson iteration. The ρ_1 axis is first searched to see if this condition is fulfilled between two points. As soon as the search indicates that a solution is present a Newton-Raphson iteration is performed to converge to the final value. With this a sequence $\{\hat{\rho}_{1m}\}$ of estimates for the ρ_1 value is calculated and this sequence converges to a limiting value which is the desired solution, i.e. $\lim_{m\to\infty} \hat{\rho}_{1m} = \rho_1$. Each member of the sequence is generated from the preceding member by the following relationship:

$$\hat{\rho}_{1,m+1} = \hat{\rho}_{1m} - \frac{F(\hat{\rho}_{1m},\rho_2)}{F'(\hat{\rho}_{1m},\rho_2)} \tag{8}$$

where now $F'(\rho_1,\rho_2)$ equals:

$$F'(\rho_1,\rho_2) = \frac{1}{\rho_1} \sum_{i,j=1}^{N} (2t_i+t_j)\, a_{ij}\rho_1^{2t_i+t_j} + \frac{1}{\rho_1} \sum_{i,j,k=1}^{N} (t_i+t_j+t_k)\, b_{ijk}\rho_1^{t_i+t_j+t_k} \tag{9}$$

Using this procedure solutions of Eq. (4) may be calculated to any accuracy. An aspect of the problem not completely understood at present is that not more than one solution of (4) has ever been found at a time, regardness of the fineness of the interval subdivision used in the search procedure. This would seem to imply that, in the restricted framework of the least-squares problem now under discussion, a uniqueness condition appears to exist for the solutions of this equation. A proof of this result, however, cannot be given at the present time and thus it must be stated as an empirical observation. This point was investigated thoroughly for numerous data sets and in no case was a contradictory result ever found.

IV. Comparison of the Procedure with Other Nonlinear Fitting Procedures

Using simulated data, least-squares values obtained with this new method were compared with those obtained using two nonlinear fit procedures which are routinely used in such problems: 1) the nonlinear fit program of MARQUARDT [1964]; 2) the nonlinear regression program in the BMDP library (Biomedical Computer Programs [1975]) which is based on a pure Gauss-Newton iteration procedure. Both of these procedures are well described in the literature (MARQUARDT [1963], DRAPER and SMITH [1966]) and need not be gone into here. They represent two of the most reliable and frequently used fitting procedures available at the present time.

For the comparison ten sets of simulated data were used. These were generated by superimposing random numbers on the function values calculated with an exact double exponential function. The random numbers were generated using a normally distributed random number generator. For each exact y_i value calculated with the double exponential function, the error values were generated from a normal distribution of the form $N(0, 0.1\ y_i)$, i.e., the distribution mean is 0 and the variance is directly proportional to the y_i value. In this manner the magnitude of a generated error is a function of the y_i value itself and it is usually less than the magnitude of y_i. A complete list of the generated data is shown in Table 1. Each data set hat ten (t_i, y_i) point pairs and the deviations of the y_i from the exact values used to generate the error terms reached magnitudes as large as 20 % of the exact values; thus one had at times to fit highly distorted double exponential data. The starting values for the iteration procedures were obtained from these data by using the peeling technique referred to earlier in this paper.

The complete results of the simulation are given in Table 2. In this one finds three sets of calculated results. The first set represents the fit parameters obtained with the present method, the second set represents those obtained with the MARQUARDT program, and the third set of parameters in the Table represent the results obtained with the BMDP program (Gauss-Newton). There are a number of interesting points to be noticed. The first is the number of cases for both the MARQUARDT and BMDP routines where either no convergence was achieved or where the routine converged to an incorrect result. With the MARQUARDT routine, when convergence is achieved, the program usually converges to at least a local minimum. In a considerable number of cases, however, the routine fails to converge to any solution. In these cases it simply returned the starting values of the parameters as the final ones and carried out no iterations which further reduce the residual sum. This result is difficult to understand since none of the starting values used represented a minimum, either local or global, of the parameter space. The BMDP routine, on the other hand, exhibited a different kind of result. This program appeared to always converge in that it always iterated to a set of parameter values different from the starting ones and with these values the residual sum was appreciably reduced. Here, however, appearances were deceiving since the final parameters often did not represent the true solution and a minimum in the residual sums was not found (compare corresponding cases in the first and third parts of Table 2). The calculated residual sums in these cases often differ only slightly from the value at the global minimum. The calculated parameters, however, may differ dramatically from the correct results, a fact which shows how large variations in the parameters can produce only minimal changes in the residual sums. This indicates how sensitive the final results can be to finding the exact global minimum. Of further interest in Table 2 are those cases where multiple solutions are found (see cases 1, 5, 8). In two of these cases two solutions of the normal equations are found; in one case three solutions of the normal equations are present. It is especially with such data that the virtues of the present method come to the fore. One surveys the entire space and the solutions which represent local minima are seen immediately. This type of information is impossible to obtain with an iteration routine which, when it converges, offers no clues as to whether a local or global minimum has been found.

The Figures 1 and 2 show two examples of typical residual curves obtained with data from Table 1. The first Figure, which was generated with the data from case 3 in this Table, shows a single well defined minimum. As one moves away from this point along the ρ_2 axis in either direction, the value of Δ increases monotonically and no further extrema are observed. Below $\rho_2 = 0.49$ the residual curve is no longer defined since no solutions of Eq. (4) appear to exist for the ρ_2 values in this region. In the Figures, the residual curves are not shown for ρ_2 values greater than 1.00, but they do, however, exist for all ρ_2 values above this point. As ρ_2 becomes infinitely large the value of Δ does not increase indefinitely, but it has been found to asymptotically approach a finite limit which one may calculate. This result is valid for all residual curves.

The curve in Fig. 2 shows a second residual curve for data of case 8 in Table 1. One sees in the Figure that there are no less than three exact solutions of the normal equations represented. To be sure the S_2 solution between the S_1 and S_3 minima is a local maximum and thus, it cannot represent a solution of the least-squares problem. For this reason such local minima are not determined when they appear; only the minima for all curves are given. The S_1 and S_3 solutions shown in the Figure are given in Table 2. Such multiple solution curves have been seen in approximately 20 % of the calculated fits to date and it is unfortunately impossible to predict in advance the number of minima that a given data set will contain. Spaces with more than three solutions have, thus far, not been observed but there is no reason to exclude such possibilities from the present description; they could in principle be handled with this method.

V. Summary of Results and Conclusions

We have reviewed the salient points of a new method for calculating least-squares fits with a sum of exponentials. Unlike the usual nonlinear fitting algorithms currently applied to such problems, the present method does not linearize the normal equations but works directly with the nonlinear ones. These are used to remove all but one nonlinear parameter from the system and one is thus left with a problem with a single degree of freedom. One may then calculate a residual curve over any desired region of the remaining parameter and at any point on the curve where the slope becomes zero an exact solution of the normal equations must exist. The method unfortunately cannot be generalized and applied to fits with all functional forms; it does, however, possess a high degree of applicability for least-squares problems with exponential functions. In these problems it offers two distinct advantages over the usual nonlinear regression algorithms: 1) no starting values of any kind are required for the calculation; 2) the complete parameter space can be scanned and thus multiple solutions may be detected. This last feature greatly increases the likelihood that the global minimum will be found.

The application of this method to the problem with three exponential functions uses essentially the same residual curve technique in which one nonlinear parameter is swept through the entire region of solution. Now, however, a complete double exponential fit calculation must be carried out for each sweep value; this entails a considerable amount of computation but, nevertheless, it is feasible. The application of this method to least-squares fits with the model

$$y = a_1 e^{k_1 t} + a_2 e^{k_2 t} - (a_1 + a_2)\, e^{k_3 t} \qquad (10)$$

is presently being studied and it is hoped that the results of this work may be presented at a later date. For this expanded type of problem, a reasonable CPU time can only be achieved by using an iteration routine to solve Eq. (4). This is not necessary for the double exponential case where very slow and primitive, but very effective and reliable interval subdivision procedures have been used for this purpose. The resulting CPU times for such a problem are then approximately 15 sec. (on an IBM 370-158 system). Projected CPU times for the three exponential problem are 45 - 60 sec. on the same system. Applications of this model to fits with four or more exponentials, while feasible in theory, are not practical because of the huge CPU times which would be required.

In conclusion it should again be stressed that this paper has only given a brief description of the basic concepts upon which the method is based. For a more complete discussion of the subject and for a number of interesting details on the computational procedure used in solving Eq. (4) the reader is referred to the paper by RANDAZZO [1976]. The possible application of the method to least-squares problems with other functional models has not been investigated up to the present time.

TABLE 1 Simulated Data Used in the Regression Procedure Comparison

t	case 1	case 2	case 3	case 4	case 5
0.5D 00	0.29444005D 01	0.30719364D 01	0.31884280D 01	0.34777689D 01	0.38028506D 01
1.0D 00	0.21503137D 01	0.25752013D 01	0.19247304D 01	0.21493331D 01	0.23302295D 01
1.5D 00	0.18123730D 01	0.15728882D 01	0.14057854D 01	0.16141078D 01	0.19626065D 01
2.0D 00	0.12438052D 01	0.13623113D 01	0.11745531D 01	0.11185975D 01	0.11821270D 01
2.5D 00	0.95410718D 00	0.93273432D 00	0.85680466D 00	0.95782233D 00	0.92517667D 00
3.0D 00	0.68967697D 00	0.69515232D 00	0.78979720D 00	0.75945559D 00	0.62061686D 00
3.5D 00	0.58457528D 00	0.62362237D 00	0.57596276D 00	0.50945864D 00	0.50112293D 00
5.0D 00	0.30120100D 00	0.26503042D 00	0.31851476D 00	0.27806626D 00	0.34374684D 00
7.0D 00	0.13379929D 00	0.12941114D 00	0.11293455D 00	0.12440849D 00	0.14596863D 00
10.0D 00	0.43449534D-01	0.43797274D-01	0.44430697D-01	0.44918358D-01	0.49062085D-01

case 6	case 7	case 8	case 9	case 10
0.35311527D·01	0.37559781D 01	0.30725127D 01	0.31879450D 01	0.33527876D 01
0.25840307D 01	0.25405958D 01	0.19782594D 01	0.19365746D 01	0.29540522D 01
0.16858559D 01	0.15506181D 01	0.18444338D 01	0.15474786D 01	0.16197435D 01
0.10961641D 01	0.12004582D 01	0.12341682D 01	0.11786243D 01	0.94150235D 00
0.11424612D 01	0.95928996D 00	0.89153430D 00	0.11848428D 01	0.10593584D 01
0.71728115D 00	0.73651161D 00	0.60021997D 00	0.68272534D 00	0.82147750D 00
0.56913219D 00	0.50318218D 00	0.61641265D 00	0.60932921D 00	0.58361465D 00
0.24707463D 00	0.27272663D 00	0.31837290D 00	0.27830534D 00	0.27931114D 00
0.13440534D 00	0.13956471D 00	0.13428139D 00	0.13970173D 00	0.15039634D 00
0.39017045D-01	0.41525480D-01	0.48727354D-01	0.46456327D-01	0.36466008D-01

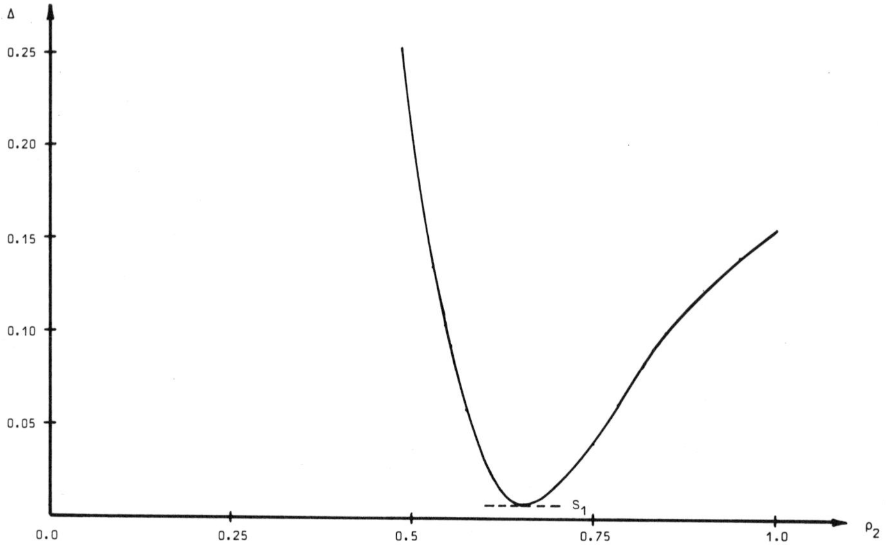

Figure 1: Residual curve for the data of case 3 in Table 1. Only one solution S_1 is found for this problem.

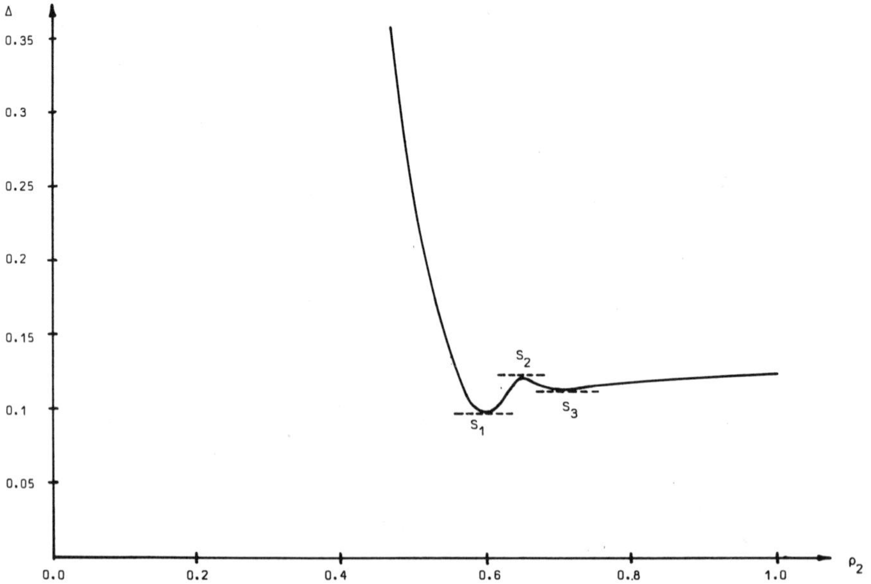

Figure 2: Residual curve for the data of case 8 in Table 1. Three separate solutions of the normal equations S_1, S_2, S_3 are clearly shown on the curve.

TABLE 2 Least-Square Parameters with the Different Fitting Routines

case	a_1	k_1	a_2	k_2	Δ	
Residual Curve Method						
1	$7.4534 \cdot 10^9$	- 46.051702	3.758239	- 0.535922	0.030785	
	0.226518	- 2.296413	3.743292	- 0.535697	0.031704	
	3.795074	- 0.581259	0.105781	- 0.087605	0.027784	
2	4.168846	- 0.607655	0.078950	- 0.051922	0.101940	
3	5.742454	- 3.393370	2.644143	- 0.426506	0.009083	
4	4.282686	- 2.856956	3.128519	- 0.489047	0.014794	
5	$0.55372 \cdot 10^{10}$	- 46.051702	4.413555	- 0.612587	0.093078	
	4.630254	- 1.015863	1.126596	- 0.293812	0.100556	
6	3.552387	- 1.016974	1.721269	- 0.375929	0.089444	
7	4.210599	- 1.300931	1.909200	- 0.381733	0.031965	
8	$0.37179 \cdot 10^{10}$	- 46.051702	3.495235	- 0.515770	0.098403	
	2.815645	- 0.862686	1.410117	- 0.340394	0.118609	
9	$1.24143 \cdot 10^{10}$	- 46.051702	3.065140	- 0.454051	0.055851	
10	4.583396	- 0.751201	0.397798	- 0.174987	0.417494	
MARQUARDT Procedure						
1	3.794956	- 0.581283	0.105921	- 0.087757	0.027784	
2					N.C.	
3	5.742245	- 3.393358	2.644142	- 0.426507	0.009083	
4					N.C.	
5					N.C.	
6					N.C.	
7	4.210518	- 1.300971	1.909318	- 0.381747	0.031965	
8	2.814590	- 0.862914	1.411276	- 0.340514	0.118609	•
9	599.87109	- 13.37877	3.063655	- 0.453872	0.055870	
10					N.C.	
BMDP (Gauss-Newton) Procedure						
1	2.424000	- 0.460136	1.504644	- 0.787775	0.030000	•
2	2.362867	- 0.484066	1.897644	- 0.761187	0.105382	•
3	5.742425	- 3.393358	2.644142	- 0.426507	0.009083	
4	4.281973	- 2.856344	3.128295	- 0.489023	0.014793	
5	4.630291	- 1.015851	1.126545	- 0.293805	0.100556	•
6	3.206141	- 1.099853	2.108000	- 0.412915	0.089702	•
7	4.210518	- 1.300971	1.909318	- 0.381747	0.031965	
8	2.160999	- 0.408339	2.134002	- 1.050295	0.118811	•
9	15.287191	- 5.946108	3.005445	- 0.447009	0.057174	
10	4.197372	- 0.812948	0.829881	- 0.279528	0.419271	•

N.C. - no convergence

• - incorrect result

TABLE 2 Least-Square Parameters with the Different Fitting Routines

case	a_1	k_1	a_2	k_2	Δ
Residual Curve Method					
1	$7.4534 \cdot 10^9$	- 46.051702	3.758239	- 0.535922	0.030785
	0.226518	- 2.296413	3.743292	- 0.535697	0.031704
	3.795074	- 0.581259	0.105781	- 0.087605	0.027784
2	4.168846	- 0.607655	0.078950	- 0.051922	0.101940
3	5.742454	- 3.393370	2.644143	- 0.426506	0.009083
4	4.282686	- 2.856956	3.128519	- 0.489047	0.014794
5	$0.55372 \cdot 10^{10}$	- 46.051702	4.413555	- 0.612587	0.093078
	4.630254	- 1.015863	1.126596	- 0.293812	0.100556
6	3.552387	- 1.016974	1.721269	- 0.375929	0.089444
7	4.210599	- 1.300931	1.909200	- 0.381733	0.031965
8	$0.37179 \cdot 10^{10}$	- 46.051702	3.495235	- 0.515770	0.098403
	2.815645	- 0.862686	1.410117	- 0.340394	0.118609
9	$1.24143 \cdot 10^{10}$	- 46.051702	3.065140	- 0.454051	0.055851
10	4.583396	- 0.751201	0.397798	- 0.174987	0.417494
MARQUARDT Procedure					
1	3.794956	- 0.581283	0.105921	- 0.087757	0.027784
2					N.C.

5					N.C.	
6					N.C.	
7	4.210518	- 1.300971	1.909318	- 0.381747	0.031965	
8	2.814590	- 0.862914	1.411276	- 0.340514	0.118609	*
9	599.87109	- 13.37877	3.063655	- 0.453872	0.055870	
10					N.C.	

BMDP (Gauss-Newton) Procedure

1	2.424000	- 0.460136	1.504644	- 0.787775	0.030000	*
2	2.362867	- 0.484066	1.897644	- 0.761187	0.105382	*
3	5.742425	- 3.393358	2.644142	- 0.426507	0.009083	
4	4.281973	- 2.856344	3.128295	- 0.489023	0.014793	
5	4.630291	- 1.015851	1.126545	- 0.293805	0.100556	*
6	3.206141	- 1.099853	2.108000	- 0.412915	0.089702	*
7	4.210518	- 1.300971	1.909318	- 0.381747	0.031965	
8	2.160999	- 0.408339	2.134002	- 1.050295	0.118811	*
9	15.287191	- 5.946108	3.005445	- 0.447009	0.057174	
10	4.197372	- 0.812948	0.829881	- 0.279528	0.419271	*

N.C. - no convergence

* - incorrect result

References

Biomedical Computer Programs [1975]. University of California Press, Berkeley, California.

CRAMER, H. [1946]. Mathematical Methods of Statistics, Princeton University Press, Princeton, New Jersey.

DRAPER, N.R. and S. SMITH [1966]. Applied Regression Analysis, Wiley, New York, 263 - 301.

FOSS, S.D. [1969]. A Method of Obtaining Initial Estimates of the Parameters in Exponential Curve Fitting, Biometrics 25, 580 - 584.

HARTLEY, H.O. [1961]. The Modified Gauss-Newton Method for the Fitting of Non-Linear Regression Functions by Least-Squares, Technometrics 3, 269 - 280.

JACQUEZ, J.A. [1972]. Compartmental Analysis in Biology and Medicine, Elsevier Book Co., Amsterdam.

MARQUARDT, D.W. [1963]. An Algorithm for Least-Squares Estimation of Nonlinear Parameters, J. Soc. Ind. Appl. Math. 11, 431 - 441.

MARQUARDT, D.W. [1964]. IBM Share Program No. S3094, Revised 1966.

RANDAZZO, D. [1976]. On a Least-Squares Fit of Data with a Sum of Exponentials, Biometrische Zeitschrift, to be published.

RESCIGNO, A. and G. SEGRE [1966]. Drug and Tracer Kinetics, Blaisdell Publishing Company, Waltham, Massachusetts.

WEI, J. and C.D. PRATER [1962]. The Structure and Analysis of Complex Reaction Systems, Advances in Catalysis, 13, 203 - 392.

A finite element solution to the neutron diffusion equation in two dimensions

D.M. Davierwalla

Abstract:

A finite element solution to the neutron diffusion equation in two dimensions is presented. Linear, quadratic and cubic Lagrangian elements are used. A direct method is substituted for the inner iterations. The rotational invariance property of the T^e matrices permits the separation of the graph-theoretical structure of the problem from the group dependent numerical values. This renders re-assembly on outer-iterations unnecessary for the multigroup case.

We consider a domain Ω with a boundary $\delta\Omega$. The equation to be solved is the diffusion equation given by

$$-\nabla\cdot D(r)\nabla\Phi(r)+\Sigma^{R}\phi(r) = G(r) \tag{1}$$

or

$$-\nabla\cdot D(r)\nabla\phi(r)+\Sigma^{R}\phi(r) = \frac{1}{k_{eff}}(\nu\Sigma_f)(r)\phi(r) \tag{1a}$$

with $r\varepsilon\Omega$ and boundary conditions

$$\phi(r)-f(r) = 0 \qquad r\varepsilon\delta\Omega_D$$

or

$$\frac{\partial\phi(r)}{\partial n}+\hat{\beta}\phi(r)+q = 0 \qquad r\varepsilon\delta\Omega_C$$

These were the monoenergetic problems. Eq.(1) is the fixed prescribed source problem and (1a) is an eigenvalue problem with fission sources only. The multigroup equations may be written as

$$-\nabla\cdot D_g(r)\nabla\phi_g(r)+\Sigma_g^{R}(r)\phi_g(r) = \sum_{\substack{g'=1\\ g'\neq g}}^{IGM}\Sigma_{g'\rightarrow g}(r)\phi_{g'}(r) +$$

$$\frac{1}{k_{eff}} \sum_{g'=1}^{IGM} \chi_{g'} (\nu\Sigma_f)_{g'} (r) \phi_{g'} (r) \tag{2}$$

with $r\varepsilon\Omega$ and g=1,2,.... IGM, the total number of energy groups with the same boundary conditions as specified before.
In addition, the solutions sought for (1), (1a) and (2) are required to satisfy the following conditions

(a) $\phi(r)$ must be continuous in $\bar{\Omega}=\Omega+\delta\Omega$ the closure of Ω

(b) $D_g \frac{\delta\phi(r)}{\delta n}$, the neutron current, must be continuous across material interfaces.

(c) $\phi(r) \geq 0$.

In equations (1a) and (2) if Dirichlet conditions, or fixed fluxes, are prescribed on a part or the whole boundary they must be zero - since the system must be autonomous. As will be seen later, conditions (a) and (b) are not difficult to satisfy, but condition (c) cannot always be satisfied by polynomial approximations so that we should expect the flux to become negative, locally, in the approximate solution.

The iteration scheme used for solving (2) for the dominant characteristic value $k = k_{eff}$ and the associated eigenfunction is the usual power method (Block Seidel). In this method (2) is rewritten as:

$$-\nabla\cdot D_g(r)\nabla\phi_g^{(n)}(r)+\Sigma_g^R(r)\phi_g^{(n)}(r) = \sum_{g'<g} \Sigma_{g'\to g}(r)\phi_{g'}^{(n)}(r) + \sum_{g'>g} \Sigma_{g'\to g}(r)\phi_{g'}^{(n-1)}(r)$$

$$+ \left[\sum_{g'=1}^{IGM} \chi_{g'} (\nu\Sigma_f)_{g'} (r) \phi_{g'}^{(n-1)}(r) \right] / k_{eff}^{(n-1)} \tag{3}$$

for g = 1,2,... IGM

The updating of the k_{eff} is performed by

$$k_{eff}^{(n)} = k_{eff}^{(n-1)} \frac{\sum_{g=1}^{IGM} (\phi_g^{(n)}, \phi_g^{(n)})}{\sum_{g=1}^{IGM} (\phi_g^{(n)}, \phi_g^{(n-1)})} \tag{3a}$$

At each outer iteration we solve IGM uncoupled self adjoint elliptic boundary value problems of the form

$$-\nabla \cdot D_g(r)\phi(r) + \Sigma_g(r)\phi_g(r) = Q_g(r) \qquad g=1,2,\dots \text{ IGM} \tag{4}$$

where $Q_g(r)$, the total source term for group g, is a known function. In passing, it should be mentioned that no problem which is not self adjoint can be treated by the minimization of a functional. Thus power iterations are not merely a convenience which permits us to treat one group at a time in core, they are dictated by the variational method which we intend to use.

Approximate Solution of Field Problems

In a field problem of one dependant variable, say, u, each governing equation (domain and boundary) is written generally as

$$F(u) = G(u). \tag{5}$$

Trial functions U_M are formed as a linear form

$$U_M(r) = \sum_{i=o}^{M} a_i\phi_i(r) \tag{6}$$

where the ϕ_i are linearly independent existing over $\overline{\Omega}$ and a_i are coefficients to be determined. Here, we distinguish between residual and variational methods.

Residual Methods

Here we choose the trial functions so that

a) The boundary values (all) are exactly satisfied but the domain equations are satisfied approximately. This is the domain, or interior method.

b) The domain equations are satisfied exactly but the boundary conditions are satisfied only approximately. This is the boundary method.

c) The mixed method, where both boundary conditions are satisfied only approximately.

The solution process consists for first forming the residues R where

$$R = G(u_M)-F(u_M) \tag{7}$$

and either minimizing these or some weighted function of them Wf(R). Of course the function f(R) is so chosen that

$$R = 0 \quad \Rightarrow f(R) = 0 \tag{8}$$

The domain method is the most commonly used and it must be borne in mind that the trial functions must satisfy all boundary conditions, both natural and essential.

Variational Methods

Here we assume both the existance and the knowledge of a variational principle. The advantage here is that the trial functions must now satisfy the essential boundary conditions only. The natural boundary conditions are taken care of by the functional itself.

We triangulate the region Ω into non overlapping elements or triangles. The boundary of Ω is approximated by a polygon. We shall refer to this approximated region by R and denote its boundary by Γ.

The approximating functions of the region R are piecewise polynomials, (bivariate) which are complete over each element. They posess the advantage of being rotationally invariant which permits us to achieve the continuity of the flux across a material interface quite easily.

We consider

$$J[u] = \sum_e J^e[u] \tag{9}$$

where

$$J^e[u] = \int_{Vol^e}\left(\frac{1}{2}D\nabla u\cdot\nabla u-\frac{1}{2}\Sigma^R u^2-Gu\right)dVol+\int_{S_c}\left(\frac{1}{2}\hat{\beta}u^2+qu\right)dS \tag{10}$$

where D, Σ^R, G, $\hat{\beta}$ and q have the same meaning as in equations (1) and D and Σ^R may be regarded as constant over one element. Of course if the particular element in question is not on that part of the boundary where Cauchy conditions are specified the second integral is omitted.

In x-y geometry the metric coefficients h_1 and h_2 are unity and the first integration is over the area of the element or triangle and the second over the side or sides which lie on a Cauchy boundary. With these assumptions (10) may be rewritten as

$$J^e[u] = \int_{A^e}\left(\frac{1}{2}D\,(u_x^2+u_y^2)+\frac{1}{2}\Sigma^R u^2-Gu\right)dA+\int_{\Gamma_c}\left(\frac{1}{2}\hat{\beta}u^2+qu\right)d\Gamma \qquad (10a)$$

and (9) as

$$\sum_e J^e[u] = \sum_e\int_{A_e}\left(\frac{1}{2}D(u_x^2+u_y^2)+\frac{1}{2}\Sigma^R u^2-Gu\right)dA \;+$$

$$+\;\sum_{e_c}\int_{\Gamma_c}\left(\frac{1}{2}\hat{\beta}u^2+qu\right)d\Gamma \qquad (9a)$$

where e_c denotes those elements which lie on a Cauchy boundary.

We take the first variation about the function $\phi(x,y)$ which renders the functional stationary. Then

$$u(x,y) = \phi(x,y)+\varepsilon\psi(x,y)$$

where $\psi(x,y)$ is chosen from an admissable class of fucntions with piecewise continuous first derivatives and which satisfy the essential boundary conditions and ε is a small parameter.

There result

$$
\begin{aligned}
u_x &= \phi_x + \varepsilon\psi_x \\
u_x^2 &= \phi_x^2 + 2\varepsilon\phi_x\psi_x \quad + O(\varepsilon^2) \\
u^2 &= \phi^2 + 2\varepsilon\phi\psi \quad + O(\varepsilon^2) \\
u_y^2 &= \phi_y^2 + 2\varepsilon\phi_y\psi_y \quad + O(\varepsilon^2)
\end{aligned}
\tag{11}
$$

$$
\begin{aligned}
\delta J[\phi,\psi] &= J[u]-J[\phi] \\
&= \sum_e \varepsilon \int_{A_e} \Big[D(\phi_x\psi_x + \phi_y\psi_y) + \Sigma^R\phi\psi - G\psi \Big] dA \; + \\
&+ \sum_{e_c} \varepsilon \int_{\Gamma_c} \Big(\beta\phi\psi + q\psi \Big) d\Gamma_c
\end{aligned}
\tag{12}
$$

with the help of Green's identity

$$
\int_A (\nabla\phi \cdot \nabla\psi)\, dA = -\int_A (\psi\nabla^2\phi)\, dA + \oint_{\Gamma_e} \psi \frac{\delta\phi}{\delta n}\, d\Gamma \tag{13}
$$

we get

$$
\begin{aligned}
\frac{\delta J}{\varepsilon} &= \sum_e \int_{A_e} \Big[-D\nabla^2\phi + \Sigma^R\phi - G \Big] \psi dA + \sum_e \oint_{\Gamma_e} D\frac{\delta\phi}{\delta n}\, \psi d\Gamma \; + \\
&\sum_{e_c} \int_{\Gamma_c} (\hat{\beta}\phi + q)\psi d\Gamma
\end{aligned}
\tag{14}
$$

Setting $\delta J=0$ and rewriting the last two summations we get

$$
\sum_e \int_{A_e} (-D\nabla^2\phi + \Sigma^R\phi - G)_e \psi dA + \sum_{\substack{\text{inter-}\\\text{faces}\\(i,j)}} \int_{\Gamma_{ij}} \psi \left(D_i \frac{\delta\phi}{\delta n} - D_j - \frac{\delta\phi}{\delta n} \right) \delta\Gamma_{ij} \; +
$$

$$+\sum_{e_c}\int_{\Gamma_c}\left(D\,\frac{\delta\phi}{\delta n}+\beta\phi+q\right)_e\psi d\Gamma_c \;=\; 0 \tag{15}$$

The first integrand is obviously zero. The second and third integrands must each be separately zero because equation (15) should be satisfied for all choices of D, $\hat{\beta}$ and q and ψ is arbitrary. We conclude, therefore, that the interface condition, the second integrand is always a natural condition and that Cauchy boundary conditions may be made natural by the addition of the second integral in the functional of equation (10). If $\hat{\beta} = q = 0$, i.e. our element was treated as an internal element, then the functional would automatically set $\frac{\delta\phi}{\delta n} = 0$ on the symmetry boundary.

Finite Elements

We now consider the elements themselves. Figs 2,3 display linear quadratic and cubic Lagrangian elements along with the local node numbering system. For triangles it is inconvenient to use cartesian co-ordinates. It is much more convenient to use simplex, or area or barycentric co-ordinates. Indeed, the numbering of the element nodes in fig.3 is just the co-ordinates of the nodes in the simplex co-ordinates system scaled by multiplying by the degree of the approximation polynomial, in order to get integers.

A triangle is a two-simplex S_2. Thus

$$S_2 \;:\; \left\{(\xi_1,\xi_2) \;:\; \xi_i \geq 0 \quad i=1,2 \;,\; \xi_1+\xi_2 \leq 1\right\}$$

We introduce a third, a dependent or slack, variable such

that $\xi_1+\xi_2+\xi_3 = 1$. The triple (ξ_1,ξ_2,ξ_3) represents a point within the element triangle in a purely local coordinate system. The coordinates of the point are invariant with respect to both rigid translations and rotations of the triangle. If (x_i,y_i) $i=1,3$ are the coordinates of the vertices of the triangle the relation between the (x,y) coordinates of a point and (ξ_1,ξ_2,ξ_3) are given by

$$\begin{vmatrix} 1 \\ x \\ y \end{vmatrix} = \begin{vmatrix} 1 & 1 & 1 \\ x_1 & x_2 & x_3 \\ y_1 & y_2 & y_3 \end{vmatrix} \begin{vmatrix} \xi_1 \\ \xi_2 \\ \xi_3 \end{vmatrix} \qquad (16)$$

The determinant of the matrix is double the area of the triangle. Hence

$$\begin{vmatrix} \xi_1 \\ \xi_2 \\ \xi_3 \end{vmatrix} = \frac{1}{2A} \begin{vmatrix} a_1 & b_1 & c_1 \\ a_2 & b_2 & c_2 \\ a_3 & b_3 & c_3 \end{vmatrix} \begin{vmatrix} 1 \\ x \\ y \end{vmatrix} \qquad (17)$$

where

$$\begin{aligned} a_j &= x_{j+1}\, y_{j+2} - x_{j+2}\, y_{j+1} \\ b_j &= y_{j+1} - y_{j+2} \qquad\qquad j=1,2,3 \\ c_j &= x_{j+2} - x_{j+1} \end{aligned} \qquad (18)$$

where the subscripts are computed modulo three.
The flux, ϕ, is expressed in terms of the point fluxes at the element nodes . Thus

$$\phi(\xi_1,\xi_2,\xi_3) = \sum_{i=o}^{N} \sum_{j=1}^{N-i} \alpha_{ijk}(\xi_1,\xi_2,\xi_3)\phi_{ijk} = \sum_{q=1}^{Nodel} \alpha_q(\xi_1,\xi_2,\xi_3)\phi_q \qquad (19)$$

where $i+j+k=N=NPROX$ $N=1,2,3$ for linear, quadratic and cubic approximations respectively and Nodel is the number of nodes in an element.

$$\left(\frac{\delta\phi}{\delta x}\right)^2 = \left(\sum_{q=1}^{Nodel} \frac{\delta\alpha_q}{\delta x}\,\phi_q\right)^2 = \sum_{i=1}^{Nodel}\sum_{j=1}^{Nodel} \frac{\delta\alpha_i}{\delta x}\,\frac{\delta\alpha_j}{\delta x}\,\phi_i\phi_j$$

$$\left(\frac{\delta\phi}{\delta y}\right)^2 = \sum_{i=1}^{Nodel}\sum_{j=1}^{Nodel} \frac{\delta\alpha_i}{\delta y}\,\frac{\delta\alpha_j}{\delta y}\,\phi_i\phi_j \qquad (20)$$

We now consider

$$J_1 = \frac{D_e}{2}\int_{A_e} \nabla\phi\cdot\nabla\phi\, dA \qquad (21)$$

i.e. that part of the functional which corresponds to the negative Laplacian and we take the first variation with respect to the point flux, ϕ_m, at node m.

$$\frac{\delta}{\delta\phi_m}(\phi_x^2) = 2\sum_{q=1}^{Nodel}\phi_q\left(\frac{\delta\alpha_m}{\delta x}\,\frac{\delta\alpha_q}{\delta x}\right)$$

$$= \frac{1}{2A^2}\sum_{q=1}^{Nodel}\phi_q\left[\sum_{i=1}^{3}\sum_{j=1}^{3} b_i b_j\,\frac{\delta\alpha_m}{\delta\xi_i}\,\frac{\delta\alpha_q}{\delta\xi_j}\right]$$

$$J=1,2,3 \qquad (22)$$

$$\frac{\delta}{\delta\phi_m}(\phi_y^2) = 2\sum_{q=1}^{Nodel}\phi_q\left(\frac{\delta\alpha_m}{\delta x}\,\frac{\delta\alpha_q}{\delta x}\right)$$

$$= \frac{1}{2A^2}\sum_{q=1}^{Nodel}\phi_q\left[\sum_{i=1}^{3}\sum_{j=1}^{3} c_i c_j\,\frac{\delta\alpha_m}{\delta\xi_i}\,\frac{\delta\alpha_q}{\delta\xi_j}\right]$$

Further using

$$\cot\Theta_i = -(b_{i+1}b_{i+2} + c_{i+1}c_{i+2})/2A$$

$$\text{and} \quad (\cot\Theta_{i+1}+\cot\Theta_{i+2}) = (b_i^2+c_i^2)/2A \qquad (23)$$

$$\frac{\delta J_1}{\delta\phi_m} = D\sum_{j=1}^{3}\cot\Theta_j \sum_{q=1}^{Nodel}\phi_q \left[\frac{1}{2A}\int_A \left(\frac{\delta\alpha_m}{\delta\xi_{j+1}} - \frac{\delta\alpha_m}{\delta\xi_{j+2}}\right)\left(\frac{\delta\alpha_q}{\delta\xi_{j+1}} - \frac{\delta\alpha_q}{\delta\xi_{j+2}}\right)dA\right]$$

$$m = 1, \text{Nodel} \qquad (24)$$

where the subscripts on ξ are computed modulo three.
We define a matrix, of order (Nodel x Nodel), Q_j^e whose (m,q)th element is defined by

$$Q_j^e = \left(q_{mq}\right)_j = \frac{1}{2A}\int_A \left(\frac{\delta\alpha_m}{\delta\xi_{j+1}} - \frac{\delta\alpha_m}{\delta\xi_{j+2}}\right)\left(\frac{\delta\alpha_q}{\delta\xi_{j+1}} - \frac{\delta\alpha_q}{\delta\xi_{j+2}}\right)dA \qquad (25)$$

$$j = 0,1,2 \bmod 3$$

Once the polynomials α_m, m=1 --- Nodel are defined the matrix Q_1^e i.e. j=1 can be evaluated. The results are displayed in Fig.4. Q_2 and Q_3 are generated by permutations applied to Q_1 where in Fig.4 we have used the same symbol P for the permutation and its matrix representation. The Q^e matrices are symmetric and have row and column sums zero. This assures the singularity of the composite matrix

$$D\left(\sum_{j=1}^{3} Q_j^e * \cot\Theta_j\right)$$

which represents the negative Laplacian in discrete form. Further ϕ behaves like a scalar potential and since the reference may be outside the element it must be possible to raise or lower the point fluxes by an arbitrary constant. This can only be done if all row and column sums are zero. Further the negative Laplacian depends only on the shape and not on the size of the element.

We now consider $J_2 = \frac{1}{2}\Sigma_e^R \int_A \phi^2 dA$ and take its variation with respect to the point flux ϕ_m at node m.

$$J_2 = \frac{1}{2}\Sigma^R \int_A \left(\sum_{j=1}^{Nodel} \alpha_j \phi_j \right) dA \tag{26}$$

$$\frac{\delta J_2}{\delta \phi_m} = \Sigma_e^R \sum \phi_j \left[\int_A \alpha_m \alpha_j \, dA \right] \qquad m=1, Nodel \tag{27}$$

This again defines an element matrix T^e multiplied by Σ_e^R and the area A of the element. The T^e matrices are displayed in Fig.5 for linear, quadratic and cubic approximations. The T^e matrices are symmetric, positive definate and further the sum of all elements is unity. One could interpret the entry t_{mj} as the effect at node j due to a unit change at node m and hence as influence numbers. There is one more property which is displayed in Fig.5 which we mention here. The T^e matrices are invariant with respect to rotations of the element. For monoenergetic computations this is not too important but in multigroup computations it is extremely important because it permits separating out the graph theoretic structure of the problem from the group dependant numerical values. This makes it unnecessary to reassemble the elements for every group during the outer iterations. We will come back to this point when we describe the code itself.

Finally we consider the term $J_3 = \int_A G\phi dA$.

Although we considered D and Σ^R to be constant over an element we permit G to vary over the element. In fact we use the same polynomial description for G, that we use for ϕ.

$$\text{Thus} \qquad G = \sum_{j=1}^{\text{Nodel}} \alpha_j G_j \qquad \text{and} \qquad \phi = \sum_{i=1}^{\text{Nodel}} \alpha_i \phi_i$$

$$\text{then} \qquad \frac{\delta J_3}{\delta \phi_m} = \sum_{j=1}^{\text{Nodel}} G_j \left[\int_A (\alpha_m \alpha_j) dA \right] \tag{28}$$

The result is a T^e matrix multiplied by the area A of the element and post multiplied by a source vector defined at the nodes of the triangle. In other words here the T^e matrix simply redistributes the source density G.

It is in the handling of the source term and the removal term that the finite element method differs from finite differences. For a linear approximation with right angled triangles the Laplacian is handled identically. But where as the finite difference would use the value of Σ^R and Q at a point the finite element tends to weight Σ^R and G.

Cauchy Boundary Terms

We consider

$$J_4 = \int_{\Gamma_c} (\hat{\beta}\phi + q\phi) d\Gamma$$

Cauchy conditions can only be prescribed on a side or sides of an element. We regard the side as a one simplex S_1. The procedure is entirely analogous to the derivation of T^e matrix for the $\hat{\beta}\phi^2$ term. We assume $\hat{\beta}$ is constant for the side in keeping with the constancy of Σ^R over the element. The result is a matrix called $(BCOEF)_i$, assuming that the conditions were prescribed on side i, multiplied by $\hat{\beta}$ and as may be expected by the length of the side i, L_i. The order of the matrix is actually 2,3 and 4 for linear, quadratic and cubic approximations. This matrix has to be superimposed on the element matrix and hence by adding rows and columns of zeros the size is made comensurate with that of the element matrix. This is only done for display purposes in Fig.6. The code operates with the actual matrices. These matrices are also symmetric. The second term gives a 2x1, 3x1 and 4x1 vector depending on the approximation used which again is multiplied by q and the length of the side. It is negated and added to any source terms that may be presented. Again for display purposes only, the vector is given as a 3x1, 6x1 and 10x1 array in Fig.6 In reactors, q is usually zero so that the contribution is zero.

Dirichlet Conditions

Here fixed values of flux are prescribed at a vertex or on one or more sides. No variation should be taken with respect to these fluxes. Hence the prescription is:
In the element matrix replace all off diagonal entries in the rows corresponding to Dirichlet nodes by zeros. Change the diagonal entry to unity. In the element column vector insert the prescribed flux in the correct row. This destroys the symmetry of the matrix. Symmetry is restored by multiplying the off diagonal entries in the Dirichlet columns by the known fluxes and subtracting the results from the element source vector. Now the off diagonal terms in the columns corresponding to Dirichlet nodes are set to zero.

The Polynomials.

The construction of the polynomial approximations is displayed in Fig.7 along with the polynomials themselves. These polynomials maintain their degree unchanged in all directions. As an example consider a quadratic approximation and consider two elements which share a common interface. Along the interface one of the variables, say ξ_i, is zero and $\xi_j+\xi_k = 1$. If we substitute $(1-\xi_k)$ for ξ_j we find that the polynomial is still quadratic in the single variable ξ_k. The solution surfaces over the two elements agree at the three nodes along the common interface and hence agree everywhere along the interface. This assures the continuity of the solution across the interfaces. This would not have been so if the polynomials had been constructed as a product of a quadratic in x with a quadratic in y unless all interfaces are parallel to either the X or the Y axes.

Integration on a Simplex

In the evaluation of the Q_i^e, T^e, $(\text{BCOEF})_i$ and QUCOEF_i arrays we need to integrate terms of the type $\xi_1^{(\nu_1-1)}\xi_2^{(\nu_2-1)}\xi_3^{(\nu_3-1)}$ where the ν_i are real and positive over the triangle A_e. In general it is required to map on to k-dimensional unit cube and then evaluate. But the integral is very well known from the Beta distribution k=2 and the Dirichlet distributions for k>2 from mathematical statistics. The result is simply

$$\int_A \xi_1^{(\nu_1-1)} \xi_2^{(\nu_2-1)} \xi_3^{(\nu_3-1)} \, dA = 2A \frac{\Gamma(\nu_1)\Gamma(\nu_2)\Gamma(\nu_3)}{\Gamma(\nu_1+\nu_2+\nu_3)} \tag{29}$$

Further, due to our scaling in the triple subscript notation the ν_i's are integers and the Gamma functions reduce to factorials.

The code

Here we give a very brief survey of those subroutines which are absolutely necessary to the understanding of the code. The Input Subroutine automatically triangulates the rectangular region, numbers the elements assigns global numbers to the nodes and computes the x-y co-ordinates of the vertices. Subroutine SHAPE takes this co-ordinate data and computes the area, lengths of each side and the cotangent of the angles of each element.

Subroutine POLTREL returns the coefficients of the Q_1^e, and T^e matrices. Only the lower triangular part stored by rows is returned in vector form.

Subroutine PERMUTE then generates Q_2^e and Q_3^e multiplies by the cotangents of the vertex angles and by the diffusion constant adds them together and stores in an array called VECTR. T^e is multiplied by the area and Σ^R and added to the contents of VECTR. Up to this point all information about the element is solely in VECTR.

Subroutine SOURCE now forms the element source column vector by multiplying the T^e matrix by the vector of element sources G, and stores the data in a one dimensional array called TEMP. From this point on an element consists of the arrays VECTR and TEMP.

Next the Subroutine CBNDRY (Cauchy Boundary) is called if needed. $(BCOEF)_i$ is multiplied by beta and the length of side i and the results added to VECTR. If $q \neq 0$, $QCOEF_i$ is multiplied by q and L_i and the results added to TEMP. Now the Subroutine DBNDRY (Dirichlet Boundary) is called if needed. It modifies the contents of VECTR and TEMP. If a node is on a Cauchy boundary and a Dirichlet boundary as can happen at a corner the latter overrides the former.

Now the assembly process is carried out by Subroutine FILL which is a linked linear list. It consists of an auxiliary vector NROW and a stack of triples. The subroutine receives as inputs, VECTR which contains the matrix coefficients, LIST which contains the global node numbers of the particular element and TEMP. NROW(I) gives the address in the stack of the first nonzero entry in row I of the system matrix. The triple in the stack at that address contains the value of the entry previously mentioned, its column index J and a variable called NXTPT i.e. next point. NEXTPT is the address in the stack of the next non-zero entry of the system matrix in the same row. The end of a row signalled by setting NXTPT equal to zero. It should be mentioned that this happens when J=I and since we deal with a positive definite matrix this entry is always positive and existant. Thus in the stack we store only the non zero elements of the system as row strings. By adding another variable, LSTPT, last-point, the list may be converted to a forward-backward list. This enables the stack to be reshuffled so that the items of a particular row string occupy consecutive places in the stack and the rows too are stored consecutively. This modification frees consecutive blocks of cells when the list is unloaded to form the actual system matrix and permits overwriting by the system matrix which is formed by Subroutine FORMA. The storage scheme is the Jenning's scheme. All elements from the first nonzero element in a row up to the diagonal element are stored. The necessary within band zeros being inserted, An auxiliary vector contains the address of the diagonal elements. The matrix is now decomposed into its Choleski factors by Subroutine VBCHOL (variable band Choleski). We have $LL^{T} = A$ and in the normal Choleski one has

$$\ell_{jj} = \left(a_{jj} - \sum_{k=1}^{j=1} \ell_{jk}^2\right)^{1/2} \qquad j=1,2,\ldots n$$

and

$$\ell_{ij} = \frac{1}{\ell_{jj}} \left(a_{ij} - \sum_{k=1}^{j-1} \ell_{jk}\ell_{ik}\right) \qquad \begin{matrix} j=1,2,\ldots n \\ i=(j+1),\ldots n \end{matrix} \qquad (30)$$

The modification that needs to be made is that the lower limit must be changed to max {JONEI, JONEJ} where JONEI and JONEJ indicate the column indices of the first nonzero in rows I and J respectively.

For a single group calculation the Subroutine BCKSUB would be called to solve the system by back substitution.

In the multigroup case the source has to be recomputed every outer iteration. We assume that down scattering occurs from the highest energy group right down to the thermal group and that upscattering extends to the next higher energy group.

Hence we have to assemble the system matrix IGM*(IGM-1)/2 times for the down scattering, IGM times for the upscattering and a further IGM times to form the fission source. In all IGM*(IGM+3)/2 times - where IGM is the total number of groups. The system matrix here consists only of the superposition of (T^e) matrices multiplied by the area of the element and by the appropriate Nu-fission or up or down scattering cross section. We note that each of these system matrices has an identical zero/nonzero structure. They have identical adjacency matrices. Let a_{IJ} denote the (I,J)th. element of the system matrix where I and J are global indices. Then

$$a_{IJ} = \sum t^e_{IJ} A^e \Sigma^e$$

where the summation extends over all elements that have both node I and J in their node sets. However, the value of t^e_{IJ} depends on its position in the T^e matrix i.e. on its local row and column indices. It is here that the rotational invariance of the T^e matrices plays a paramount role. It implies that the value of t^e_{IJ} is identical for all the elements that come in question!

Hence, we can write $a_{IJ} = t_{IJ} \sum A^e \Sigma^e$ where the summation is as before. So in the Subroutine STRUCT (Structure) when we assemble the elements we simply write $a_{IJ} = t_{IJ}$ and in a separate word denoted by NCODE pack the designations (labels) of the elements over which the summation extends. Since no more than six elements can meet at one point three octal digits are reserved for each label. This limits as to at most 511 elements. STRUCT also only stores row-strings up to the diagonal element of row I. But the flux has to be multiplied by the whole row of the matrix. Hence, one has to search all succeeding row strings for elements having a column index equal to I. This is too time consuming so Subroutine COLINK (Co or column linkage) works out column linkages for J >1. Both subroutines STRUCT and COLINK are called once in a run irrespectively of the number of groups or the number of outer iterations. With the information provided by these two subroutines, subroutine FISCAT (Fission or Scattering) works out the sources as needed and BCKSUB is called to compute the fluxes. Next subroutine INPROD works out the requisite inner products of the fluxes and subroutine NORMFLX normalizes the flux.

Some Results

A one group fixed source problem is depicted in Fig. 8 which a very simplified model of SAPHIR. The example is of interest because of very large flux gradients which occour. Figs 9, 10 and 11 depict the triangulations used. These cases were considered before the writing of the automatic triangulation input subroutine. Figs 9 and 10 depict the SE quadrant, while Fig II depicts the lower half of Fig. 8. Fig. 9 divides the region into thirty six and Fig. 10 into seventy two elements.

Fig. 11 depicts a mixture of Quadratic, cubic and linear elements with mesh refinements in the region of high flux gradients. In this case the continuity of the flux is violated accross some element boundries. However, the consequences are not serious. We may, however, point out that we have on another occasion, violated the rule in the region of high gradients between the zones with sources and the source free zones and the results have been catastrophic. Table 1 displays our results and Table 2 gives the results of computing the same problem with some finite difference codes at our disposal. It may be noted that the results of the finite difference and finite elements are comparable in zones 1 and 3 (see Fig. 8) which contain the uniform sources ie.where the flux is relatinely flat and at a maximum. The results differ, however, in the source free zones 2 and 4. A subsequent computation with a transport theory code confirmed the results of the values in zones 2 and 4 achieved by the finite element computation. It will be noted that finite differences can only achieve an accuracy comparable with finite elements by employing a very fine mesh and hence at large execution times and cost. The current state of our finite element program has, however, not been optimized with respect to core utilization. Relabelling algorithms have still to be applied so as to reduce the number of temporary zones in the core which should enable us to handle larger problems or reduce the computational work or smaller problems.

2nd Example

A simple two group homogenous k_{eff} problem was chosen for the second example. This choice was prompted by the fact that k_{eff} can be determined analytivally and also because the computed values for k_{eff} determined by the finite element code HOD (Higher Order Diffusion) have been published by the Argonne National Laboratory.(7). It was not possible to use the same triangulation used in the publication but we give for comparison two cases Argonne's computation which bracket our case. Fig. 12 displays the triangulation and the cross sections for the problem.

The equations are given by:

$$-D_1\nabla^2\phi_1 + \Sigma_1^R\phi_1 = \chi_1\left[(\nu\Sigma_f)_1\phi_1+(\nu\Sigma_f)_2\phi_2\right]/k_{eff} \qquad (31)$$

$$-D_2\nabla^2\phi_2 + \Sigma_2^R\phi_2 = \chi_2\left[(\nu\Sigma_f)_1\phi_1+(\nu\Sigma_f)_2\phi_2\right]/k_{eff} + \Sigma_{1\to2}\phi_1 \qquad (32)$$

for $(x,y)\varepsilon\Omega$ with the boundary conditions

$$\frac{\partial\phi_g}{\partial n}(o,y) = \frac{\partial\phi_g}{\partial n}(x,o) = 0$$

$$\phi_g(L,y) = \phi_g(x,L) = 0 \qquad L = 50.05$$

for $(x,y)\varepsilon\delta\Omega$, $g = 1,2$

Assuming a flux of the form

$$\phi_g = A_g \cos\left(\frac{\Pi x}{2L}\right)\cos\left(\frac{\Pi x}{2L}\right) \qquad g = 1,2$$

and $\alpha = A_1/A_2$ and further setting

$$E_g = D_g\left(\frac{2\Pi}{L}\right)^2 + \Sigma_g^R \qquad g = 1;2$$

we get

$$\alpha = \chi_1E_2/(\chi_2E_1+ \chi_1\Sigma_{1\to2})$$

and

$$k_{eff} = \left[\chi,(\nu\Sigma_f)_1 E_2+(\chi_1\Sigma_{1\to2}+\chi_2E_1)(\nu\Sigma_f)_2\right]/E_1E_2$$

$$= 1.4653\ 8738\ 4104$$

HOD (Argonne's Finite Element Diffusion Program) for cubic approximations with 127 and 271 nodes per group gave values

k_{eff} = 1.46538691930 and

k_{eff} = 1.46538734216 respectinely.

FINELM-2D with a cubic approximation and 169 nodes per group gave

k_{eff} = 1.4653872112

Conclusion

The preliminary testing showed that the method to be extremely promising. At this time the code has been inserted into our RSYST-system and is being tested on more realistic problems. However, much still remains to be done, especially, with respect to better core utilisation and we hope to take up this problem in the very near future.

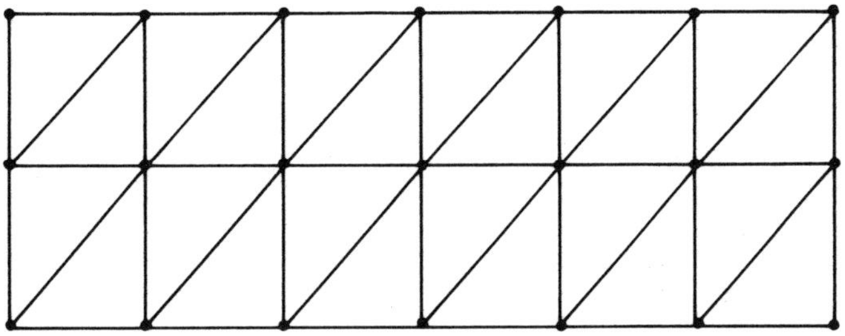

Fig. 1 Basic Triangulation of a Rectangular Region.

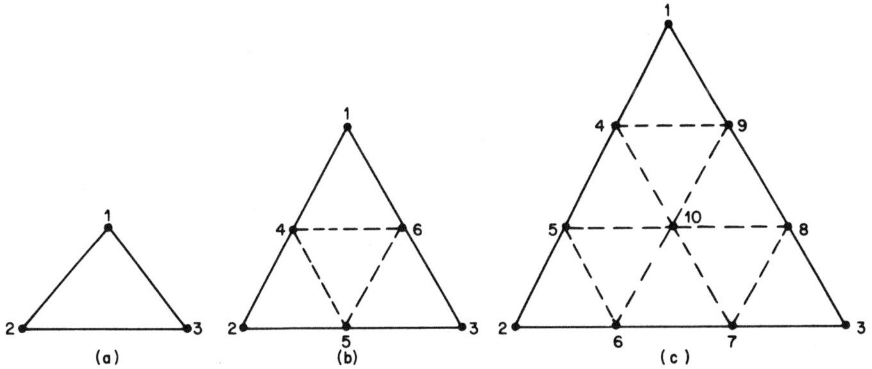

Fig. 2 Local numbering of nodes on a (a) linear, (b) quadratic, (c) cubic element.

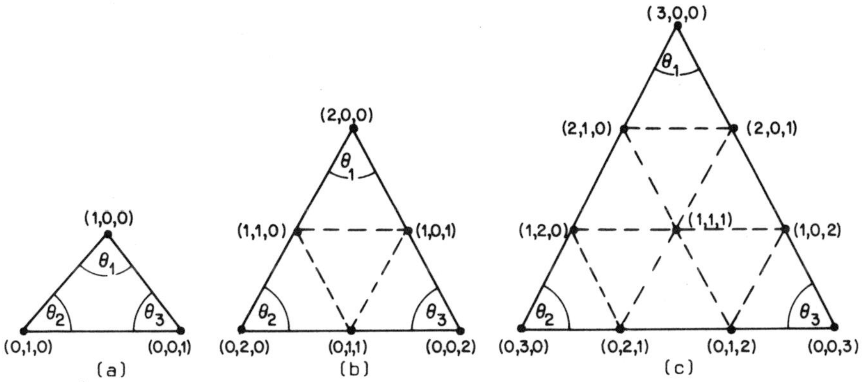

Fig. 3 Langrangian (a) linear, (b) quadratic, (c) cubic elements numbered with the triple subscript notation.

$2*(Q_1^e)$: 0/0,1/0,-1,0/ (3x3)

$(Q_{1+i}) = (P^i)(Q_1^e)(P^i)^\tau$ $i=1,2$

where P : (1,2,3)

Linear Approximation

$6*(Q_1^e)$: 0/0,3/0,1,3/0,0,0,8/0,-4,-4,0,8/0,0,0,-8,0,8/ (6x6)

$(Q_{1+i}^e) = (P^i)(Q_1^e)(P^i)^\tau$ $i=1,2$

where P : (1,2,3)(4,5,6)

Quadratic Approximation

$80*(Q_1^e)$: 0/0,34/0,-7,34/0,3,-3,135/0,3,-3,-27,135/
0,-54,27,0,0,135/0,27,-54,0,0,-108,135/
0,-3,3,27,27,0,0,135/0,-3,3,-135,27,0,0,-27,135/
0,0,0,0,-162,0,0,-162,0,324/ (10x10)

$(Q_{1+i}^e) = (P^i)(Q_1^e)(P^i)^\tau$ $i=1,2$

where P : (1,2,3)(4,6,8)(5,7,9)

Cubic Approximation.

Fig. 4 : The lower triangular parts of the Q_i^e matrices used to construct the negative Laplacian for an element.

$12*(T^e)$: 2/1,2/1,1,2/ (3x3)

$(P^i)(T^e)(P^i)^\tau = (T^e)^\tau$ $i \geq 1$

where P : (1,2,3)

Linear Approximation

$180*(T^e)$: 6/-1,6/-1,-1,6/0,0,-4,32/-4,0,0,16,32/0,-4,0,16,16,32/

(6x6)

$(P^i)(T^e)(P^i) = (T^e)$ $i \geq 1$

Quadratic Approximation

$6720*(T^e)$: 76/11,76/11,11,76/18,0,27,540/0,18,27,-189,540/

27,18,0,-135,270,540/27,0,18,-54,-135,-189,540/

0,27,18,-135,-54,-135,270,540/18,27,0,270,-135,-54,-135,-189,540/

36,36,36,162,162,162,162,162,162,1944/

(10x10)

$(P^i)T^e)(P^i)^\tau = T^e$ $i \geq 1$

Where P : (1,2,3)(4,6,8)(5,7,9)

Cubic Approximation

Fig. 5 : The lower triangualr part of the T^e matrices used to construct the fixed, fission and scattering sources and the removal terms for an element.

$$(CB^e) = Beta * L_i * (BCOEF)_i$$
$$CV_i = QCOEF_i * Qu * L_i$$

$$(BCOEF)_{i+1} = (P^i)(BCOEF)_1(P^i)^\tau \qquad i=1,2$$
$$QCOEF_{i+1} = (P^i)QCOEF_1$$

a) $6*(BCOEF)_1$ = 0/0,2/0,1,2/ (3x3)

$2*QCOEF_1$ = 0,-1,-1 (3x1)

P : (1,2,3)

b) $30*(BCOEF)_1$ = 0/0,4/0,-1,0/0,0,0,0/0,2,2,0,16/0,0,0,0,0,0/ (6x6)

$6*\ QCOEF_1$ = 0,-1,-1,0,-4,0 (6x1)

P : (1,2,3)(4,5,6)

c) $1680*(BCOEF)_1$ = 0/0,128/0,19,128/0,0,0,0/0,0,0,0,0/0,99,-36,0,0,648/
0,-36,99,0,0,-81,648/0,0,0,0,0,0,0,0/0,0,0,0,0,0,0,0,0/
0,0,0,0,0,0,0,0,0,0/
(10x10)

$8*QCOEF_1$ = 0,-1,-1,0,0,-3,-3,0,0,0 (10x1)

P : (1,2,3)(4,6,8)(5,7,9)

Fig. 6 : (CB^e), the contribution to the element matrix and CV_i, the contribution to the element vector due to (a) linear, (b) quadratic (c) cubic approximations to Cauchy boundary conditions, $\frac{\delta\phi}{\delta n} + \hat{\beta}\phi + Q = 0$ prescribed on the ith side of the element.

$$P_m(\xi) = P_{m-1}(\xi) * (NPROX*\xi-m+1)/m$$

$$P_o(\xi) = 1$$

$$\alpha_{ijk}(\xi_1,\xi_2,\xi_3) = P_i(\xi_i)*P_j(\xi_2)*P_k(\xi_3) \qquad i+j+k = NPROX$$

$$\xi_1+\xi_2+\xi_3 = 1$$

Linear Approximation - NPROX=1

$$P_o(\xi) = 1 \,, \qquad P_1(\xi) = \xi$$

$$\phi(\xi_1,\xi_2,\xi_3) = \xi_1\phi_1 + \xi_2\phi_2 + \xi_3\phi_3$$

Quadratic Approximation - NPROX=2

$$P_o(\xi) = 1 \,, \quad P_1(\xi) = 2\xi \,, \quad P_2(\xi) = (2\xi^2-\xi)$$

$$\phi(\xi_1,\xi_2,\xi_3) = (2\xi_1^2-\xi_1)\phi_1+(2\xi_2^2-\xi_2)\xi_2+(2\xi_3^2-\xi_3)\phi_3 + 4\xi_1\xi_2\phi_4 + 4\xi_2\xi_3\phi_5 + 4\xi_1\xi_3\phi_6$$

Cubic Approximation - NPROX=3

$$P_o(\xi)=1 \,, \; P_1(\xi)=3\xi \,, \; P_2(\xi)=\frac{1}{2}(9\xi^2-3\xi) \,, \; P_3(\xi)=\frac{1}{2}(9\xi^3-9\xi^2+2\xi)$$

$$\begin{aligned} 2*\phi(\xi_1,\xi_2,\xi_3) = {} & (9\xi_1^3-9\xi_1^2+2\xi_1)\phi_1+(9\xi_2^3-9\xi_2^2+2\xi_2)\phi_2+(9\xi_3^3-9\xi_3^2+2\xi_3)\,\phi_3 \\ & + (27\xi_1^2\xi_2-9\xi_1\xi_2)\phi_4+(27\xi_1\xi_2^2-9\xi_1\xi_2)\phi_5+(27\xi_2^2\xi_3-9\xi_2\xi_3)\phi_6 \\ & + (27\xi_2\xi_3^2-9\xi_2\xi_3)\phi_7+(27\xi_1\xi_3^2-9\xi_1\xi_3)\phi_8+(27\xi_1^2\xi_3-9\xi_1\xi_3)\phi_9 \\ & + 27\xi_1\xi_2\xi_3 \end{aligned}$$

Fig. 7 : Polynomial Approximations for the fluxes.

2. COMPUTED PROBLEMS

Benchmark Problem No. 1

Source problem

One energy group, isotropical scattering, 5 materials, 5 zones each with material of the same number.

Source : : flat, isotropical.
In zones 1 and 3, Q = 1,
in zones 2,4 and 5, Q = 0

Boundary condition : vacuum

X-Y Geometry:

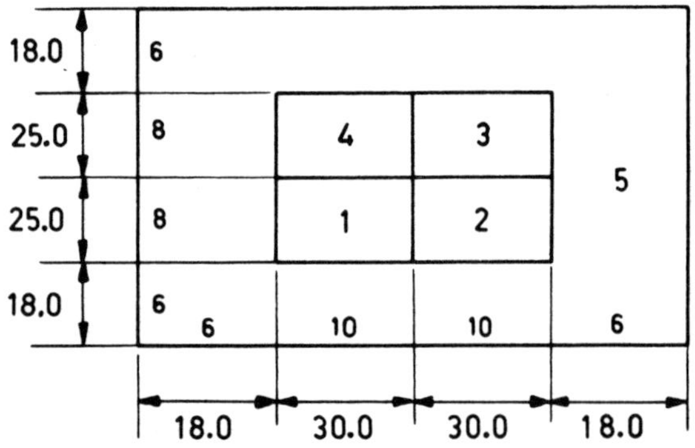

Fig. 8

Cross Sections:

Material	Σ_a	$\nu\Sigma_f$	Σ_t	Σ_{gg}
1	0.07	0.0	0.60	0.53
2	0.28	0.0	0.48	0.20
3	0.04	0.0	0.70	0.66
4	0.15	0.0	0.65	0.50
5	0.01	0.0	0.90	0.89

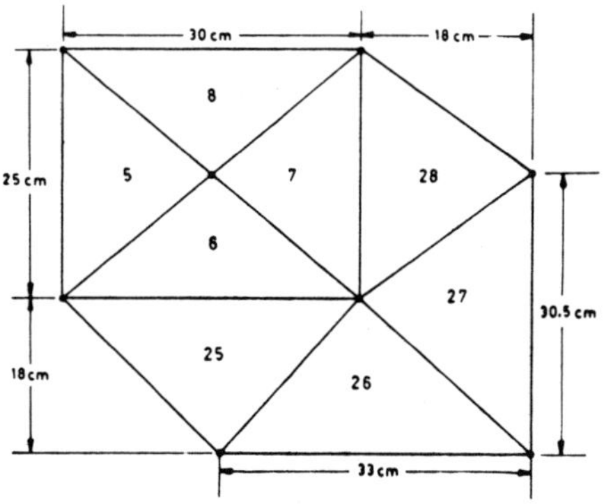
30 cm
18 cm
25 cm
18cm
30.5 cm
33cm

Fig.

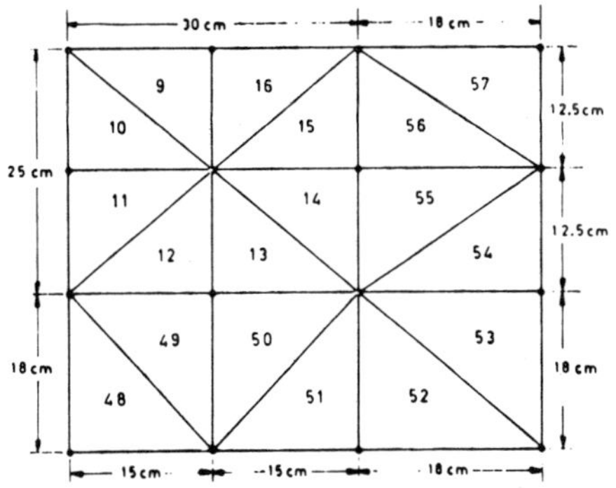
30 cm
18 cm
25 cm
18 cm
12.5cm
12.5cm
18 cm
15cm
15cm
18cm

Fig.

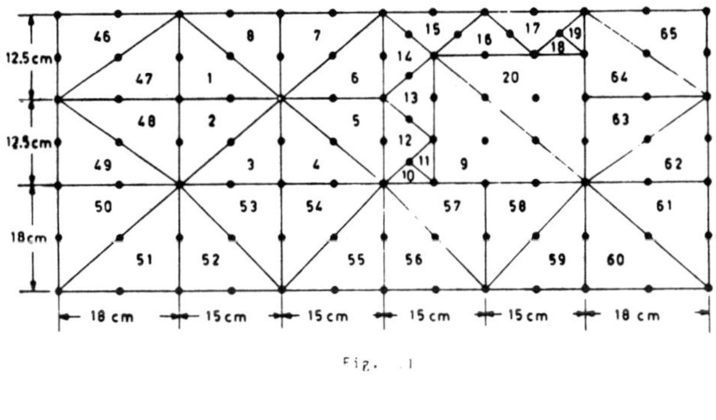
12.5cm
12.5cm
18cm
18 cm
15cm
15cm
15cm
15cm
18 cm

Fig.

Code	Number of Intervals	Average Flux Ratios Φ_n/Φ_1 in Zone n				Time (sec
		2	3	4	5	
CODIFF	16 x 14	2.8163-2	1.6350	4.3503-2	1.0224-1	2.8
	32 x 28	3.9249-2	1.6137	6.0280-2	1.2033-1	10.7
	64 x 56	--	--	--	--	--
DIFFUS	16 x 14	2.8162-2	1.6349	4.3504-2	1.0225-1	3.7
	32 x 28	3.9246-2	1.6138	6.0283-2	1.2006-1	13.0
	64 x 56	--	--	--	--	--
DIFF-2D	16 x 14	2.8163-2	1.6350	4.3504-2	1.0232-1	5.9
	32 x 28	3.9249-2	1.6137	6.0280-2	1.2041-1	22.4
	64 x 56	4.5129-2	1.6065	6.8998-2	1.2717-1	105.8
PHADGA	16 x 14	9.2817-2	1.5830	1.3090-1	2.3570-1	1.9
	32 x 28	1.2120-1	1.48526	1.7706-1	3.8581-1	3.6
	64 x 56	--	--	--	--	--

Tab. 1: Problem Nr. 1: Given volumic source
($Q_1 = Q_3 = 1$, $Q_2 = Q_4 = Q_5 = 0$, "vacuum" boundary)

Item		Case 1	Case 2	Case 3	Case 4	Case 5
Approx Type-No.Elements/ Poly.degree		36/Quadratics	36/Cubics	72/Quadratics	72/Cubics	80/Quadratics & Cubics (Fig.3)
Avg. Flux in Zone 1		11.69997	11.79263	11.62513	11.81733	11.69459
Avg. Flux Ratios Φ_n/Φ_1 in Zone n	2	0.05333	0.04996	0.05424	0.04916	0.05232
	3	1.57795	1.60300	1.60095	1.60337	1.60265
	4	0.08241	0.07544	0.08141	0.07458	0.07976
	5	0.13090	0.13020	0.13299	0.12968	0.13021
H.Stepsize x V.Stepsize cm x cm Zone	1	12.5 x 15	10 x 8.3	6.25 x 7.5	5 x 4.16	6.25 x 7.5
	2	12.5 x 15	10 x 8.3	6.25 x 7.5	5 x 4.16	3.75 x 3.125 &(7.5 x 6.25)
	3	12.5 x 15	10 x 8.3	6.25 x 7.5	5 x 4.16	6.25 x 7.5
	4	12.5 x 15	10 x 8.3	6.25 x 7.5	5 x 4.16	3.75 x 3.125 &(7.5 x 6.25)
	5	15 x 18 &(18 x 18)	10 x 12 &(12 x 12)	9 x 7.5 &(9 x 9)	5 x 6 &(6 x 6)	9 x 6.25 &(9 x 9)
(Exec./Total) CP secs		2.048/6.565	4.132/8.594	4.255/8.670	10.503/14.907	5.742/9.814
Degrees of freedom or Syst. Matrix Order		85	181	169	361	227
No. Coupling Coeffs.		482	1513	944	3025	1312
Storage for coupling Coeffs. plus temporary zeros		1291	5239	3320	13717	5456

Tab. 2: Given volumic Source (FINELM Computations) ($Q_1 = Q_3 = 1$, $Q_2 = Q_4 = Q_5 = 0$, Vacuum boundary)

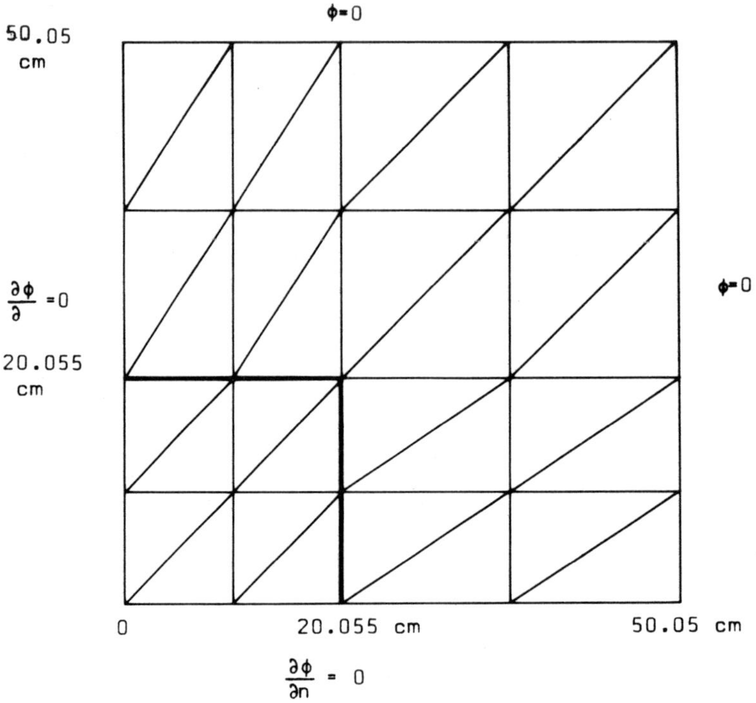

Group	Dg	Σ_{r}^{R}	$(\nu\Sigma_f)_g$	Σ 1→2	χ_g
1	2.68000451313	$5.45770376809 10^{-2}$	$3.083448\cdot 10^{-2}$		.575
2	1.57876722277	$1.44960876\cdot 10^{-2}$	$2.52\cdot 10^{-2}$	$4.07920706831\cdot 10^{-2}$	.425

Fig.12 : Geometry and cross-sections for a homogeneous, two group reactor.

REFERENCES

(1) Forsythe & Wasow, Finite difference methods for Partial Differential Equations.

(2) Hansen & Kang, Advances in Nuclear Science and technology Vol.8 (1975)

(3) Protter, Weinberg, Maximum Principles in Differential Equations

(4) I. Stackgold, Boundary Value problems in Mathematical Physics.

(5) O. Zienkiewicz, The Finite Element Method.

(6) Strang & Fix, Analysis of the Finite Element Method.

(7) Kaper, Leaf & Lindeman, A Timing study for same high order Finite Element Approximation Procedures and a Low Order Finite Difference Approximation Procedure for the Numerical Solution of the Multigroup Neutron Diffusion Equation - Nucl. Sci. and Eng. 49 (27-48) 1972

(8) J.J. Goel, Construction of Basic Functions for Numerical Utilization of Ritz's Method, Numer. Math. 12, 435-447 (1968)

(9) Dupuis & Goel, Finite Element with high degree of regularity, International Journal for Numerical Methods in Engr. Vol.2, (563-577) 1970.

(10) Kratochvil, Zenisek, Zlamal, A simple algorithm for the stiffness matrix of triangular plate Bending Elements, International J. for Num. Methods in Engr. Vol.3, (553-563) 1971.

(11) Bramble & Zlamal, Triangular Elements in the Finite Element Method, Math. of Computation Vol. 24 Nr. 112, Oct. 1970.

(12) J. Descloux, On finite Element Matrices SIAM, J. Num.Anal. Vol 9, No.2, June 1972.

(13) Délèze & Goel, Tetraèdre comme Elément Fini de classe C', a seize paramètres contenant les polynômes de degree deux - Institut de Mathématique, Université de Fribourg Jan. 1972.

(14) Davierwalla, Hager, Köhler, Stepanek - Two dimensional X-Y Diffusion, Benchmark Problem Study TM-PH-582.

D.M. Davierwalla
Eidg. Institut für Reaktorforschung
CH-5303 Würenlingen

COMPUTER CALCULATION OF THE MAGNETIC EFFECTS IN THE ALUMINIUM ELECTROLYTIC CELLS

Jean-Marc BLANC
Aluminium Suisse SA

Abstract

Electromagnetic effects produced in the electrolytic cells during the production of aluminium are known to exist. In particular, these effects bring about movements in the liquid metal, as well as interface variations in level, that are detrimental to efficiency and energy consumption. An experimental study of these effects would raise a number of problems particularly difficult to solve technically at present. For this reason, it is advisable to have recourse to an electronic computer for working out the electric, magnetic, force and velocity field distributions within the liquid in the cell. This paper outlines the methods that we proposed and applied for the computing of the electric and magnetic fields.

Introduction

Nowadays aluminium is essentially produced according to the Hall-Héroult process, in other words, by electrolysis of alumina Al_2O_3 desolved in molten cryolite Na_3AlF_6 at a temperature of about 950 ^oC. In a reduction plant cells are connected in series. For technical and economical reasons, it is advisable to choose large nominal currents (150 kA). For such intensities, the electromagnetic effects in the cells become important. In particular, these effects bring about movements in the liquid metal, as well as interface variations in level, that are detrimental to efficiency and energy consumption [1,2]. For an optimal design, it is necessary to predetermine the electromagnetic behaviour of each new typ of cells. It is specially necessary to calculate the repartition of the current density in each point of the cell (electric problem), and the magnetic induction produced in the liquid metal by the currents circulating in the cell itself, in the near cells and in the external conductors (magnetic problem).

Electric problem formulation

Stationary electric phenomena are described by the equations

$$\vec{rot}\vec{E}=0 \qquad (1)$$

$$div\vec{J}=0 \qquad (2)$$

$$\vec{E}=\rho\vec{J} \qquad (3)$$

The first equation can be replaced by

$$\vec{E}=-\overrightarrow{grad}U \qquad (4)$$

where U is the electric potential.

We can eliminate $\vec{E}$ and $\vec{J}$ between the equations above. In an homogeneous material, we obtain a Laplace's equation

$$\Delta U=0 \tag{5}$$

On surfaces separating material of different resistivities, the electric field $\vec{E}$ and the current density $\vec{J}$ cannot be continuous (refraction of the current lines), and the differential operators $\vec{rot}$ and div become irrelevant. The equations (1) and (2) must be replaced by the expression of continuity of the tangential components of $\vec{E}$ and of the normal component of $\vec{J}$.

$$\vec{E}_{1t} = \vec{E}_{2t} \tag{6}$$

$$J_{1n} = J_{2n} \tag{7}$$

If we introduce the electric potential, we must write

$$U_1 = U_2 \tag{8}$$

The differential formulation of the electric problem, as shown above, is not practical for numeric applications: the only method we have to integrate such an elliptic equation, consists in solving a system of finite differential equations. The system is etablished with the help of an orthogonal network. In most practical problems, the geometry of the region of integration is so complicated that the method becomes impossible. Moreover, the continuity relations (6), (7) and (8), that should be used on the surfaces separating materials of different resistivities, would involve unmountable difficulties. For these reasons, we are obliged to consider another formulation.

We name V the area in which circulate the currents that we want to study, and S the surface limiting V. The region V is divided in a finite number of partial regions V_i, limited by surfaces S_i, in which we have an uniform resistivity ρ_i.

The value of the potential U is given at least on a part of S. On the rest of S, its normal derivative is equal to zero.

We name D the set of scalar functions

- that comply to the above conditions on S
- of the class C^1 in the V_i
- continuous on the S_i

We define the functional

$$G\left[U\right] = \iiint_V \frac{\overrightarrow{\mathrm{grad}U}\;\overrightarrow{\mathrm{grad}U}}{2\varrho}\,dV \qquad (9)$$

We define thereafter as electric potential the function U, member of the set D, which makes $G[U]$ extremum. It could be demonstrated that this extremal formulation is similar to the above differential formulation. Moreover, there are good methods to solve such problems.

Numerical solution of the electric problem

In order to keep computer costs low we restrained ourselves, up to now, to bidimensional problems: transversal and longitudinal sections through a cell divulge usefull informations.

We elaborated some programs for bidimensional problems, using the finite elements method. We chose triangular elements of the first order: the complexity of the geometry makes imperative a great number of small elements. High-order finite elements would increase the density of the matrix of the system, without any reduction of its order.

For solving large systems, it is advisable to take advantage of the low density of the matrix: the numbering of the mesh points can therefore be made in a way that the non-zero terms are concentrated in a few partial matrices grouped near the principal diagonal, as shown below.

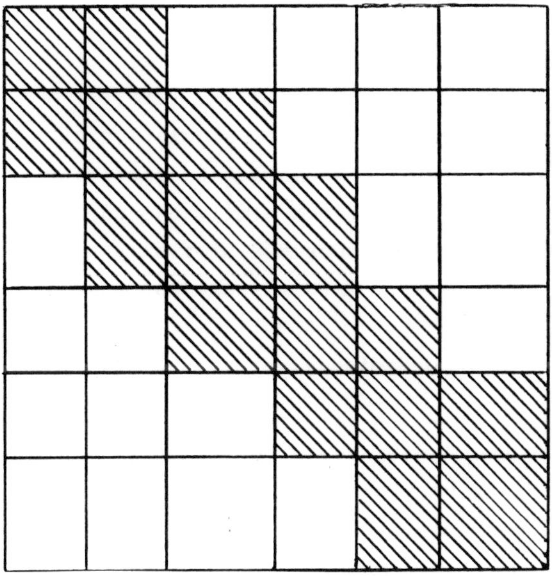

To solve such a system, we used a modified Choleski's method [3,4], that gave excellent results. Many applications have been so treated. In most cases, the question was to etablish the map of the electric potential in the transversal section of a cell. In a first stage, we plotted this map for an existing "reference" cell, upon which we could plot maps for any proposed modification.

The use of the actual version of the program has made clear that some extensions are usefull:

- the magnitude of the input requires extensive error diagnostics. Moreover, a partial automatisation of the preparation of the input would notably reduce the costs
- the plot of the current lines would say more than the

equipotential lines

- the extension to tridimensional problems should be possible almost without increase of the nead of core memory, but with an important increase in computing time and number of disk accesses.

The problem of the holes

In some cases, there are areas of isolating material inside of the studied section. For the calculation of the potential repartition, such areas don't contribute to the integral (9) . They should be simply excluded from the domain of integration. For the plot of the current lines, we have to make extremal the functional

$$H[I] = \iint \frac{\varrho}{2} (\partial_x I)^2 + (\partial_y I)^2 \, dxdy \qquad (10)$$

The contribution of the "hole" would be infinite. It is possible to use a trick, that we demonstrate here for a section with one hole.

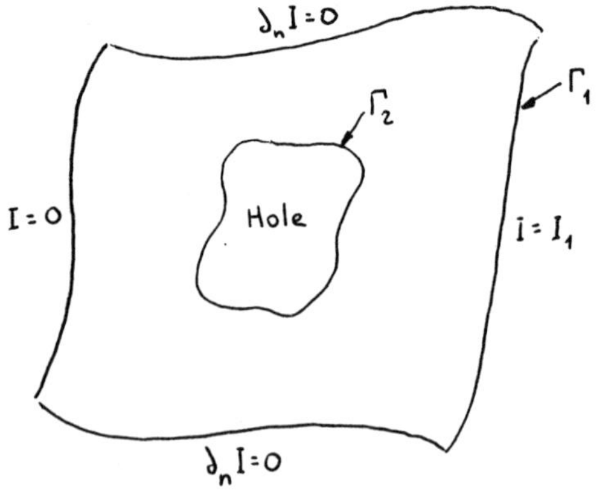

It is evident that Γ_2 is an equi-I line, but the value I_2 of I on Γ_2 is unknown. The functional $H[I]$ is a quadratic function of I_1 and I_2

$$H[I] = \alpha I_1^2 + \beta I_2^2 + 2\gamma I_1 I_2$$

We can calculate $H[I]$ for three typical boundary conditions:

1 on the right side of Γ_1 and 0 on Γ_2

0 on the right side of Γ_1 and 1 on Γ_2

1 on the right side of Γ_1 and 1 on Γ_2

and determine α, β and γ. If $H[I]$ is extremum for $I=I_2$ on Γ_2, we have

$$\frac{\partial H}{\partial I_2}=2(\beta I_2+\gamma I_1)=0$$

The value of I_2 is now known, and we can calculate I. The method can be extended to more than one hole.

<u>The magnetic problem</u>

Stationary magnetic phenomena are described by the equations

$$\overrightarrow{\mathrm{rot}}\vec{H}=\vec{J} \qquad (11)$$

$$\mathrm{div}\vec{B}=0 \qquad (12)$$

$$\vec{B}=\mu\vec{H} \qquad (13)$$

The equation (12) can be replaced by

$$\overrightarrow{\mathrm{rot}}\vec{A}=\vec{B} \qquad (14)$$

where $\vec{A}$ is the magnetic vector-potential, with

$$\mathrm{div}\vec{A}=0 \qquad (15)$$

On the surfaces between materials of different permeabilities, we have

$$\vec{H}_{1t}=\vec{H}_{2t} \qquad (16)$$

$$B_{1n}=B_{2n} \qquad (17)$$

$$\vec{A}_1=\vec{A}_2 \qquad (18)$$

We can eliminate $\vec{E}$ an $\vec{J}$ between (11), (13) and (14). In an homogeneous material, we obtain a Poisson's equation:

$$\vec{\Delta} A = -\mu \vec{J} \quad (19)$$

If we neglect the effect of ferromagnetic materials, we have overall

$$\mu = \mu_0$$

and we can write

$$\vec{A} = \frac{\mu_0}{4\pi} \iiint \frac{1}{r} \vec{J} dV \quad (20)$$

The value of the magnetic vector-potential can be easily calculated according to the relation (20).

References

1 J.-P. Givry: Le calcul sur ordinateur des effets magnétiques dans les cuves d'électrolyse à aluminium. AIME-Meeting, 1967.

2 T. Iuchi: Rise and flow of molten metal in aluminium reduction cells. AIME-Meeting, 1970.

3 Centre de Calcul de l'EPF-Lausanne: Programme SL7, systèmes tridiagonaux par blocs.

4 G. Dupuis et J.-J. Goël: Calcul numerique des plaques fléchies. Bulletin technique de la Suisse Romande, 1966, n°s 4 et 5.

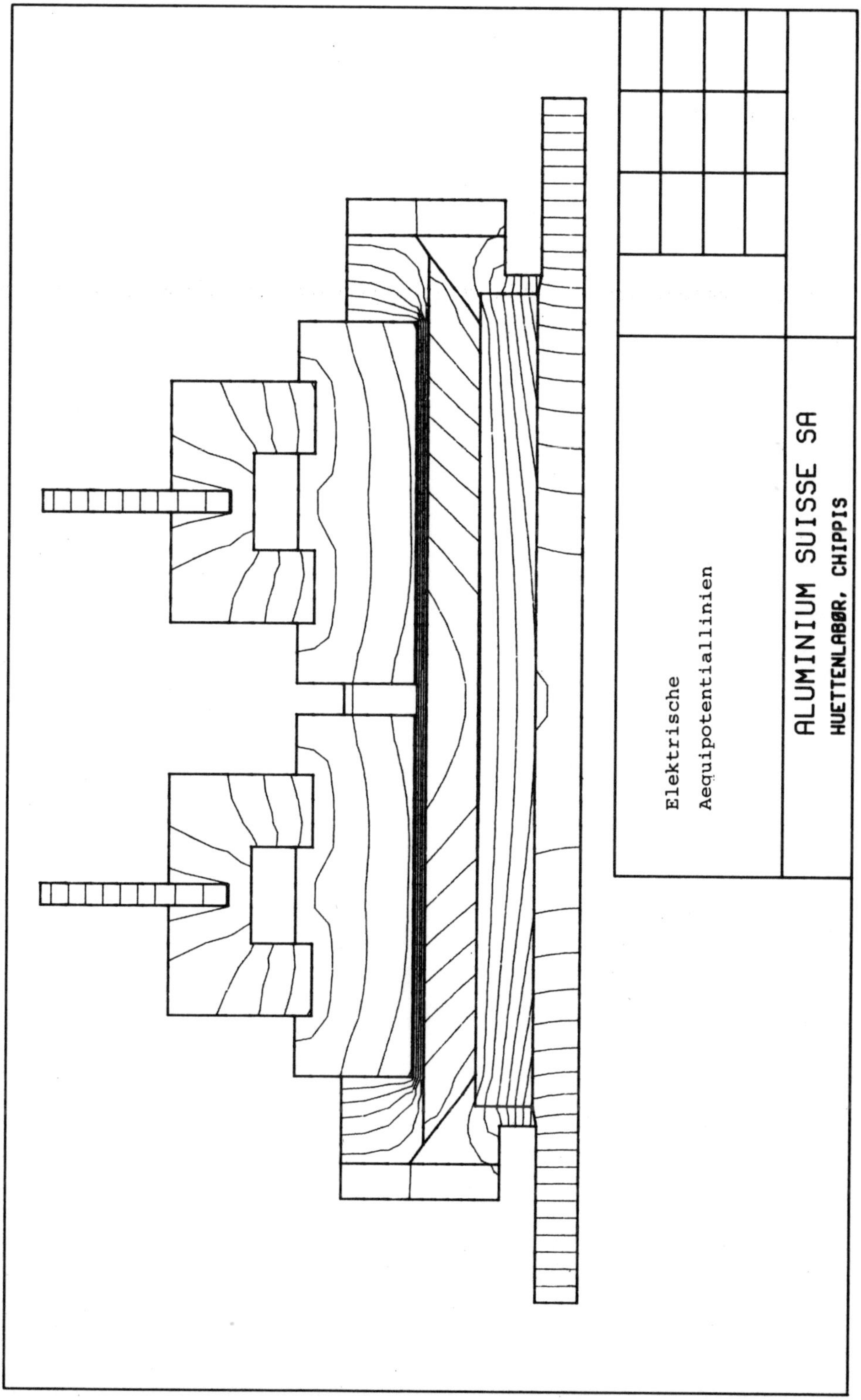
Elektrische
Aequipotentiallinien
ALUMINIUM SUISSE SA
HUETTENLABOR, CHIPPIS

ISNM 37 Birkhäuser Verlag, Basel und Stuttgart, 1977

NUMERICAL METHODS FOR THE CALCULATION OF MOLECULAR DYNAMICS:

1. Integration of the Equations of Motion;
2. Calculation of Correlation Functions.

R.H. Morf* and E.P. Stoll

IBM Zurich Research Laboratory, 8803 Rüschlikon, Switzerland

Abstract: The calculation of molecular dynamics requires the numerical solution of many coupled differential equations. We present an efficient and stable method for numerical integration. Further we discuss a procedure for calculating time-correlation functions and spectral densities by means of the Fast Fourier Transform.

October 5, 1976

---

*On leave from the Theoretical Physics Institute of the University of Basel, Switzerland.

1. Integration of the Equations of Motion

In order to study the thermodynamical properties of physical systems, the method of computer simulation has been increasingly used and developed. On the one hand, the method of Monte Carlo simulation is used to determine some of the static properties while, on the other hand, the method of molecular-dynamics calculation is suitable to obtain information on both statical and dynamical properties of the system. Hereby, the Newtonian equations of motion are numerically solved for a large number of particles. The integration times have to be quite long so as to ensure that the system gets into a thermodynamic state independent of the initial conditions. Also, the physical quantities (e.g., correlation functions) are calculated as time averages, and, in order to keep the statistical errors small, the averaging period must be much longer than the relaxation time of the slowest cooperative motions [1]. So, one is faced with two problems which make the numerical solution difficult: i) the large number of coupled differential equations; ii) the long integration times.

Furthermore, in practically all interesting systems, the differential equations are strongly nonlinear, which imposes high requirements on the stability of the numerical procedure used to solve Newton's equations. In particular, we must be able to reproduce stationary or equilibrium states so the energy of the system must neither decrease nor blow up during the numerical integration.

It may be useful to illustrate this by means of a simple example. Consider the well-known harmonic oscillator

$$\ddot{X}(t) = -\omega_0^2 X(t) \tag{1}$$

subject to the initial conditions

$$X(t{=}0) = 1, \tag{2}$$

$$\dot{X}(t{=}0) = i\omega_0. \tag{3}$$

The well-known exact solution

$$X(t) = e^{i\omega_0 t} \tag{4}$$

always lies on the unit circle.

Numerical methods can be classified according to their behavior when applied to Eq.(1):

a) amplitude true

b) non-amplitude true.

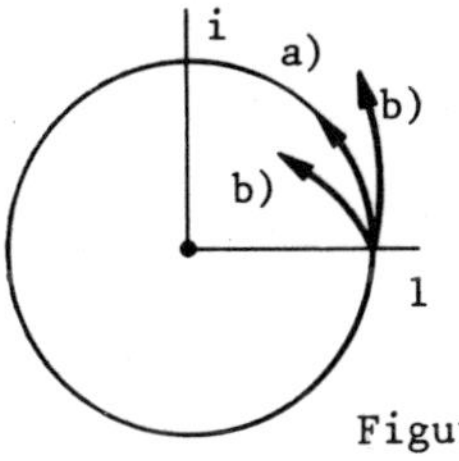

Figure 1

In Fig. 1, these cases are illustrated. Of the non-amplitude true methods, the particuarly dangerous ones are those which lead out of the unit circle and eventually blow up. The stability properties of a particular numerical method will, in general, depend upon the type of differential equation as well as the integration step size, as will be seen below.

In the following, we shall describe a numerical integration procedure which has proved to be particularly useful in all cases where a high level of stability is required. We shall apply these to two different problems, namely, the solution of the pure Newtonian equations of motion as well as equations of motion in the presence of damping and stochastic forces used to describe coupling of the system to a heat bath.

1.1 *Newtonian Equations of Motion*

We write our system of coupled differential equations in the following form:

$$m_i \ddot{\vec{X}}_i = - \nabla_i V(\vec{X}_1, \vec{X}_2, \ldots, \vec{X}_N, t), \tag{5}$$

where the subscript i refers to particle i with mass m_i. Owing to the presence of external forces the potential V may be explicitly time dependent. In this section, however, we confine ourselves to conservative forces. Thus, V is taken to be independent of the particle velocities $\dot{\vec{X}}_i$. This suggests the use of a numerical scheme which does not require the knowledge of first derivatives.

A simple formula (see, for example, Godunov *et al.*[2]) can be derived from a Taylor expansion of $X(t \pm \Delta)$ up to third derivatives

$$X(t+\Delta) = X(t) + \Delta\dot{X}(t) + \frac{\Delta^2}{2} \ddot{X}(t) + \frac{\Delta^3}{6} \dddot{X}(t) + 0(\Delta^4) \tag{6}$$

and

$$X(t-\Delta) = X(t) - \Delta\dot{X}(t) + \frac{\Delta^2}{2} \ddot{X}(t) - \frac{\Delta^3}{6} \dddot{X}(t) + 0(\Delta^4). \tag{7}$$

Adding these two quantities, we get as in Ref.[3]

$$X(t+\Delta) = 2X(t) - X(t-\Delta) + \Delta^2 \ddot{X}(t) + 0(\Delta^4) \tag{8}$$

Let us investigate its stability properties for the harmonic oscillator problem (1) and study the solutions to the finite difference equation (8) analytically. Using the Ansatz

$$X(t) = e^{i\alpha t + \beta t}, \tag{9}$$

where α and β are real constants, we obtain together with the equation of motion (8)

$$e^{i\alpha\Delta + \beta\Delta} = - e^{-i\alpha\Delta - \beta\Delta} + 2 - \Delta^2 \omega_0^2, \tag{10}$$

or looking at its real and imaginary parts

$$\cos \alpha\Delta \cdot \cosh \beta\Delta = 1 - \frac{\Delta^2 \omega_0^2}{2} \tag{11}$$

and

$$\sin \alpha\Delta \cdot \sinh \beta\Delta = 0. \tag{12}$$

To study the solutions to these equations we have to consider three different cases:

i) $\alpha \neq n\pi \qquad n = 0, \pm 1, \pm 2, \ldots$

In this case, β has to be zero and the solution is thus stable. Thus, the approximation only leads to phase errors which result in a frequency shift. The frequency α is found to be

$$\alpha = \frac{1}{\Delta} \text{ arc cos}\left(1 - \frac{\Delta^2 \omega_0^2}{2}\right) \tag{13}$$

and for small $\Delta\omega_0$

$$\alpha \approx \omega_0 \left(1 + \frac{1}{24} \Delta^2\omega_0^2\right). \tag{14}$$

ii) $\alpha = 2n\pi, \quad n = 0, \pm 1, \ldots$

Equation (11) in this case becomes

$$\cosh \beta\Delta = 1 - \frac{\Delta^2\omega_0^2}{2} \tag{15}$$

which for non-zero ω_0 has no real solution for β. For $\omega_0 = 0$ we get the correct result $\beta = 0$.

iii) $\alpha = (2n + 1)\pi, \qquad n = 0, \pm 1, \pm 2, \ldots$

In this case, Eq.(11) reads

$$\cosh \beta\Delta = \frac{(\Delta\omega_0)^2}{2} - 1 \tag{16}$$

which has no real solutions as long as $\Delta\omega_0 < 2$. For $\Delta\omega_0 > 2$ we find unstable solutions with $\beta > 0$.

Thus, the stability limit is given by

$$\Delta\omega_0 = 2. \tag{17}$$

The finite difference approximation is thus stable as long as

$$\Delta < \frac{T}{\pi}, \tag{18}$$

where T is the period of the oscillation. One comment which we have to make at this point is that the numerical procedure defined by Eq.(8) is not self starting but requires the knowledge of both $X(-\Delta)$ and $X(0)$. In initial value problems, where $X(0)$ and its derivative are defined, some method must be used to calculate $X(-\Delta)$. For this purpose, the Taylor expansion is quite practical, especially if higher-order derivatives can be calculated analytically. Otherwise, a suitable method is to initially take a smaller step size $\Delta_i (\Delta_i = \Delta/n)$ for which the second-order Taylor expansion is accurate enough.

A third way of satisfying some physical properties is to start with a scheme including damping and random noise, described in the Section 1.*3*, and after a certain time to switch off these properties.

1.*2* *Equations of Motion with Damping*

In contrast to the situation considered above, in this case the equations of motion explicitly depend on the velocities

$$m_i \ddot{\vec{X}}_i = - \nabla_i V(\vec{X}_1, \ldots, \vec{X}_N, t) - \Gamma m_i \dot{\vec{X}}_i . \tag{19}$$

Two principally different methods can be used in this case:

i) The velocities are treated as additional variables which are integrated numerically.

ii) The velocities are eliminated from the equations of motion by a suitable transformation.

We shall use the latter procedure in order to employ the very practical method described in Section 1.*1*.

To eliminate the first derivative term in Eq.(19), we introduce new variables

$$\vec{y}_i = e^{\Gamma t/2}\, \vec{X}_i. \tag{20}$$

Then Eq.(19) becomes

$$\ddot{\vec{y}}_i = \frac{\Gamma^2}{4}\, \vec{y}_i - e^{\Gamma t/2} \cdot 1/m_i \nabla_i V\,(\vec{X}_1, \vec{X}_2, \ldots \vec{X}_N, t). \tag{21}$$

This equation can now be integrated by means of Eq.(8),

$$\vec{y}_i(t+\Delta) = 2\vec{y}_i(t) - \vec{y}_i(t-\Delta) + \Delta^2 \ddot{\vec{y}}_i(t) + O(\Delta^4), \tag{22}$$

or inserting the definition of y,

$$\begin{aligned}\vec{X}_i(t+\Delta) = {} & 2\vec{X}_i(t)\, e^{-\Gamma\Delta/2} - e^{-\Gamma\Delta}\, \vec{X}_i(t-\Delta) \\ & + \Delta^2 e^{-\Gamma\Delta/2} \left[\frac{\Gamma^2}{4}\, \vec{X}_i(t) - 1/m_i \nabla_i V(\vec{X}_1, \ldots, \vec{X}_N, t) \right] + O(\Delta^4).\end{aligned} \tag{23}$$

This equation, although of order Δ^4 like Eq.(8) has a serious deficiency as it is not translationally invariant. Consider the special case

$$\ddot{X} = -\Gamma \dot{X} + C, \quad C = \text{const.} \tag{24}$$

The stationary solution is given by

$$X(t) = \frac{C}{\Gamma}\, t + X(0). \tag{25}$$

The equation of motion (24) is clearly invariant under the transformation $X'(t) = X(t) + \text{const.}$ On the other hand, it is easy to see that the finite difference formula (23) is invariant against translation only up to third order in Δ, the fourth-order term violating translational invariance. However, this can be corrected quite easily by rewriting Eq.(23) as

$$\begin{aligned}\vec{X}_i(t+\Delta) = {} & \vec{X}_i(t) + \left(\vec{X}_i(t) - \vec{X}_i(t-\Delta)\right) e^{-\Gamma\Delta} \\ & - \Delta^2 e^{-\frac{\Gamma\Delta}{2}} \cdot 1/m_i \nabla_i V\,(\vec{X}_1, \ldots, \vec{X}_N, t) + O(\Delta^4).\end{aligned} \tag{26}$$

Up to third order in Δ this equation is identical to Eq.(23) and it obviously displays the translational invariance property we require.

1.3 *Equations of Motion with Stochastic Forces*

If a system is coupled to a heat bath, this effect can be taken into account by the well-known method due to Onsager and Machlup [4],

$$m_i\ddot{\vec{X}}_i = - m_i\Gamma\dot{\vec{X}}_i - \nabla_i V(\vec{X}_1,\ldots,\vec{X}_N,t) + \vec{\eta}_i(t), \tag{27}$$

where the stochastic force $\vec{\eta}_i(t)$ is a Gaussian distributed random vector with the property of its α - component

$$\langle\eta_i^\alpha(t)\ \eta_k^\alpha(t+\tau)\rangle = 2\ m_i k_B T\ \Gamma\delta_{ik}\delta(\tau). \tag{28}$$

Here, k_B denotes the Boltzmann constant, and T stands for the temperature of the heat bath.

In the discrete case, Eq.(28) takes the form

$$\langle\eta_i^\alpha(t_1)\ \eta_k^\alpha(t_2)\rangle = 2\ m_i k_B T\ \Gamma\ \delta_{ik}\ \delta_{t_1,t_2}\ \frac{1}{\Delta}, \tag{29}$$

where Δ is the time interval between subsequent actions of the stochastic force. Thus, $\vec{\eta}(t)$ can be simulated numerically by means of Gaussian distributed random numbers $\gamma(t)$ with unit variance through

$$\eta_i^\alpha(t) = \sqrt{\frac{2m_i k_B T\ \Gamma}{\Delta}}\ \gamma(t). \tag{30}$$

It is well known that kinks in the derivatives as they are produced by the stochastic forces can seriously affect the stability of a numerical integration procedure. As a general rule, methods of high order in Δ must be applied cautiously because in the presence of stochastic forces, higher-order derivatives will be increasingly pathological. For this reason, Runge-Kutta methods as well as predictor-corrector methods, e.g., those in

Ref. [1] or the Adams method, should not be used. From practical experience, we recommend use of the method outlined in Section 1.2.

2. Calculation of Correlation Functions

For the fast Fourier method, we adopt the notation of Cooley and Tukey [5]. Consider the problem of calculating the complex Fourier series

$$X(j) = \sum_{k=0}^{N-1} A(k)\, W^{jk}, \quad j = 0,1\dots,N-1, \tag{31}$$

where N is the dimension of the vector to be transformed. The complex Fourier coefficients are denoted by $A(k)$, and W is the principal Nth root of unity

$$W = e^{2\pi i/N}. \tag{32}$$

A straightforward calculation using (31) would require N^2 operations where "operation" means, as it will throughout this paper, a complex multiplication followed by a complex addition.

The algorithm described here iterates on the array of given complex Fourier amplitudes and yields the result in less than $2N \log_2 N$ operations without requiring more data storage than is required for the given array A. To derive the algorithm, suppose N is a composite, i.e., $N = r_1 r_2$. Then let the indices in (31) be expressed

$$j = j_1 r_1 + j_0, \quad j_0 = 0,1,\dots,r_1 - 1, \quad j_1 = 0,1,\dots,r_2 - 1, \tag{33}$$

$$k = k_1 r_2 + k_0, \quad k_0 = 0,1,\dots,r_2 - 1, \quad k_1 = 0,1,\dots,r_1 - 1.$$

Then one can write

$$X(j_1,j_0) = \sum_{k_0} \sum_{k_1} A(k_1,k_0)\cdot W^{jk_1 r_2} W^{jk_0}. \tag{34}$$

Since

$$W^{jk_1r_2} = W^{j_0k_1r_2}, \tag{35}$$

the inner sum, over k_1, depends only on j_0 and k_0 and can be defined as a new array,

$$A_1(j_0,k_0) = \sum_{k_1} A(k_1,k_0) \cdot W^{j_0k_1r_2}. \tag{36}$$

The result can then be written

$$X(j_1,j_0) = \sum_{k_0} A_1(j_0,k_0) \cdot W^{(j_1r_1+j_0)k_0}. \tag{37}$$

There are N elements in the array A_1, each requiring r_1 operations, giving a total of Nr_1 operations to obtain A_1. Similarly, it takes Nr_2 operations to calculate X from A_1. Therefore, this two-step algorithm, given by (36) and (37), requires a total of

$$T = N(r_1 + r_2) \tag{38}$$

operations.

It is easy to see how successive applications of the above procedure starting with its application to (36), give an m-step algorithm requiring

$$T = N(r_1 + r_2 + \ldots + r_m) \tag{39}$$

operations, where

$$N = r_1\, r_2 \ldots\, r_m. \tag{40}$$

Guided by these ideas, very efficient computer programs have been developed (e.g., Ref. [6]).

Now, let us investigate how this powerful method can be applied for the calculation of time-correlation functions in molecular-dynamics calculations. We shall confine the discussion to the autocorrelation functions $\phi_{XX}(t)$, defined by

$$\phi_{XX}(t) = \langle X(0)\ X(t)\rangle . \tag{41}$$

Assuming the system to be ergodic, the canonical averages $\langle\ \rangle$ may be replaced by time averages $\langle\ \rangle_t$, (Ref. [1] and [7]),

$$\phi_{XX}(t) = \langle X(t')\ X(t+t')\rangle_t ,$$

$$= \lim_{\tau\to\infty} \frac{1}{\tau - t} \int_0^{\tau - t} dt' X(t')\ X(t'+t). \tag{42}$$

Here, τ is the total time during which the observables $X(t)$ have been measured.

In all practical cases, the time variable is discretized into intervals of length Δt. Thus, t may be expressed as $k\ \Delta t$ and τ as $n\ \Delta t$. Equation (42) then takes the form

$$\phi_{XX}(t) = \lim_{n\to\infty} \frac{1}{n-k} \sum_{j=0}^{n-1-k} X(j)\ X(j+k) = \lim_{n\to\infty} f_n(k), \tag{43}$$

where $f_n(k)$ is defined by

$$f_n(k) = \frac{1}{n-k} \sum_{j=0}^{n-1-k} X(j)\ X(j+k). \tag{44}$$

If this function has to be calculated for all possible k values, the sum can be computed very efficiently by means of the Fast Fourier-Transform method. Recall the well-known fact that the Fourier transform of a convolution integral

$$f(\tau) = \int g(t)\ h(t+\tau)\ dt \tag{45}$$

is given by

$$F(\omega) = G(\omega) \cdot H(\omega), \tag{46}$$

where capital letters denote the Fourier-transformed functions. Thus, the convolution integral can be written as

$$f(\tau) = \frac{1}{2\pi} \int_{-\infty}^{+\infty} G(\omega)\ H(\omega)\ e^{-i\omega\tau}\ d\omega. \tag{47}$$

To apply this method for the discrete case of Eq.(42), we follow the suggestions by Bertora *et al.* [8], and write Eq.(44) for $f_n(k)$ as

$$f_n(k) = \frac{1}{n-k} \sum_{j=0}^{n-1} \sum_{j'=0}^{n-1} X(j)\, X(j')\, \delta_{k+j,j'} \; . \tag{48}$$

Now, the Kronecker δ symbol can be decomposed into the form

$$\delta_{k+j,j'} = \frac{1}{2n} \sum_{\ell=0}^{2n-1} W^{\ell(k+j-j')}, \tag{49}$$

where W is the $2n$-th principal root of unity, defined by

$$W = e^{2\pi i/2n} = e^{i\pi/n}. \tag{50}$$

The validity of Eq.(49) can be checked quite easily by observing that for $k+j \neq j'$ the sum over ℓ can be arranged in pairs of opposite sign which cancel each other. Inserting Eq.(49) for the δ symbol in Eq.(48), we obtain

$$f_n(k) = \frac{1}{2n(n-k)} \sum_{\ell=0}^{2n-1} W^{\ell k} \sum_{j=0}^{n-1} X(j)\, W^{\ell j} \sum_{j'=0}^{n-1} X(j') W^{-\ell j'}. \tag{51}$$

For real observables $X(j)$ the last two sums conjugate to each other, so we may write

$$f_n(k) = \frac{1}{2n(n-k)} \sum_{\ell=0}^{2n-1} W^{\ell k}\, |A(\ell)|^2, \tag{52}$$

where $A(\ell)$ is the Fourier transform of $X(j)$,

$$A(\ell) = \sum_{j=0}^{n-1} X(j)\, W^{-\ell j}. \tag{53}$$

While $X(j)$ is given at n different time points, $A(\ell)$ must be known for $2n$ frequencies. To make use of the Fast Fourier technique, one requires $X(j)$ at $2n$ time points. This is easily accomplished by writing

$$A(\ell) = \sum_{j=0}^{2n-1} X(j)\, W^{-\ell j} \tag{54}$$

with

$$X(j) \equiv 0 \quad \text{for} \quad j \geq n. \tag{55}$$

So using Eqs.(52) and (54), the autocorrelation function $\phi_{XX}(\tau_k) = \lim_{n\to\infty} f_n(k)$ can be calculated by means of two Fast Fourier Transformations. While the direct calculation of $f_n(k)$ according to Eq.(44) involves $1/2\ n(n-1)$ multiplications, the Fast Fourier technique leads to an n log n dependence, which for large n will result in a considerable saving in computing time.

To predict the computer time t_{comp} of one transformation as a function of the manner in which N can be divided into prime factors j, we can use the following empirical formula [6]:

$$N = \prod_j j^{k_j}, \tag{56}$$

$$S_2 = 2\cdot k_2, \tag{57}$$

$$S_F = \sum_{j>2} j\cdot k_j, \tag{58}$$

$$n_F = \sum_{j>2} k_j, \tag{59}$$

For $j = 2$ in Eq.(56), r_2 in Eq.(36) is 2, and the sum can be evaluated without restoring the data in an auxiliary array. This storing time for all other j gives a larger t_3 than t_2 and is the reason for t_4.

$$t_{comp} = t_0 + N(t_1 + t_2\cdot S_2 + t_3\cdot S_F + t_4\cdot n_F), \tag{60}$$

where $t_0 \ldots t_4$ are computer-type dependent time constants.

We conclude from this formula that it is very favorable to choose N as a power of 2, or to let S_F and n_F be as small as possible by choosing an N only containing other, few and small, prime factors. If, on the other hand, N is a prime number , the Fast Fourier procedure can never save computer time, owing to the overhead times t_0, t_1 and t_4.

Using all these tools, we can calculate the coordinates of a many-particle system by the appropriate numerical integration method on the one hand, and using the Fast Fourier Transform it becomes easy, on the other hand, to compute $\phi_{XX}(t)$ and its Fourier transform $S_{XX}(q,\omega)$ which can be compared with experimental data.

References

[1] T. Schneider and E. Stoll, Phys. Rev. B13, 1216-37 (1976).

[2] S.K. Godunov and V.S. Ryabenki, "Theory of Difference Schemes, An Introduction" (North-Holland, Amsterdam, 1964) p.47.

[3] L. Verlet, Phys. Rev. 159, 98-103 (1967).

[4] S. Machlup and L. Onsager, Phys. Rev. 91, 1512-15 (1953).

[5] J.W. Cooley and J.W. Tukey, Math. Comp. 19, 297-301 (1965).

[6] N. Brenner, "Cooley-Tukey Fast Fourier Transform", FFTT 44.3 44.0 SHARE program library agency, COSMIC, University of Georgia.

[7] E. Stoll, K. Binder and T. Schneider, Phys. Rev. B8, 3266-89 (1973).

[8] F. Bertora, C. Braccini, G. Gambardella and G. Musso, "Study on the Use of the Fast Fourier Transform in Spectral Analysis", (Report ESRO-CR(P) 469 (1973), University of Genoa, Vol.3).

ISNM 37 Birkhäuser Verlag, Basel und Stuttgart, 1977

"The Mechanical Response of Brittle Materials to Intense Impulsive Loading" - L.A. Glenn

(an invited paper to be presented at the colloquium on numerical methods of analysis, EPFL, 11-13 October 1976)

Abstract

The main features are outlined of a finite difference method to solve multi-dimensional problems in continuum mechanics. The application of this method to the prediction of the fracture zone growth in impacted glass blocks is described and good agreement with experiment is demonstrated.

INTRODUCTION

Perhaps the most common analytical approach to brittle fracture begins with the crack-free state of a system, for which it is assumed that the field is elastic and known. The prior stress distribution uniquely determines the crack energetics. The entire crack growth history may, in principle, be predetermined by the existing stress state before propagation has begun.

It is well known, however, that this cannot be the case when the system is loaded impulsively such that the applied forces displace the system boundary at a rate comparable with that of sonic velocities [1]. Actually, it can be shown that, even when the imposed boundary velocity is much less than any wave speed in the medium, the influence of the propagating crack on the stress field in the surrounding "virgin" material can be important. A good example is Figure 1. A 100 x 100 x 19 mm soda glass plate was impacted with a 15 mm D x 15 mm length cylindrical steel projectile at nominal velocity of 25 m/s; the impact stress Hugoniot ($\sigma_H = U_0 I_T / (1 + I_T/I_P)$, where U_0 is the projectile speed, and I_T and I_P respectively the target and projectile impedance) is approximately 250 MPa (2.5 kb). The photo sequences illustrated were taken with an image converter (IMA-CON) camera and polariscope, a detailed description of which is given in [2]. In the upper sequence, (a), the glass target had been acid-etched prior to the test to remove surface flaws, long known to have important influence on the strength. The lower left-hand frame, marked "1" was taken roughly 3 μs after impact of the projectile, seen as the dark rectangle at the top, and each subsequent photo occurs at 5 μs intervals. The plate did not fracture and the isochromatic fringe pattern describes the evolution of the stress field. In the lower sequence, (b), a similar unetched plate was impacted in like manner. A well-defined crack is observed under the left "toe" of the projectile in frame 3 and continues to grow in subsequent frames. The effect on the fringes is evident already in frame 4 and, in the time for the first crack "information" to traverse the plate, roughly 20 μs (frame 7), the stress field is markedly different than for the uncracked specimen.

Thus, it is not enough to know the material state prior to fracture. In fact, the development of the fracture zone itself is strongly influenced by a feedback effect from the interaction of the (elastic) solution in the virgin material with signals propagating forward from the existing fracture zone.

An analytical method for describing this feedback process is the subject of this report. The main features are outlined and good agreement with experiment is demonstrated when the method is applied to the prediction of crack growth in impacted glass blocks.

METHOD OF ANALYSIS

A stress wave itself may be viewed as a time dependent process transferring momentum and energy from point to point in a medium due to a feedback loop that exists between the various physical properties of the medium that are changed as a result of the transfer (Figure 2). The equations of motion provide a functional relation between the applied stress field and the resulting acceleration of each point in the medium. Accelerations, allowed to act over a small time increment, produce new velocities (strain rates) which, in turn, produce displacements (strains) and these complete the loop by producing a new stress field; sometimes the latter depends directly as well on the strain rate and material history, as shown schematically by the dashed line in Figure 2. The two critical areas in such a loop are the manner in which the stress field produces the motion and the manner in which the material displacement is coupled to the stress field, to wit - the equations of state of the medium.

Equations of Motion

Finite difference analogs of the integral statements of mass and momentum conservation, and the first law of thermodynamics, have been written which imply an exactly conservative finite difference equation for the total energy [3]. These equations form the basis of the AFTON computer codes which, given appropriate equations of state,provide a description of the propagation of a stress wave of arbitrary amplitude through a medium.

The method is, in principle, three-dimensional. Attention is limited here, however, to axi-symmetric (2D) geometry. Even with this limitation, the code structure is far too voluminous for elaboration here; the details may be found in [3] and [4]. The most important aspects for the problem at hand are the spacial discretization (zoning) and the momentum calculation and these are outlined below.

The equations of motion take simplest form and usually provide the most accurate results for a closed, finite region whose bounding surfaces move with the local velocity of matter and which, therefore, always contain the same material particles. This description of continuum motion is termed Lagrangian and is the one adopted here, as particle displacement is normally small in comparison to zone size. It is noted in passing that the AFTON codes also permit motion in an arbitrary, time dependent,coordinate frame and several applications of this feature can be found in [5] and [6].

For convenience, zones are taken to be elementary quadrilaterals, actually the projection of quadrilateral wedges onto an azimuthal symmetry plane. A typical wedge, together with its projection onto the x-y (symmetry), y-z and z-x planes is shown in Figure 3. The wedge is a polyhedron bounded by two nearly-parallel azimuthal planes and having similar quadrilateral cross-section in all azimuthal planes contained between the two. Four trapezoidal faces normal to the central quadrilateral (formed by the lines joining the points 1, 2, 3 and 4 and shaded in the figure) complete the polyhedron.

The calculation of the momentum increment is outlined as follows: A "momentum zone" is constructed at each vertex from the intersection of quadrilaterals which share the vertex in common. An interior momentum zone is then a polyhedron of 10 faces; Figure 4(a) illustrates a typical momentum zone projected into the symmetry plane. Forces exerted on the 8 trapezoidal faces and 2 wedge faces (a wedge face is the shaded area in Figure 4(a)) produce an acceleration of the momentum mass. Conservation of momentum for the zone centered at point 1 in Figure 4(a) is expressed by the equation

$$\underline{M}_1^n - \underline{M}_1^{n-1} = \Delta^{n-\frac{1}{2}}t \left[\underline{F}_{1a}^{n-\frac{1}{2}} + \underline{F}_{2b}^{n-\frac{1}{2}} + \underline{F}_{3c}^{n-\frac{1}{2}} + \underline{F}_{4d}^{n-\frac{1}{2}}\right]. \tag{1}$$

The sense of the force vectors is shown in Figure 3(b). Each of the force vectors in (1) is composed of three terms, for example

$$\underline{F}_{1a}^{n-\frac{1}{2}} = \underline{\underline{\sigma}}_a^{n-\frac{1}{2}} \cdot \left(\underline{A}_{\underline{a}a}^{n-\frac{1}{2}} + \underline{A}_{\underline{d}a}^{n-\frac{1}{2}} + \underline{A}_{w_1}^{n-\frac{1}{2}}\right) \tag{2}$$

$\underline{\underline{\sigma}}_a^{n-\frac{1}{2}}$ is the stress tensor defined within the quadrilateral zone centered at point a and the $\underline{A}^{n-\frac{1}{2}}$ are appropriate vector areas. The first two terms of (2) are force components acting on 2 of the 4 interior trapezoidal faces shaded in Figure 4(b), whereas the last term arises from the wedge faces (whose projection on the x-y plane is the quadrilateral joining the points 1, $\underline{d}$, a, $\underline{a}$ in Figure 4).

Having updated the momentum with (1), the particle velocity vector at t^n is found as

$$\underline{U}_1^n = \underline{M}_1^n / m_1 \tag{3}$$

where m_1 is the mass of the momentum zone centered at point 1.

Equation of State

Given the velocity field at t^n, the velocity at $t^{n+\frac{1}{2}}$ is determined in explicit fashion by forward extrapolation,

$$\underline{U}_1^{n+\frac{1}{2}} = 2\underline{U}_1^n - \underline{U}_1^{n-\frac{1}{2}} \tag{4}$$

and the displacement is found as

$$\underline{\delta}_1^{n+1} = \underline{U}_1^{n+\frac{1}{2}} \Delta^{n+\frac{1}{2}}t + \underline{\delta}_1^n \tag{5}$$

The displacement field, together with the initial particle coordinate positions, allows computation of the deformation tensor in the quadrilateral zones, from which the strain field immediately results. The equation of state, or constitutive model, provides the stress field $\underline{\underline{s}}^{n+1}$ and the loop is completed by calculating the stress tensor at $t^{n+\frac{1}{2}}$:

$$\underline{\underline{\sigma}}^{n+\frac{1}{2}} = \frac{1}{2}\left(\underline{\underline{s}}^{n} + \underline{\underline{s}}^{n+1} + \underline{\underline{Q}}^{n+\frac{1}{2}}\right) \tag{6}$$

where $\underline{\underline{Q}}^{n+\frac{1}{2}}$ is the artificial viscosity tensor; a discussion of the latter may be found, for example in [4] or [7]. A very simple and intuitive constitutive model of brittle fracture has been advanced to account for the observed growth of the fracture zone, including crack branching and opening and re-closing of crack surfaces. The model is illustrated in Figure 5. Material is assumed locally elastic until such time as <u>any</u> principal stress exceeds in tension some small prescribed value, Y_T, the nominal tensile strength (A). When such a condition is satisfied, a "crack" is assumed to open and relieve the tensile stress such that no forces or tractions continue to exist on the crack surfaces. The stress relief is here taken to be instantaneous but relaxation over finite time is not necessarily excluded; earlier experiments with glass suggest that, at least for this material, relaxation effects can be ignored [2]. When fully relieved, the local fracture zone (LFZ) has zero normal and shear stress on the crack surface (B).

Material in the LFZ can, however, continue to sustain tensile stresses,up to the limiting value, in directions parallel to the crack surface (C). If the tensile failure condition is subsequently satisfied in a direction perpendicular to the original crack (either in an azimuthal plane or in the hoop direction), a second crack can develop. The presence of two cracks is treated in analogous fashion, i.e., zero normal and shear stress on the surface of both cracks. If a third crack develops, the LFZ is considered to be pulverized.

It is possible for cracks to reclose under normal compressive stress. When this occurs, the elastic moduli in reloading are assumed identical to those of the virgin material. The subsequent tensile strength, normal to the crack surface, is zero.

It should be noted that the finite difference method per se is not limited to such simple material representation and in fact much more complex constitutive relations have been used to study phenomena such as hysteresis, strain hardening, plastic dilatation, etc. (see, for example, [2], [8] and [9].

SOME RESULTS

Axisymmetric (2D) calculations with the simple tensile failure model have been made to simulate steel projectile impact on flat glass targets [2] and symmetric impacts of granite bars [10]. We describe here some previously unpublished work with steel projectiles impacting in shallow holes which have been pre-drilled into cubical glass targets.

Figure 6 illustrates a typical experiment. A 16 mm diameter hole, 16 mm long was drilled in a 100 mm cube of 20% PbO Rejmyra (Swedish) glass. A 30 mm (length) cylindrical steel projectile was then fired into the hole at 25 m/s. As in Figure 1, the framing interval between each view of the IMA-CON photo sequence was 5 μs, frame number 1 commencing at ∿ 14 μs after impact. The last frame, marked "∞" is a static view of the glass block after the experiment. The dark rectangular shape at the top of each frame is the projectile protruding out of the target; it was removed for the static picture. The dark trapezoidal-shaped region is the spreading fracture zone, in reality the surface of a conical crack. After intersecting the free surface of the cube, the crack was partially arrested but did manage to reflect from at least 2 corners, as seen in the last frame.

Figure 7 illustrates the results of a calculation of a similar experiment; the projectile was only half as long as in the above experiment and the speed was 100 m/s, but many of the observed features are present. Figure 7(a) displays the instantaneous particle velocity vector field 12 μs after impact ($\bar{t} = C_\ell t/R = 8$, where C_ℓ is the dilatational wave speed in the glass, $\sim$ 5 mm/μs, and R is the projectile radius), assuming both projectile and target to be elastic. The center of impact is at coordinate (0,0) and, employing the symmetry, only half of the azimuthal plane is displayed. The spacial coordinates are scaled to the projectile radius. Each arrow represents the material particle velocity at a zone vertex, the length of the arrow being taken proportional to the magnitude, with unity referenced to the velocity Hugoniot, $U_H = \sigma_H/I_T$. Note that at this (still rather early) time, projectile rebound is already well in evidence, as witnessed by the upward pointing arrows in the hole region.

The elastic solution depicted in Figure 7(a) can be contrasted with the solution obtained assuming the dynamic tensile strength of the glass to be about 200 MPa (2kb) [2]. The latter is illustrated in Figure 7(b). In this case, the velocity field in the target near the top (impact) surface is very much reduced since the cone crack, spreading from the impact corner, cannot sustain the tensile stresses necessary for the downward displacement. The predicted crack speed and direction were found to be in remarkable agreement with the experiment.

Another aspect, the reclosing of crack surfaces, is illustrated in Figures 6 and 7. The "wing"-shaped region above the main cone crack on the left-hand side in the photo sequence is observed to grow continuously until frame 6. In the next 10 μs, the wing disappears to return again in frame 9. The disappearance of the wing is indicative of the re-mating of previously opened crack surfaces. The simulated event also develops temporary crack closure. Figure 7(c) shows the particle velocity field at $\bar{t} = 24$ with the main boundaries of the cracked region indicated. Part of the crack surface has reclosed, as evidenced by the smooth velocity field overlying the main cone crack.

CONCLUSION

The computational method exemplified in the AFTON codes can be very useful in studying the dynamic constitutive behavior of materials. It has also been used extensively to calculate free field ground motion resulting from explosions or earthquakes, to design pressure vessels subjected to dynamic loading, to evaluate armor protection against impact, and for many other purposes.

The employment of finite difference codes like AFTON to solve multi-dimensional continuum mechanics problem has been limited in the past by the cost of such calculations and by the fact that large and expensive computer installations were required. Recent advances in computer technology have radically altered this picture. The impact calculation described in the preceding section was made on an HP-3000, a 16-bit, disc-based machine. It required about 11 hours of central processor time (about 4 times the figure for a CDC-6500) and was run overnight.

REFERENCES

1) Lawn, B.R. & Wilshaw, T.R.; "Fracture of Brittle Solids", Cambridge University Press, 1975 (p. 105).

2) Glenn, L.A.; "The Fracture of a Glass Half-Space by Projectile Impact", J. Mech. and Phys. of Solids, 24, June 1976.

3) Trulio, J.G.; "Theory and Structure of the AFTON Codes", AFWL TR-66-19, June 1966.

4) Niles, W.J., Germroth, J.J. & Shuster, S.H.; "Numerical Studies of AFTON 2A Code Development and Applications", AFWL TR-70-22, vol. II, February 1971.

5) Glenn, L.A.; "On the Dynamics of Hypervelocity Liquid Jet Impact on a Flat Rigid Surface", J. App. Math. and Phys. (ZAMP), 25, 1974 (pp. 383-398).

6. Glenn, L.A.; "The Mechanics of the Impulsive Water Cannon", Int. J. of Computers and Fluids, 3, 1975 (pp. 197-215).

7) Alder, B., Fernbach, S. & Rotenberg, M., (ed.); "Methods in Computational Physics, volume 3", Academic Press, 1964.

8) Trulio, J.G., Carr, W.E., Germroth, J.J. & McKay, M.W.; "Numerical Ground Motion Studies, vol.III - Ground Motion Studies and AFTON Code Development", AFWL-TR-67-37, vol. III, June 1968.

9) Isenberg, J.; "Material Properties for AFTON Code", Defense Atomic Support Agency Report DASA 2178, December 1968.

10) Glenn, L.A. & Janach, W.; "Failure of Granite Cylinders under Impact Loading", to be published in Jl. Geophys. Res., 1976.

FIGURE 1

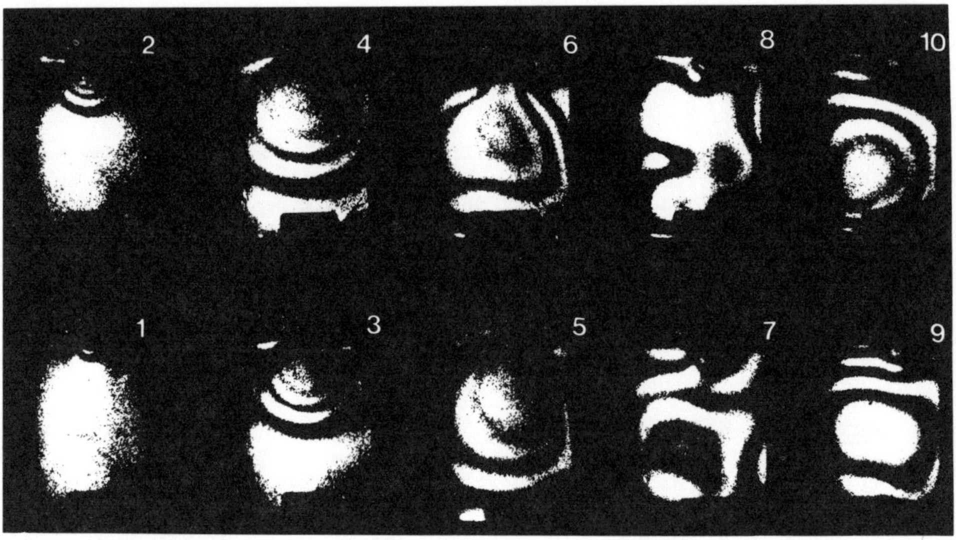

a) STEEL PROJECTILE IMPACT ON UPPER EDGE OF ACID-ETCHED SODA GLASS PLATE. FRAME 1 @ 3 μs AFTER IMPACT. FRAMING INTERVAL IS 5 μs. NO FRACTURE.

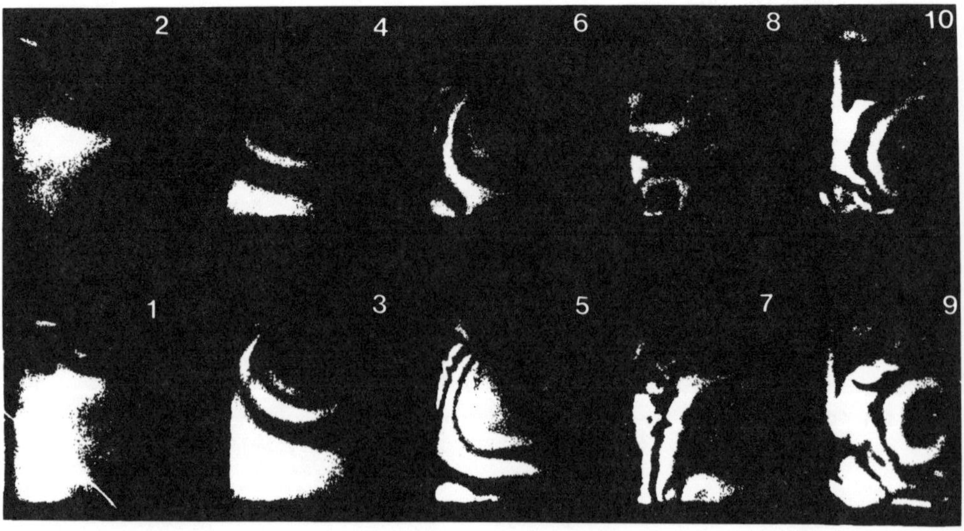

b) STEEL PROJECTILE IMPACT ON UPPER EDGE OF UNETCHED SODA GLASS PLATE. CRACK GROWTH BEGINS UNDER LEFT "TOE" OF PROJECTILE.

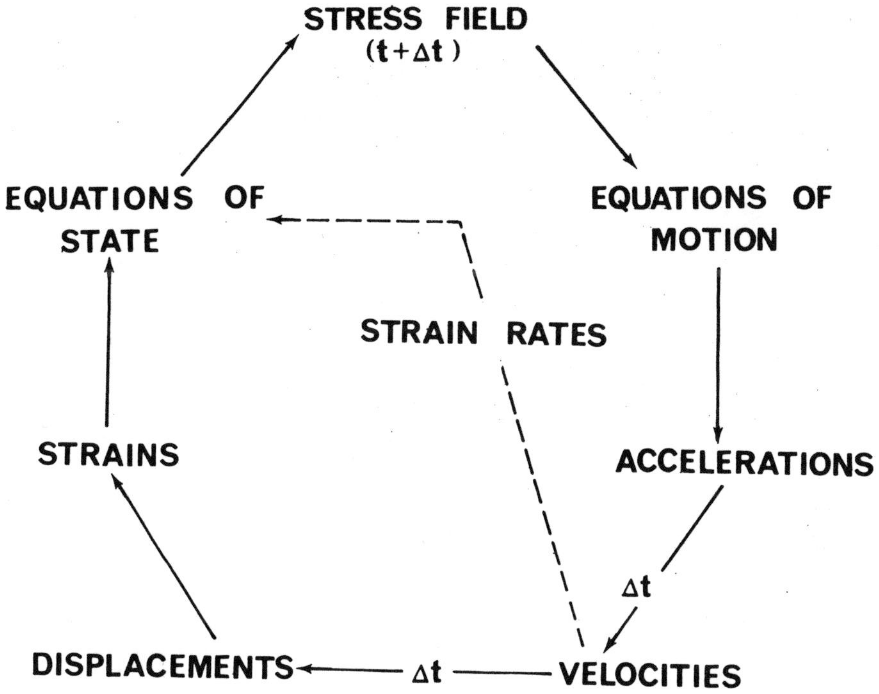

FIGURE 2 - FEEDBACK LOOP REPRESENTATION FOR A STRESS WAVE

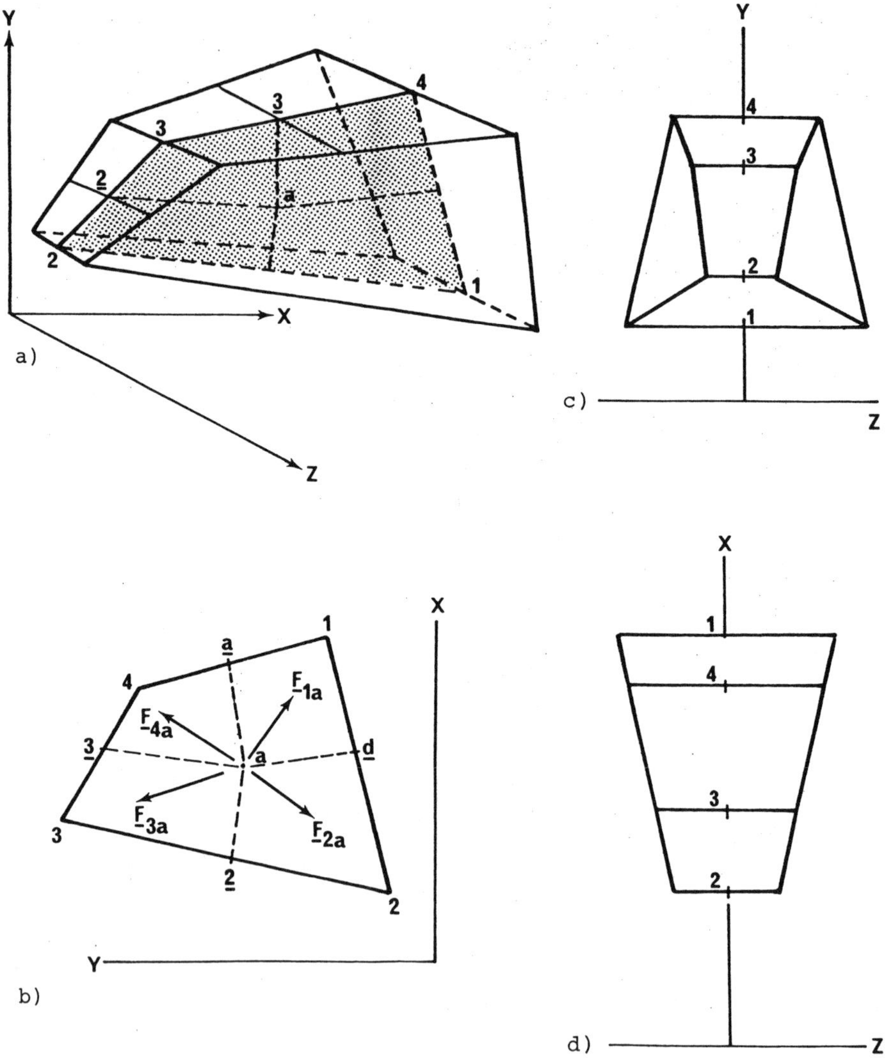

FIGURE 3 - QUADRILATERAL WEDGE (a) AND ITS PROJECTION ONTO THE x-y(b), y-z(c) and x-z(d) PLANES. FIGURE 3(b) ALSO SHOWS THE SENSE OF THE FORCE VECTORS IN EQUATION (1).

FIGURE 4

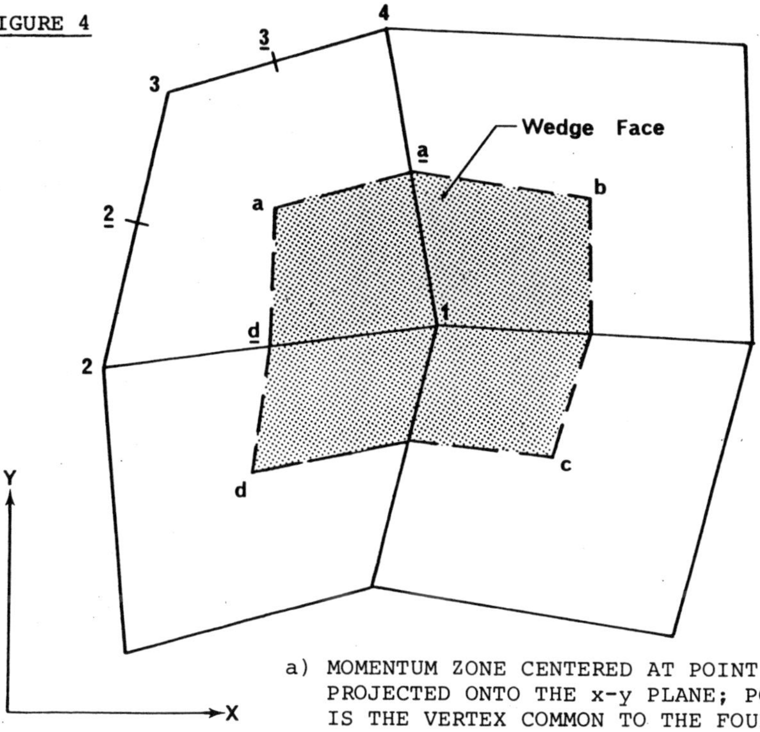

a) MOMENTUM ZONE CENTERED AT POINT 1 PROJECTED ONTO THE x-y PLANE; POINT 1 IS THE VERTEX COMMON TO THE FOUR QUADRILATERAL ZONES LABELED a, b, c, d.

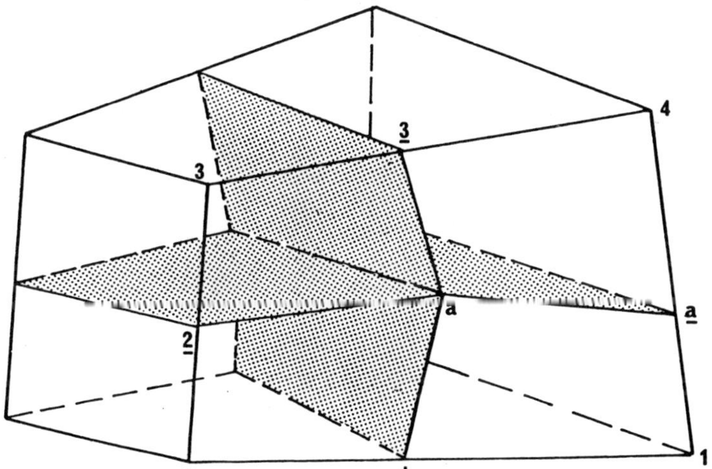

b) INTERIOR AREAS OF QUADRILATERAL WEDGE CENTERED AT a.

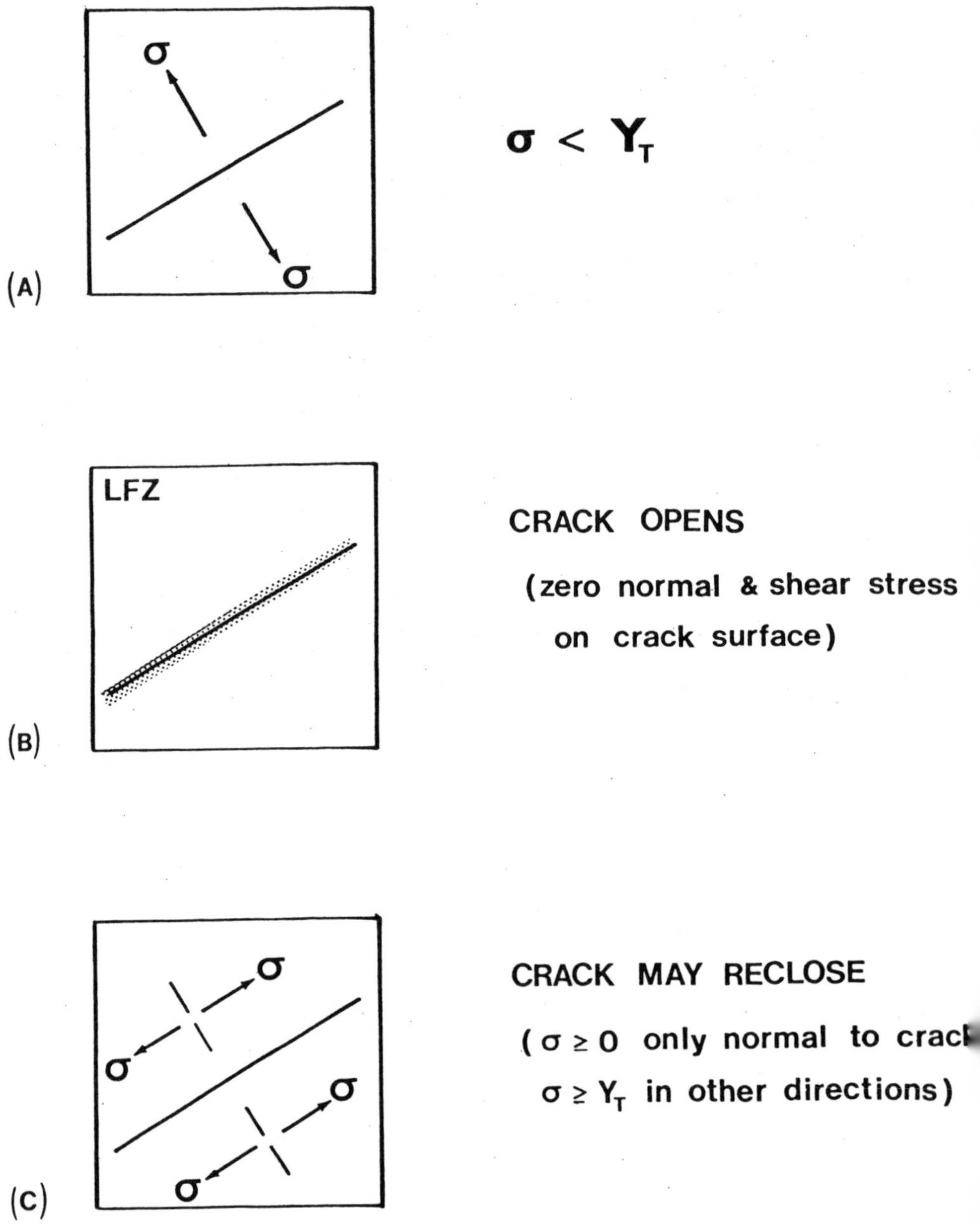

FIGURE 5 - SCHEMATIC ILLUSTRATION OF THE SIMPLE (TENSILE) BRITTLE FRACTURE MODEL

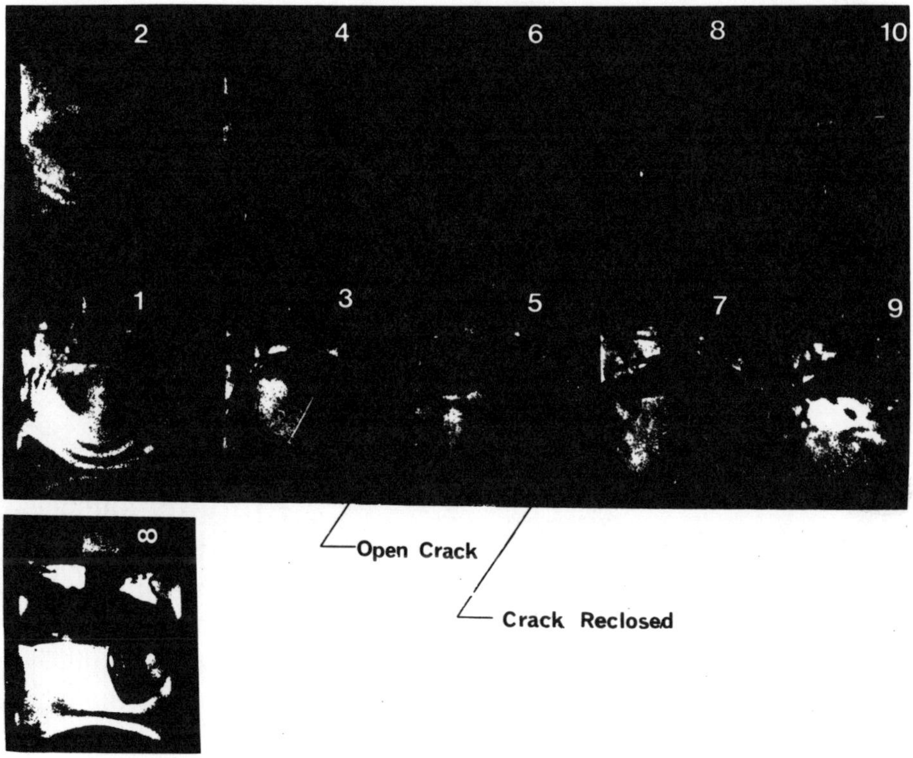

FIGURE 6 - CYLINDRICAL STEEL PROJECTILE FIRED INTO HOLE DRILLED IN GLASS CUBE. FRAME 1 @ $\sim$ 14 μs AFTER IMPACT. FRAMING INTERVAL is 5 μs.

FIGURE 7

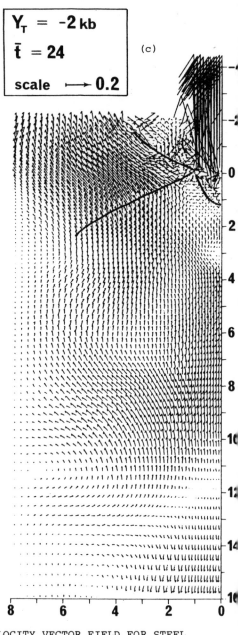

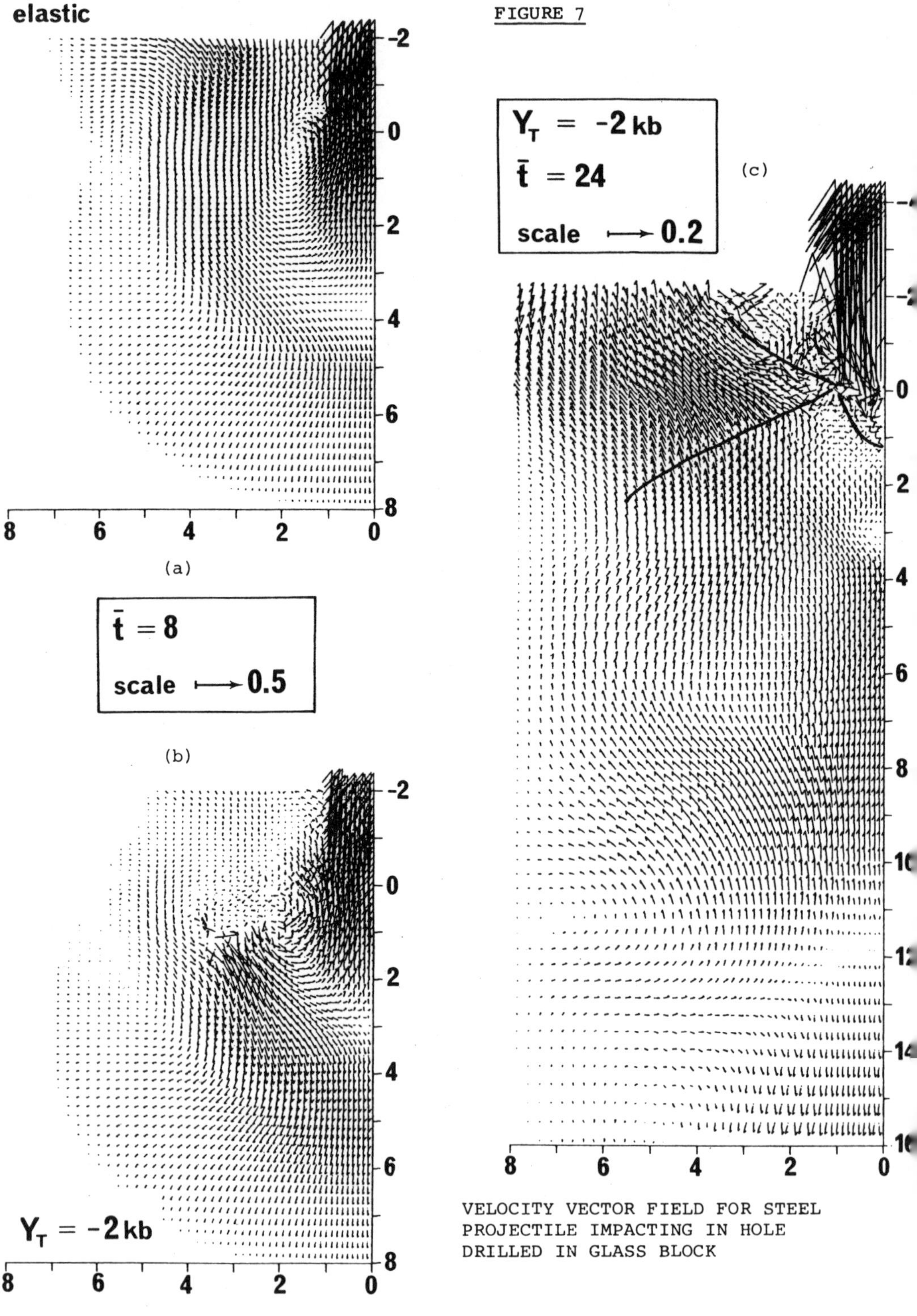

VELOCITY VECTOR FIELD FOR STEEL PROJECTILE IMPACTING IN HOLE DRILLED IN GLASS BLOCK

VISCOELASTIC STABILITY OF SHELLS - NUMERICAL ASPECTS

by

Silvio Merazzi

Swiss Federal Institute of Technology, Lausanne, Switzerland

Peter Stehlin

The Aeronautical Research Institute of Sweden, Stockholm, Sweden

List of symbols

a_{i1}, a_{i2}, a_{i3} / b_{i1}, b_{i2}, b_{i3}	polynome coefficients (Appendix II)
$\{a\}_k$	vector of relaxation moduli at t_k
α	decay factor in exponential series
b	half distance between arch supports
$C(t)$, $C_{ij}(t)$	relaxation functions
C_{ij}^{o}, C_{ij}^{k}	relaxation moduli in series
C_o	initial arch displacement
$D_{ij}(t)$	creep compliances
δ	convergence parameter
$[D]_k$	matrix of creep compliances at $t_n - \tau_k$
$\{d\}_k$	mean value of relaxation moduli (k-th interval)
E	Young's modulus
ε, ε_i	strains
κ_k	constants in exponential series
λ	constant for the first time interval predictor step
p	external pressure
p_{cr}	critical external pressure (according to linear buckling theory)
q_1, q_2, q_3	creep law constants
r_o	initial arch radius
$r(t)$	radius in deformed state
σ, σ_i	stresses

t,τ	time variables
ξ,η	surface coordinates of shell
$w(\xi,\eta,t)$	shell displacement perpendicular to surface
$\bar{w}(\xi,\eta)$	imperfection of shell surface (deviation from initial shape)
w_o	imperfection amplitude

1. INTRODUCTION

This paper describes some results of a current work on viscoelastic behaviour of composite structures made in collaboration with the Aeronautical Research Institute of Sweden.

The non-linear behaviour of structures [1], [2] as well as the characterisation of viscoelastic materials forces us to refer to numerical methods. However, these methods should be adapted to the computing tools we dispose of. The following chapters describe some of these possibilities.

In the first part, we discuss the basic concepts using a very simple model. It exhibits the type of material behaviour we are investigating. The two following chapters deal with material characterisation, i.e. numerical transformation of creep laws and approximation of relaxation curves by exponential sums. Finally, in the last part, we show how the theory is implemented in a computer program in order to determine the viscoelastic stability of shells, and an example is discussed.

2. VISCOELASTIC STABILITY

In order to illustrate the general concepts of computation let us consider a very simple one-degree-of-freedom model which consists of a shallow arch under external pressure (fig. 1). It is assumed that the arch deforms again into an arch increasing it's radius. The following assumption hold :

1) The material is linear-viscoelastic, i.e.
   - proportionality
   - superposition (each new response can be added to the total response)

2) The load is applied at t=0 and then held constant

3) The strain-displacement relations are non-linear. This also leads to non-linear load-displacement relations.

It is now possible to find a relation between the radius r and p, t. The elongation of the arch

$$\varepsilon\,(r) = \frac{S\,(r)}{S_o(r)} - 1 \qquad (2.1)$$

simply is the difference between the length of the arch in the undeformed state $S_o(r)$ and in the deformed state $S(r)$ divided by $S_o(r)$, and

$$S\,(r) = 2\alpha r \qquad (2.2.1)$$

$$= 2r \text{ arc sin } \frac{b}{r} \qquad (2.2.2)$$

Development of arc sin $\frac{b}{r}$ into a series and retaining the first two terms finally leads to

$$\varepsilon\,(r) = C_1 \cdot (1 - \frac{C_2}{r^2}) - 1 \qquad (2.3)$$

with

$$C_1 = \frac{1}{1 - \frac{b^2}{6\,r_o^2}} \qquad (2.3.1)$$

$$C_2 = \frac{b^2}{6} \qquad (2.3.2)$$

Due to absence of bending forces the equilibrium relation reduces to

$$\sigma(r) = -\frac{p}{A} \cdot r \tag{2.4}$$

The elastic solution is found by combining (2.2) and (2.4) through Hooke's law

$$C_1 \cdot (1-\frac{C_2}{r^2}) + \frac{p}{A \cdot E} \cdot r-1 = 0 \tag{2.5}$$

In order to find the viscoelastic solution we introduce the viscoelastic strain-stress law

$$\varepsilon(t) = \int_o^t D(t-\tau)d\sigma(\tau) \tag{2.6}$$

Integrating (2.6) by parts leads to

$$\varepsilon(t) = C(o)\,\sigma(t) - \int_o^t \frac{\partial D(t-\tau)}{\partial \tau}\,\sigma(\tau)d\tau \tag{2.7}$$

Both equations (2.6) and (2.7) can be substituted into (2.3) together with (2.4) to get integral equations

$$C_1(1-\frac{C_2}{r^2(t)}) - \frac{p}{A}\int_o^t D(t-\tau)dr(\tau) -1 = 0 \tag{2.8}$$

$$C_1(1-\frac{C_2}{r^2(t)}) - \frac{pD(o)}{A}\,r(t) + \frac{p}{A}\int_o^t \frac{\partial D(t-\tau)}{\partial \tau}\,r(\tau)d\tau -1 = 0 \tag{2.9}$$

some methods to solve (2.8) and (2.9) are now discussed.

a) The Newmark-β method [3], [4], [5]

This method is widely used to integrate the equations of motion of a system. Although equations (2.8) and (2.9) do not contain mass terms (it is assumed that there are no dynamic forces and that the creep speed $\frac{d\varepsilon}{dt}$ is very small compared to the wave velocity) it may be used to integrate (2.8).

The integration scheme starts from the assumption that the acceleration within an interval (t_{n-1}, t_n) is a function of the nodal point accelerations at t_{n-1} and t_n. To solve (2.8) we take

$$r(t_n) = r(t_{n-1}) + (t_n - t_{n-1})\dot{r}(t_{n-1}) + \frac{(t_n - t_{n-1})^2}{4}(\ddot{r}(t_n) + \ddot{r}(t_{n-1})) \quad (2.11)$$

This means that the acceleration $\ddot{r}(t)$ within the interval is constant

$$\ddot{r}(t) = \frac{1}{2}\left[\ddot{r}(t_{n-1}) + \ddot{r}(t_n)\right] \quad (2.12)$$

By substituting (2.10) and (2.11) into (2.8) we obtain a nonlinear equation in $\ddot{r}(t_n)$. This equation is solved until $\ddot{r}(t_n)$ satisfies a convergence criterion. The initial conditions at t=0 are readily found by differentiating (2.8) at t=0.

b) Predictor-corrector methods [4]

A way to solve equation (2.9) consists of predicting a first value $r_o(t_n)$ by fitting a polynomial through some previous points $r(t_{n-i})$. This value, together with points $r(t_{n-i})$, again defines a polynomial which is used to compute the integral in (2.9). The resulting iteration is of the form

$$f\left[r_k(t_n)\right] = \int_o^{t_n} \frac{\partial D(t_n - \tau)}{\partial \tau} \cdot r\,(r(t_{n-i}), r_{k-1})t_n)) \cdot d\tau \quad ;i=1,2 \quad (2.13)$$

In order to simplify the integration in (2.13) we choose the material function such that

$$f(r_k(t_n)) = g(t_n) \cdot \left[\int_o^{t_{n-1}} \frac{\partial D(t_{n-1}-\tau)}{\partial \tau} \cdot r(\tau) \cdot d\tau\right.$$

$$\left.+ \int_{t_{n-1}}^{t_n} \frac{\partial D(t_n - \tau)}{\partial \tau} \cdot r(r(t_{n-i}), r_k(t_n)) \cdot d\tau\right] \quad (2.14)$$

Now the integration in eq. (2.13) has no more to be done over the whole domain for each new time step.

Several polynomes have been tried out. One of them, the quadratic approach, will be examined more in detail :
The first step is to predict a new solution

$$r_o(t_n) = f\left[r(t_{n-i})\right] \quad i = 1,2,3 \tag{2.15}$$

by fitting a parabola through the three previous solutions.
Special care has to be taken for the first interval

$$r_o(t_1) = \lambda \cdot r(t_o) \qquad \lambda > 1.0 \tag{2.16}$$

and for $t = t_2$, where we use a linear extrapolation.

Then, by use of $r_o(t_n)$, we construct a new parabola

$$r(\tau) = f\left[r_o(t_n),\ r(t_{n-1}),\ r(t_{n-2})\right] \tag{2.17}$$

which is substituted into the second integral of eq. (2.14). Eq. 2.14 is solved with the Newton method until a convergence criterion, say

$$\left[\frac{r_k(t_n) - r_{k-1}(t_n)}{r_{k-1}(t_n)}\right] \leq \delta \tag{2.18}$$

is satisfied. If convergence does not occur, then the time step is cut by a certain factor and the whole procedure starts again with eq. (2.15). If the solution converges well for a certain number of time steps the time steps become bigger.

The example in fig. 1 has been computed numerically for a creep function which reflects linear viscoelastic-plastic behaviour in it's simplest form

$$D(t) = q_1 + q_2(1-e^{-\kappa t}) + q_3 t \tag{2.19}$$

and assuming some numerical values

$b = 500$ mm

$r_o = 1300$ mm

$c_o = 10$ mm

$p = 0.02$ kp/mm^2

$q_1 = 0.00322$ mm^2/kp

$q_2 = 0.000161$ mm^2/kp

$\kappa = 0.01$ 1/sec

$q_3 = 5.613 \cdot 10^{-6}$ mm^2/kp sec

Fig. 2 shows the elastic behaviour of the arch, i.e. $q_2 = q_3 = 0$. The time integration methods have been tried out for the linear viscoplastic case with $q_2 = 0$ (fig.3) and for the viscoelastic solution (fig.4). The extrapolation method with parabolic functions is closest to the exact solution (fig.3), even with a very big time step. It's use is simpler than the Newmark method, because only the variable itself must be retained.

3. NUMERICAL TRANSFORMATION OF CREEP LAWS

The linear viscoelastic stress-strain law of an orthotropic sheet is of the form

$$\sigma_i(t) = \int_0^t C_{ij}(t-\tau)\cdot d\varepsilon_j(\tau) \quad i,j = 1,3 \tag{3.1}$$

where the $C_{ij}(t)$ are material functions which could be determined by step-function relaxation tests.

The inverse of (3.1), i.e. the strain-stress relation

$$\varepsilon_i(t) = \int_0^t D_{ij}(t-\tau)\cdot d\sigma_j(\tau) \tag{3.2}$$

is more often used to determine the viscoelastic behaviour, because the creep compliances $D_{ij}(t)$ are quite suitably obtained by the step function creep test.

Let us consider the simple traction or compression test. Then we have

$$\left.\begin{aligned} \sigma_1 &= \begin{cases} 0 : t \leqslant 0 \\ \sigma_1 : t > 0 \end{cases} \\ \sigma_2 &= \sigma_3 = 0 \end{aligned}\right\} \tag{3.3}$$

and equation (3.2) becomes

$$\varepsilon_i(t) = D_{i1}(t)\cdot\sigma_1 \tag{3.4}$$

Integration by parts of (3.1) and substitution of (3.4) into it yields

$$\sigma_i = C_{ij}(o)\cdot\varepsilon_j(t) - \int_0^t \frac{\partial C_{ij}(t-\tau)}{\partial\tau}\cdot D_{j1}(\tau)\cdot\sigma_i\cdot d\tau \tag{3.5}$$

Equation (3.5) is also called volterra equation of the second kind and may be transformed into a volterra equation of the first kind

$$\int_0^t C_{ij}(\tau)\cdot D_{j1}(t-\tau)\cdot d\tau = T_i \tag{3.6}$$

with $T_1=t$ and $T_2=T_3=0$. This equation is now well suited for direct numerical integration in order to get the functions $C_{ij}(t)$ from experimentally determined discrete values $D_{i1}(t)$.

For the isotropic tensile specimen we have

$$\left.\begin{array}{l} D_{11} = D_{22} \\ D_{12} = D_{21} \\ D_{13} = D_{31} = D_{23} = D_{32} = 0 \end{array}\right\} \tag{3.7}$$

such that C_{33} is independent and may be treated separately (torsional test). The functions $C_{ij}(t)$ are now discretized by taking the mean value

$$C_{ij}'(t) = \tfrac{1}{2}(C_{ij}(t_k) + C_{ij}(t_{k+1})) \qquad t_k \leq t \leq t_{k+1} \tag{3.8}$$

Introducing (3.8) into (3.6) leads to a system of the form

$$\sum_{k=0}^{n-2} [D]_k \cdot \{d\}_k + [D]_{n-1} \cdot \left(\{a\}_n + \{a\}_{n-1}\right) - \{T\}_n = 0 \tag{3.9}$$

$$n = 2,N$$

which we solve straightforward for each value n. All matrices and vectors are defined in appendix I. The unknown values $\{a\}_n$ at time t_n are obtained by solving (3.9).

$$\{a\}_n = [D]_{n-i}^{-1} \left[\{T\}_n - \sum_{k=0}^{n-2} [D]_k \cdot \{d\}_k\right] \tag{3.10}$$

and the central difference values become

$$\{d\}_n = \tfrac{1}{2}(\{a\}_{n-1} + \{a\}_n) \tag{3.11}$$

Special case has to be taken for the initial values $\{a\}_o$ and for $t = t_1$

$$\{a\}_o = [D]^{-1} \cdot \begin{Bmatrix} 1 \\ o \end{Bmatrix} \tag{3.12}$$

which is simply the inverse of (3.2) (elastic solution). At the end of the first interval we get

$$\{a\}_i = [D]_o^{-1} \cdot \{T\}_1 - \{a\}_o \tag{3.13}$$

since the sum term in (3.10) is zero.

Fig. 5.1 shows creep curves C_{11} (t) and C_{12} (t) obtained by a computer-controlled creep test of a tensile specimen. The creep curves are inverted on-line by the above mentioned method and the corresponding relaxation curves are displayed in fig. 5.2.

4. APPROXIMATION OF RELAXATION CURVES

Due to the advantages already mentioned the relaxation functions are described by exponential series of the form

$$C_{ij}(t) = C_{ij}^{o} - \sum_{k=1}^{n} C_{ij}^{k} \cdot (1-e^{-\kappa_k \cdot t}) \qquad (4.1)$$

The expansion in this form or other forms related to it has been used by several authors [6], [7]. Equation (4.1) contains 2n unknowns, namely C_{ij}^{k} and κ_i (C_{ij}^{o} is a constant which reflects instant elasticity).
A suitable method [2] is to choose the values κ_k

$$\kappa_k = \frac{\alpha}{t_k} \qquad (4.2)$$

at intervals

$$t_k = 10^{k-k_o} \qquad (4.3)$$

in order to get a linear system of equations by means of a least square fit. α is a decay factor and k_o the exponent of the first time decade. The resulting linear system then becomes

$$c_{lk} \cdot C_{ij}^{k} = C_{ij}^{o} - C_{ij}(t_k) \qquad l,k=1,n \qquad (4.4)$$

where

$$c_{lk} = 1-e^{-\alpha \cdot \frac{t_l}{t_k}}$$

and substituting (4.3) into (4.5)

$$c_{lk} = 1-e^{-\alpha \cdot 10^{l-k}} \qquad (4.5)$$

The series of values C_{ij}^{k} is not necessarily increasing or decreasing. Some values may even become negative, although this is, from physical points of view, contradictory. However, it is possible to determine the C_{ij}^{k} such that they are growing but then the α_k are no more the same for all coefficients C_{ij}.

The computed relaxation curves for C_{11}, C_{12} and C_{33} have been approximated by this method using 4 terms in the series (4.1) at the collocation points 10^i sec, where i=0,3, and for α=0,5. Table 1 shows the corresponding terms of the series (4.1). The plots of C_{ij} (t) in fig. 6 exhibit good agreement between computed (measured) and approximated values within the limits of validity.

A more rigorous solution is achieved by means of dynamic programming. Optimizing the values C_{ij}^k under the constraint that the κ_i for all series must be the same yields quite better results.

5. VISCOELASTIC BUCKLING OF SHELLS

The extrapolation method has been implemented in the STAGS-program [8], [9]. This code already performs elastic and plastic collapse analysis of shells using a finite difference approach and employing the Newton-Raphson iteration to solve the non-linear equations. The solution method will be briefly reviewed here. Assume again that the stress-strain relations are of the form

$$\sigma_i(t) = C_{ij}(o)\cdot\varepsilon_j(t) - \int_o^t \frac{\partial C_{ij}(t-\tau)}{\partial\tau}\cdot\varepsilon_j(\tau)\cdot d\tau \tag{5.1}$$

and that we consider a discrete point of the shell.

In order to avoid repeated summation of the integral in (5.1) we take

$$C_{ij}(t) = C_{ij}^{o} - \sum_{k=1}^{n} C_{ij}^{k}\cdot(1-e^{-\kappa_k\cdot t}) \tag{5.2}$$

and substitute it into (5.1)

$$\sigma_i(t) = C_{ij}^{o}\cdot\varepsilon_j(t) - \sum_{k=1}^{n}\kappa_k\cdot e^{-\kappa_k t}\cdot C_{ij}^{k}\cdot\int_o^t e^{\kappa_k t}\cdot\varepsilon_j(\tau)\cdot d\tau \tag{5.3}$$

Equation (5.3) consists of an elastic part $C_{ij}^{o}\cdot\varepsilon(t)$ and an anelastic part. We may then split up (5.3) to get

$$\sigma_i^{l}(t_n) = C_{ij}^{o}\cdot\varepsilon_j^{l}(t_n) - \sum_{k=1}^{n}\kappa_k\cdot e^{-\kappa_k t_n}\cdot C_{ij}^{k}\cdot\int_o^{t_n} e^{\kappa_k\tau}\cdot\varepsilon_j^{l-1}(\tau)\cdot d\tau \tag{5.4}$$

The second right-hand term of (5.4) can thus be considered a pseudo-load and be added to the load vector. The numerical evaluation of this part will now be described.

At the beginning of a new time step $\Delta t_n = t_n - t_{n-1}$ a new solution

$$\varepsilon_i^{o}(t_n) = a_{i1}\cdot t_n^2 + a_{i2}\cdot t_n + a_{i3} \qquad i=1,3 \tag{5.5}$$

is extrapolated. Refer to appendix II for the coefficients a_{i1}, a_{i2}, a_{i3}. This first approximation defines, together with $\varepsilon_i(t_{n-1})$ and $\varepsilon_i(t_{n-2})$, a parabola

$$\varepsilon_i^{l-1}(\tau) = b_{i1}^{l-1}\cdot\tau^2 + b_{i2}^{l-1}\cdot\tau + b_{i3}^{l-1} \qquad l=1,3 \tag{5.6}$$

with coefficients b_i defined in appendix II. The integral J_i in (5.4) is separated into two parts

$$J_i = - \sum_{k=1}^{n} \kappa_k \cdot e^{-\kappa_k t_n} \cdot C_{ij}^{k} \cdot \left[\int_0^{t_{n-1}} e^{\kappa_k \cdot \tau} \cdot \varepsilon_j(\tau) \cdot d\tau + \int_{t_{n-1}}^{t_n} e^{\kappa_k \tau} \varepsilon_j^{l-1}(\tau) \cdot d\tau \right] \quad (5.7)$$

The first integral in (5.7) is the final sum obtained during the previous integration step, and the second integral in (5.7) can be computed with (5.6)

$$\int_{t_{n-1}}^{t_n} e^{\kappa_k \tau} \cdot \varepsilon_j^{l-1}(\tau) \cdot d\tau = \int_{t_{n-1}}^{t_n} (b_{i1}^{l-1} \cdot \tau^2 + b_{i2}^{l-1} \cdot \tau + b_{i3}^{l-1}) \cdot e^{\kappa_k \tau} \cdot d\tau \quad (5.8)$$

Equations (5.5) - (5.8) must be computed at each mesh point of the shell through several points over the shell thickness. Thus the anelastic stresses of eq. (5.4) may be integrated over the shell thickness to get pseudo-loads. A new solution $\varepsilon_i^{l}(t_n)$ is found and the iteration continues with l=l+1 at eq. (5.6) until convergence of the shell displacements are achieved.

We should briefly comment on strategy [7] during a viscoelastic analysis. The Newton-Raphson iteration reuses the inverted Jacobian matrix. This means that the new load vector is substituted for each iteration step using a previous solution. The STAGS program offers several possibilities to control the convergence behaviour. If convergence has been good for previous time steps, the next step becomes bigger by a specified factor. On the other hand, if convergence is bad, the new time step is cut by a factor. A recomputation of the Jacobian only occurs after a specified number of time step cuts. We should therefore separate a problem into several parts. Firstly, the non-linear solution at t=0 must be found, which itself involves all the strategy parameters. Then a small number of time steps are evaluated in order to get an idea of the magnitude of the steps. A restart is made, which automatically includes the refactorisation of the Jacobian. If the creep rate $\dot{\varepsilon}(t)$ now is not changing too rapidly, the time step is increased and integration goes on with larger time steps until we get into a region where $\dot{\varepsilon}(t)$ starts to increase drastically just before collapse. Here a more frequent recomputation of the Jacobian is necessary.

Let us illustrate this by an example. A cylindrical panel (fig.7) under external pressure is analyzed. Due to symmetry, one quarter of the shell is considered. The segment is divided into a finite difference mesh of 7x9. At first we compute the linear bifurcation load p_{cr}. Then we determine the non-linear elastic solution taking as initial load p a fraction of p_{cr}.

Both solutions use elasticity coefficients $\overset{o}{C}_{ij}$. The corresponding displacement-load curve is displayed in fig. 8 for the displacement w_A (perpendicular to the surface) at point A of fig. 7.

In order to obtain the viscoelastic solution we use the coefficients $\overset{k}{C}_{ij}$ of chapter 4 for an isotropic shell. The load $p = 0{,}8\ p_{cr}$ is applied at t=0 and held constant. Thus, the first step consists of computing the nonlinear elastic solution, i.e. we move on the curve in fig.8 until $p = 0{,}8\ p_{cr}$ and thereafter the time starts to run. The corresponding displacements $w_A(t)$ and $w(\xi=0,\eta,t)$ are displayed in figs. 9 and 10. Restarts are made after the primary creep stage and just before the collapse where convergence difficulties occur. Note the influence of an imperfection of the form

$$\bar{w}(\xi,\eta) = w_o \cdot \sin \frac{\pi \cdot \eta}{\theta} \tag{5.9}$$

with $w_o = -1.0$ mm.

Appendix I

Summary of matrices and vectors used in chapter 3.

$$[D]_k = \begin{bmatrix} D_{11}(t_k^*) & D_{12}(t_k^*) \\ D_{12}(t_k^*) & D_{11}(t_k^*) \end{bmatrix} \cdot (t_{k+1} - t_k)$$

$$t_k^* = t_n - \tfrac{1}{2}(t_{k+1} + t_k)$$

$$[D] = \begin{bmatrix} D_{11}(o) & D_{12}(0) \\ D_{12}(0) & D_{11}(0) \end{bmatrix}$$

$$\{a\}_k = \begin{Bmatrix} C_{11}(t_k) \\ C_{12}(t_k) \end{Bmatrix}$$

$$\{d\}_k = \tfrac{1}{2}\left[\{a\}_k + \{a\}_{k+1}\right]$$

$$\{T\}_k = \begin{Bmatrix} 2 \cdot t_k \\ 0 \end{Bmatrix}$$

Appendix II

The extrapolated solution $\varepsilon_i^o(t_n)$ is obtained by writing the quadratic equation at the three last solutions

$$\begin{bmatrix} t_{n-3}^2 & t_{n-3} & 1 \\ t_{n-2}^2 & t_{n-2} & 1 \\ t_{n-1}^2 & t_{n-1} & 1 \end{bmatrix} \cdot \begin{Bmatrix} a_{i1} \\ a_{i2} \\ a_{i3} \end{Bmatrix} = \begin{Bmatrix} \varepsilon_i(t_{n-3}) \\ \varepsilon_i(t_{n-2}) \\ \varepsilon_i(t_{n-1}) \end{Bmatrix} \qquad \text{II.1}$$

Solving eq. II.2 we find

$$\varepsilon_i^o(t_n) = a_{i1} \cdot t_n^2 + a_{i2} \cdot t_n + a_{i3} \qquad \text{II.2}$$

The same procedure

$$\begin{bmatrix} t_{n-2}^2 & t_{n-2} & 1 \\ t_{n-1}^2 & t_{n-1} & 1 \\ t_n^2 & t_n & 1 \end{bmatrix} \cdot \begin{Bmatrix} b_{i1}^{l-1} \\ b_{i2}^{l-1} \\ b_{i3}^{l-1} \end{Bmatrix} = \begin{Bmatrix} \varepsilon_i(t_{n-2}) \\ \varepsilon_i(t_{n-1}) \\ \varepsilon_i^{l-1}(t_n) \end{Bmatrix} \qquad \text{II.3}$$

leads to

$$\varepsilon_i^l(\tau) = b_{i1}^{l-1} \cdot \tau^2 + b_{i2}^{l-1} \cdot \tau + b_{i3}^{l-1} \qquad \text{II.4}$$

which is used to compute the integral in (5.8).

Index

[1] B.O. Almroth, D.O. Brush; Buckling of Bars, Plates and Shells; Mc Graw-Hill; New-York, 1974.

[2] B.O. Almroth; Nonlinear Behaviour of Shells; Lockheed Palo Alto Research Laboratory.

[3] N.M.Newmark; A Method of Computation for Structural Dynamics; Journal of the Engineering Mechanics Division ASCE; Vol. EM3 p. 67-94; 1959.

[4] C.W. Grear; Numerical Initial Value Problems in Ordinary Differential Equations; Prentice-Hall, Englewood Cliffs, N.J., 1971.

[5] R.E. Nickell; On the Stability of Approximation Operators in Problems of Structural Dynamics; Int. Journal of Solids and Structures, Vol.7, 1971.

[6] R.A. Schapery; A simple Collocation Method for Fitting Viscoelastic Models to Experimental Data, California Institute of Technology; 1961.

[7] M.H. Gradowczyk & F. Moavenzadeh; Characterisation of linear viscoelastic Materials; Trans. of the Society of Rheology 13:2; 1969.

[8] P. Stehlin, F. Brogan, S. Merazzi; Viscoelastic Buckling of layered orthotropic Shells; The Aeronautical Research Institute of Sweden Report HU-1807:0, Stockholm 1976.

[9] B.O. Almroth et al.; Collapse Analysis for Shells of General Shape, Lockheed Palo Alto Research Laboratory Report AFFDL TR-71-8, 1973.

		C_{11}° [kp/mm^2]	C_{12}°	C_{33}°
		354	138	108
t_i [sec]	$\kappa_i \left[\frac{1}{\text{sec}}\right]$	$C_{11}^{k}(t_i)$ [kp/mm^2]	$C_{12}^{k}(t_i)$	$C_{33}(t_i)$
1	0.5	14.7	5.22	5.95
10	0.05	39.31	17.19	11.32
100	0.005	53.05	18.62	19.11
1000	0.0005	69.38	28.19	20.20

Table 1

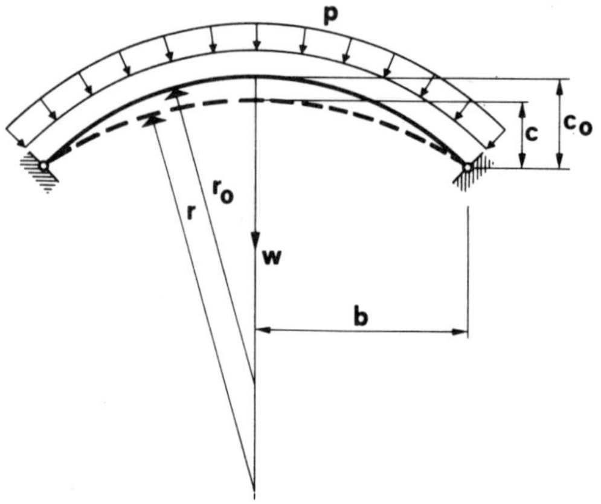

Fig. 1 Cylindrical Arch

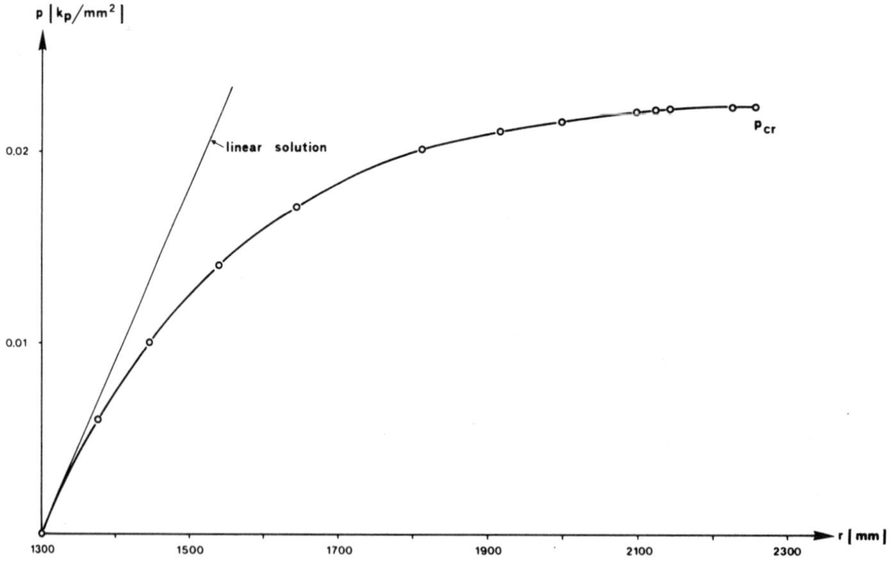

Fig. 2 Arch- Elastic Solution

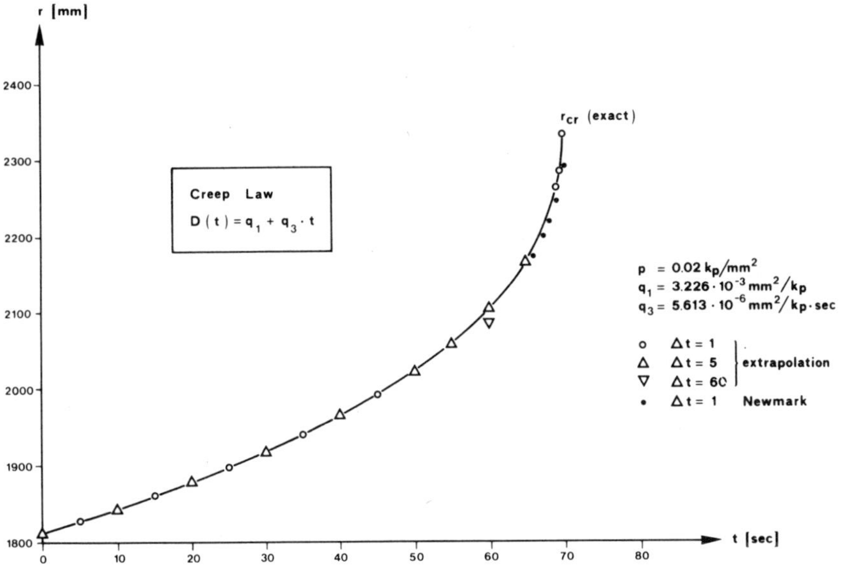

Fig. 3 Arch- Viscoplastic Solution

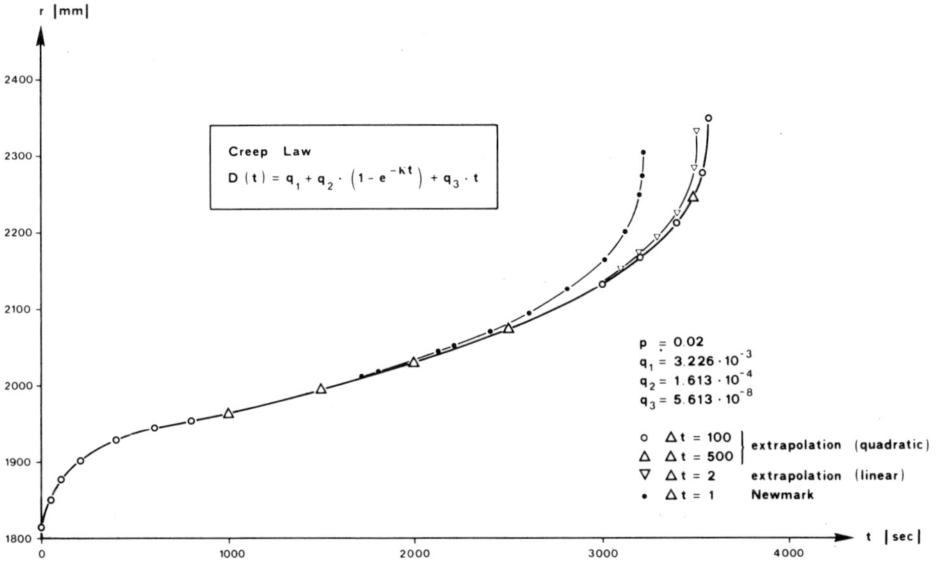

Fig. 4 Arch- Viscoelastic Solution

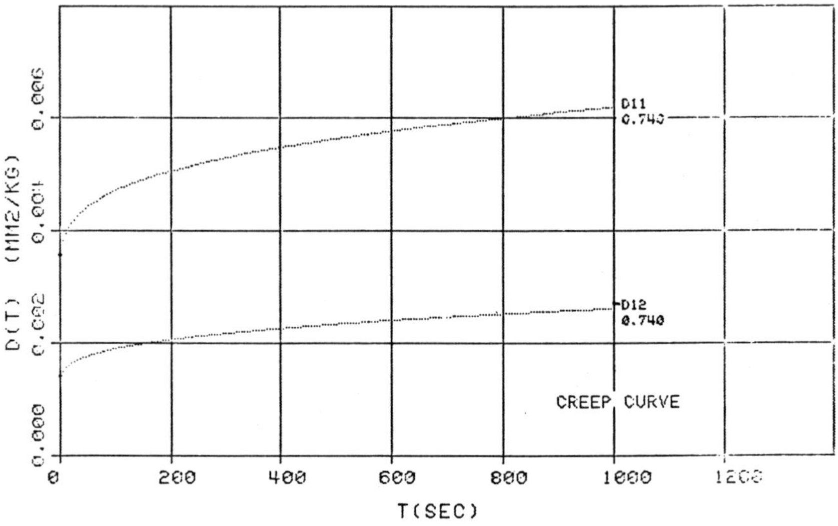

Fig. 5.1 Creep Curves D_{11} and $-D_{12}$

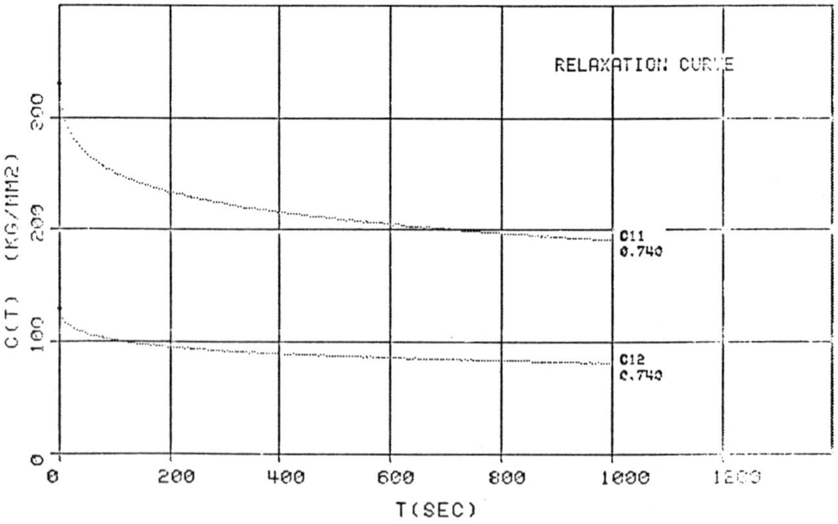

Fig. 5.2 Relaxation Moduli C_{11} and C_{12}

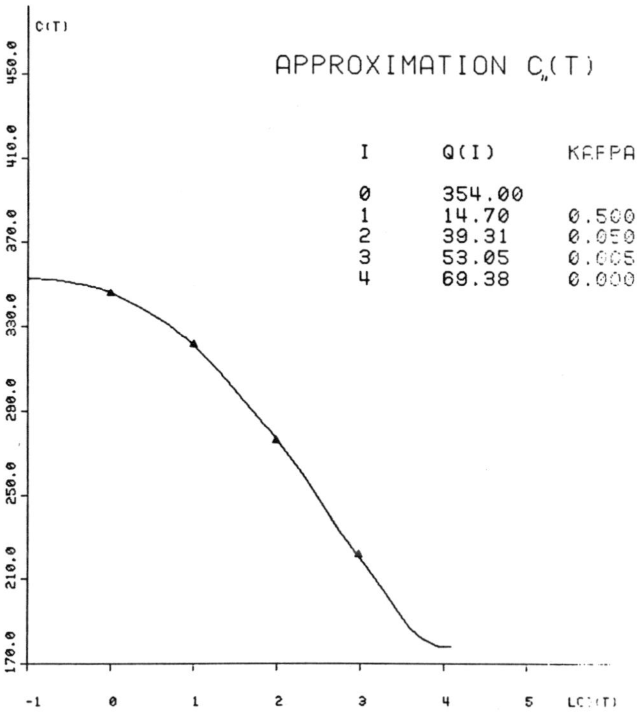

Fig. 6 Approximation of C_{11} (t) Δ exact values

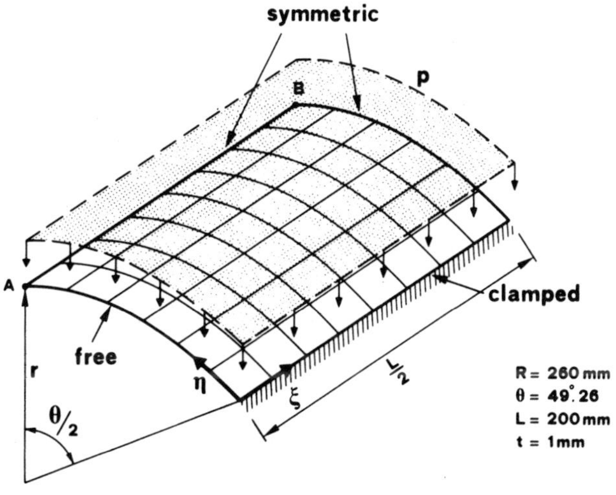

Fig. 7 Cylindrical Panel

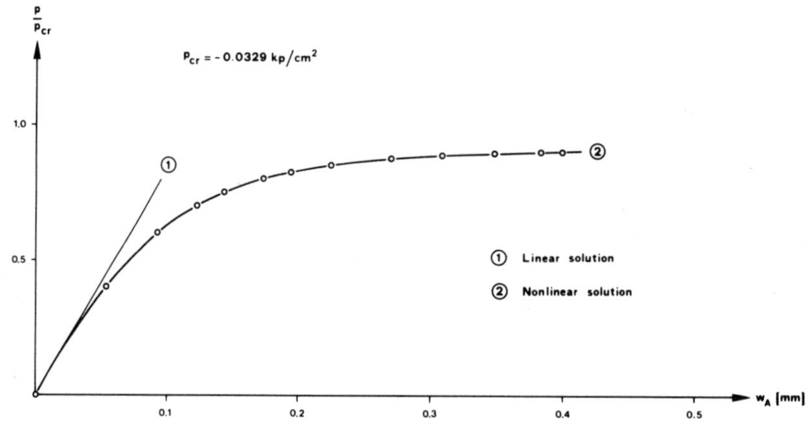

Fig. 8 Panel -Elastic Solution

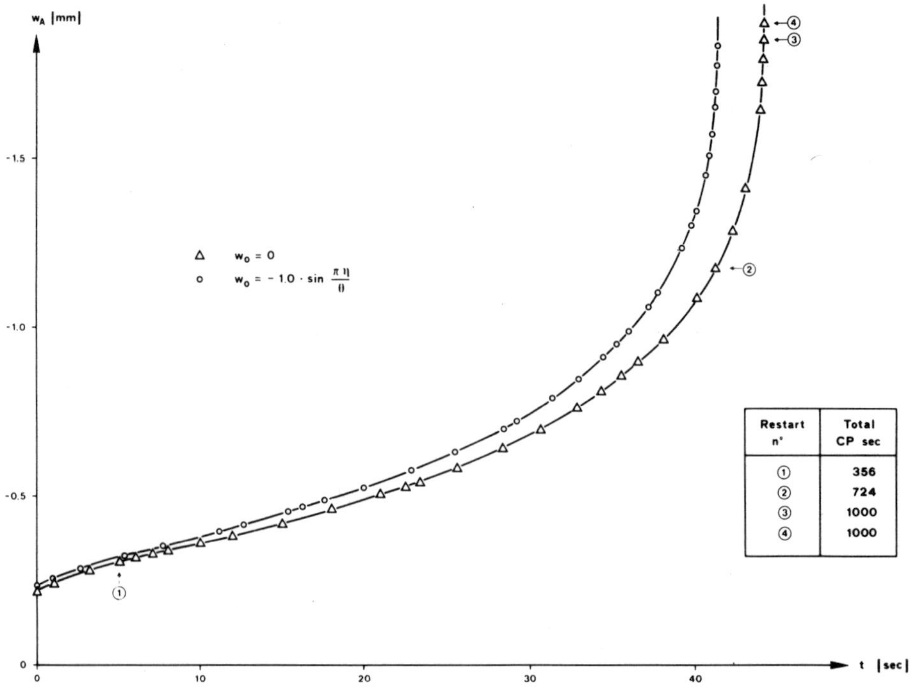

Fig. 9 Cylindrical Panel- Viscoelastic Solution

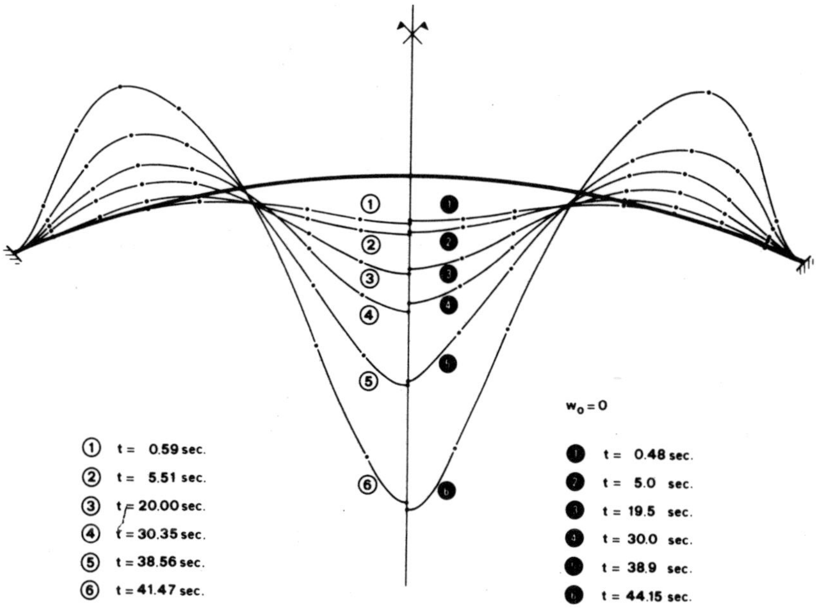

Fig. 10 Cylindrical Panel Viscoelastic Solution $w(o, \eta, t)$

COMBINATION OF ANALYTICAL AND NUMERICAL CALCULATION METHODS

by: P. Bremi
Computer Centre, Ko.St. 1506
Sulzer Brothers Ltd.
8400 Winterthur

0. Introduction

Before computers became so widespread, the calculation engineer always tried to solve his problems analytically if he could. Only as a last resort did he turn to numerical methods, because they usually call for very extensive arithmetical calculations that had to be churned through more or less by hand.

Since the advent of the computer, which uses a program to run through these arithmetical calculations extremely rapidly and reliably, the calculation engineer finds himself in a totally new situation. Now he has learned to solve his problems with the computer. With it, he can even handle highly complex problems.

But problems often crop up that do not lend themselves to purely numerical solutions. As the following examples will show, there can be a number of different reasons for this. Neither can many of these problems be solved purely analytically, however. But combining analytical and numerical methods will often make possible very sound solutions with relatively little effort. The object of these examples is to demonstrate this and to show how broad the range of combination possibilities is. The first example is intended as an introduction to the subject. Unlike the subsequent ones, it has not been taken from everyday practice.

1. Singular integral

a.) Problem

To calculate the integral

$$\int_0^{\pi/2} \ln(\sin x)\,dx$$

b.) Analytical solution

The integral cannot be calculated analytically.

c.) Numerical solution

For $x \to 0$ $(x \geq 0)$, the integrand approaches $-\infty$ (see Fig. 1.1). Hence the integral is singular, and a purely numerical solution would be very troublesome.

d.) Combined solution

One can transform the integral this way:

$$\begin{aligned}\int_0^{\pi/2} \ln(\sin x)\,dx &= \int_0^{\pi/2} \ln\left(x \cdot \frac{\sin x}{x}\right) dx \\ &= \int_0^{\pi/2} \ln x \, dx + \int_0^{\pi/2} \ln\left(\frac{\sin x}{x}\right) dx \\ &= \frac{\pi}{2}\left[\ln\frac{\pi}{2} - 1\right] + \int_0^{\pi/2} \ln\left(\frac{\sin x}{x}\right) dx\end{aligned}$$

The remaining integral is no longer singular (see Fig. 1.1), and so can be integrated numerically with ease, e.g. with Simpson's method. The value obtained for the integral sought is -1.089045... . Rather imprecisely, you could say that the singularity has been integrated analytically, the rest numerically.

2. Plane potential flow

a.) Problem

In the middle of a plane canal (see Fig. 2.1) $2 \cdot b$ wide, there is a round obstacle with the radius $r = 1$. We wish to calculate a potential flow in the canal, the velocity and potential of which are denoted by $\vec{V}$ and φ respectively, for which $\vec{V} = \nabla\varphi$. For $|x| \to \infty$, the following should be true: $V_x = V_\infty = 1$, $V_y = 0$. Above all we need to establish $V_0 = V_x(0, 1)$ for various $b \geq 2$.

b.) Analytical solution

An analytical solution is possible only for the case $b = \infty$. If we mark all variables for this special case with an *, the following applies for $b = b^* = \infty$:

$$\varphi^* = \left[1 + \frac{1}{x^2 + y^2}\right] \cdot x$$

$$V_x^* = 1 + \frac{1}{x^2 + y^2}\left[1 - \frac{2x^2}{x^2 + y^2}\right]$$

$$V_y^* = \frac{-2xy}{[x^2 + y^2]^2}$$

thus, in particular

$$V_0^* = 2$$

c.) Numerical solution

The problem can only be solved numerically with a program based on difference methods or finite element methods. Instead of the infinitely long canal, one assumes a canal of finite length, namely 2a (with "a" sufficiently large). Because of symmetry considerations, only one-fourth of the canal has to be calculated. For φ, one has boundary conditions as shown in Fig. 2.2 (n indicates the direction of the extreme boundary normals). The higher the accuracy with which one determines V_0, the greater the computation expense.

d.) Combined solution

The field φ^* (for b = b* = ∞) is an approximation of the field φ we are seeking (for finite b). Because φ and φ^* are satisfied by the same linear differential equation, the difference field $\varphi - \varphi^*$ will also be satisfied by the same differential equation. The boundary conditions for $\varphi - \varphi^*$ are given in Fig. 2.3. The difference field can be calculated numerically in the manner described in c.) above. Adding the know field φ^* to the result yields the desired field φ . If we assume that the relative error of V_0 in the purely numerical calculation c.) is equal to ρ , i.e. that the absolute error is ρV_0 , the absolute error of V_0 under the combined calculation is approximately $\rho(V_0 - V_0^*)$ with roughly the same calculating effort; thus it is smaller, and one can show that for b $\geqslant$ 2 it is less than about 1/5 as great. Fig. 2.4 presents the result of the combined calculation graphically.

3. Vapour bubble formation in liquids

a.) Problem

A spherical vapour bubble of radius R exists in a liquid with density ρ. If one assumes that the liquid is incompressible and satisfies the Navier-Stokes differential equation, that the equation

$$p_D - p_R = \frac{2\sigma}{R}$$

applies to the vapour bubble (p_D being the vapour pressure, p_R the pressure in the liquid at the bubble surface, and σ the surface tension), and that we are dealing with spherical geometry, R yields the differential equation

$$\ddot{R} = \left[\frac{p_D - p_\infty(t)}{\rho} - \frac{2\sigma}{\rho} \cdot \frac{1}{R} - \frac{3}{2} \dot{R}^2 \right] \frac{1}{R}$$

in which derivatives based on time are denoted conventionally with dots and $p_\infty(t)$, the (static) pressure in the liquid, is an infinite distance away from the bubble. We want to integrate this differential equation assuming that p_D, ρ and σ are constant and that $p_\infty(t)$ does not change either. The initial conditions given are

$$R(0) = R_0$$
$$\dot{R}(0) = \dot{R}_0 = 0$$

b.) Analytical solution

The given equation cannot be solved analytically.

c.) Numerical solution

The given equation can be integrated numerically without difficulty (e.g. by describing it as a 1st order system and then integrating with the Runge-Kutta method). But together with its initial conditions the differential equation contains three parameters, namely $\frac{p_D - p_\infty}{\rho}$, $\frac{\sigma}{\rho}$ and R_0 , so that one would have to run through a great many numerical calculations to find the solution for various values of these parameters.

d.) Combined solution

If one substitutes

$$y = \frac{R}{R_0}$$

for the dimensionless radius y and

$$x = \sqrt{\frac{2\sigma}{R_0^3 \rho}}\, t$$

for the dimensionless time x in the differential equation and the initial conditions, one obtains the differential equation

$$y'' = \left[\frac{R_0}{2\sigma}(p_D - p_\infty) - \frac{1}{y} - \frac{3}{2}(y')^2 \right] \frac{1}{y}$$

and the initial conditions

$$y(0) = 1$$

$$y'(0) = 0$$

Now the 3 parameters have been reduced to a single one, namely the variable $\frac{R_0}{2\sigma}(p_D - p_\infty)$. This sharply reduces the number of numerical calculations required and makes the solutions much more manageable.

This particular investigation involved bubble formation in water pumps, in which the parameter $\frac{R_0}{2\sigma}(p_D - p_\infty)$ varied between 2 and 40. Fig. 3.1 provides a graphic presentation of the numerical solutions of the differential equation for y for parameter values in this range.

It is striking that for x greater than about 2, $y' \approx const.$, $y'' \approx 0$. If one inserts this into the differential equation and makes sure $\frac{1}{y}$ is not constant, the result is

$$\frac{R_0}{2\sigma}(p_D - p_\infty) - \frac{3}{2}(y')^2 \approx 0$$

Reversing the variable substitution again yields

$$\dot{R} \approx \sqrt{\frac{2}{3}\,\frac{p_D - p_\infty}{\rho}}$$

Calculating the time t belonging to x = 2 yields such a small value (order of magnitude 10^{-7}s) that it can be said that the approximation formula derived for $\dot{R}$ is valid for virtually any time t. Based on the curve (see Fig. 3.1), the approximation obtained for R is

$$\sqrt{\frac{2}{3}\,\frac{p_D - p_\infty}{\rho}}\; t < R < R_0 + \sqrt{\frac{2}{3}\,\frac{p_D - p_\infty}{\rho}}$$

4. Statistical measurement of amplitude

a.) Problem

Two compressor blades are installed a distance c apart. The tip of one of them vibrates sinusoidally in the installation plane with the amplitude a_{10} and the period T_1, the tip of the other in the same plane with the amplitude a_{20} and the period T_2. It is assumed that the two blades vibrate independently of each other. If the location a_{1k} of the first blade tip and the location a_{2k} of the second are measured at n randomly (uniformly distributed) chosen time-points t_k, $k = 1, \dots, n$, the expression

$$\max_{k=1}^{n} (a_{1k} - a_{2k}) - c$$

will represent an approximation of $a_{10} + a_{20}$ (see Fig. 4.1). What needs to be calculated is the probability W that the above expression will be greater than $(1-\varepsilon)\cdot(a_{10} + a_{20})$. W depends upon ε, n and the amplitude ratio $\alpha = a_{10}/a_{20}$, but not on c and the amplitudes a_{10} and a_{20} per se. W should be calculated for ε in the interval 0 to 0.05; n = 100, 200, 300, ... 1000, and $\alpha = 0, \frac{1}{2}, 1$.

b.) Analytical solution

If one sets up an analytical formula for W, the result is

$$W = 1 - [g(\varepsilon, \alpha)]^n$$

with

$$g(\varepsilon,\alpha) = \frac{1}{\pi^2} \int_{-(1+\alpha)}^{(1-\varepsilon)(1+\alpha)} \left[\int_{\max[-1, \frac{x-1}{\alpha}]}^{\min[1, \frac{x+1}{\alpha}]} \frac{1}{\sqrt{1-y^2}} \cdot \frac{1}{\sqrt{1-(x-\alpha y)^2}} \, dy \right] dx$$

This double integral is singular in complicated fashion, and can only be integrated closed for the special case of $\alpha = 0$ (one blade not vibrating):

$$g(\varepsilon, 0) = \frac{1}{2} + \frac{1}{\pi} \arcsin(1-\varepsilon)$$

For $\alpha \neq 0$, there is no analytical solution.

c.) Numerical solution

An attempt could be made to integrate the double integral given in b.) numerically. As noted, though, this integral is very comlicatedly singular, so it would be extremely time-consuming.

Another possibility is this: getting around the double integral by simulating the original problem directly with the aid of a random number generator. This is possible with a quite simple, short computer program. But because the convergence is very poor for a large n, the computation becomes very expensive in order to obtain satisfactory results.

d.) Combined solution

From the formula given in b.) for calculating W, it follows that

$$g(\varepsilon, \alpha) = \sqrt[n]{1 - W}$$

Thus it is possible to run through the simulation mentioned in c.) with n = 1, and then to use the W obtained to calculate $g(\varepsilon, \alpha)$. This provides the following advantages: in the numerical calculation it is necessary to vary only the parameters ε and α, while n always remains 1. Because n = 1, the convergence of the simulation is relatively good, making the overall computation work considerably less than for purely numerical computation.

The result of the calculations for n = 100 is plotted in Figure 4.2. In this (logarithmic) plot the ordinates are proportional to n, making it a relatively simple matter to use the case of n = 100 to deduce values for n ≠ 100 as well. For α = 0 two curves are plotted. The solid-line curve represents the result of the combined solution method, the broken-line curve that of the analytical solution as described in b.).

5. Conclusions

The following inferences can be drawn from the examples treated: Combined methods

- often make it possible to solve problems that are insoluble with a purely analytical approach.
- usually yield more easily understood and universally applicable solutions than purely numerical ones.
- usually yield considerably more accurate results than numerical methods, assuming an equal amount of computation effort.
- usually require much less computation effort for the same degree of accuracy.

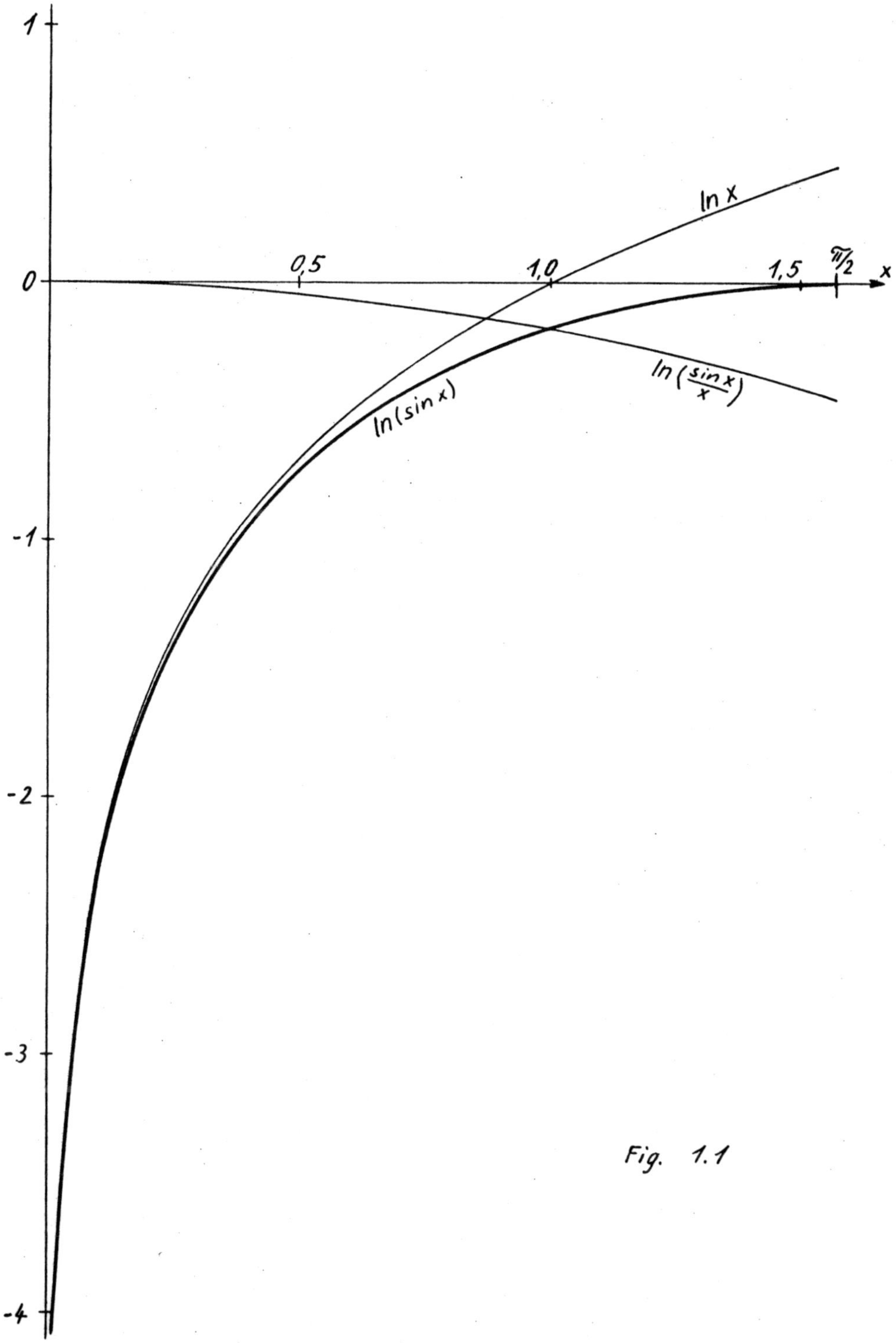

Fig. 1.1

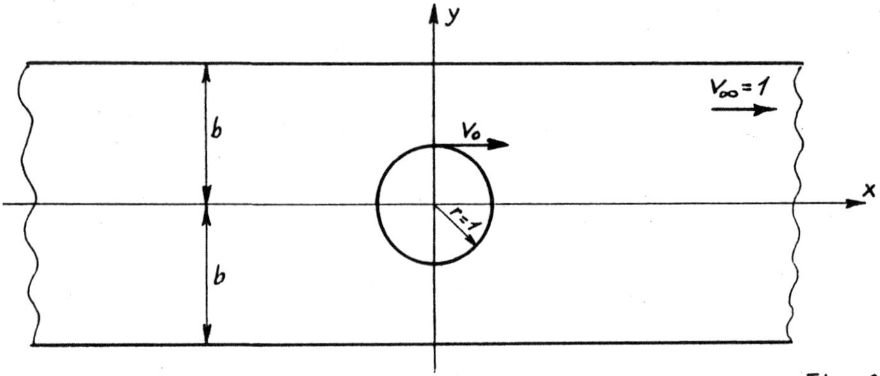

Fig. 2.1

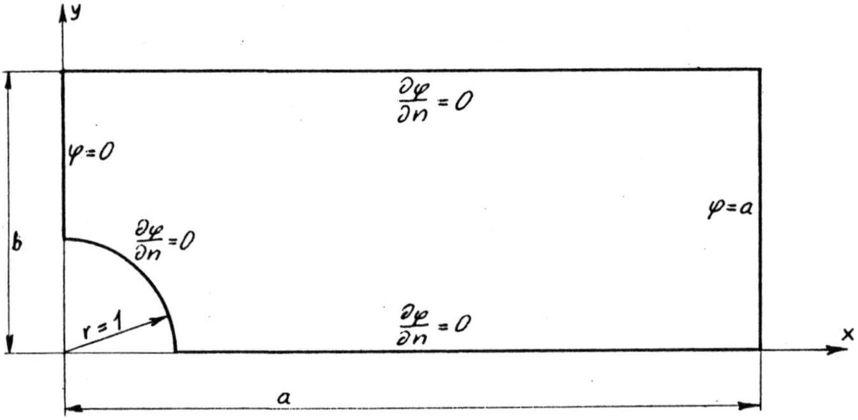

Fig. 2.2

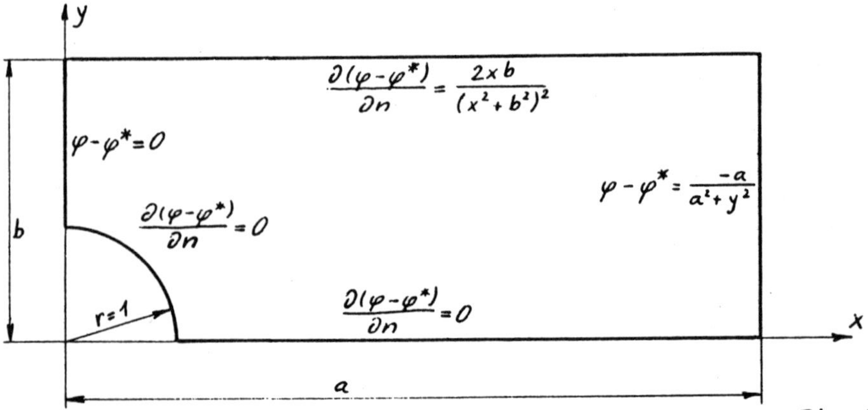

Fig. 2.3

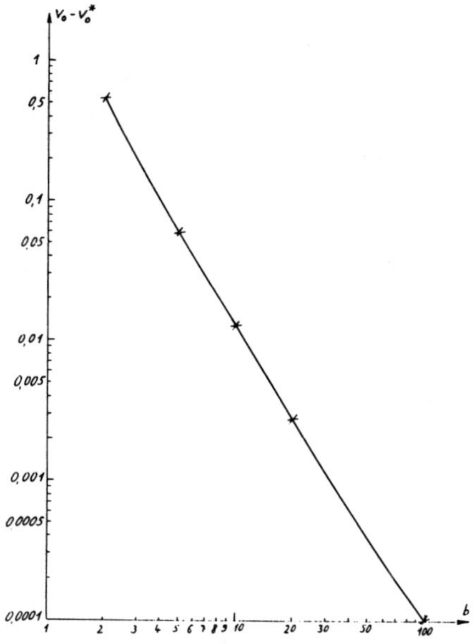
$V_0 - V_0^*$
1
0,5
0,1
0,05
0,01
0,005
0,001
0,0005
0,0001
1
2
3
4
5
6
7
8
9
10
20
30
50
100
b

Fig. 2.4

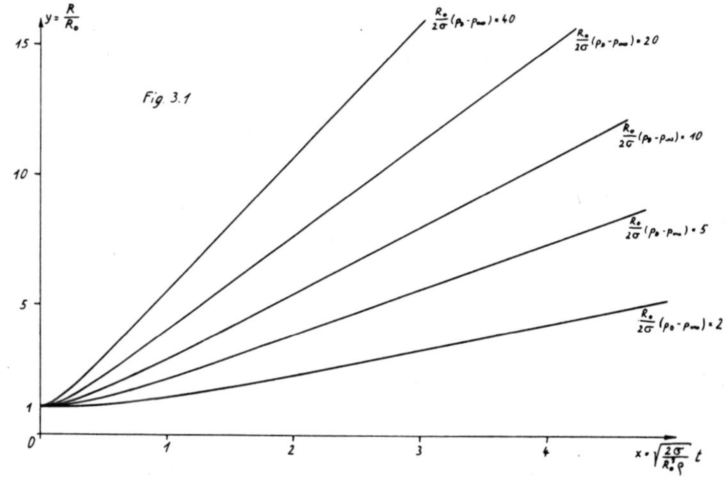
$y = \frac{R}{R_0}$
15
10
5
1
0
1
2
3
4
$x = \sqrt{\frac{2\sigma}{R_0^3 \rho}}\, t$
$\frac{R_0}{2\sigma}(p_0 - p_\infty) = 40$
$\frac{R_0}{2\sigma}(p_0 - p_\infty) = 20$
$\frac{R_0}{2\sigma}(p_0 - p_\infty) = 10$
$\frac{R_0}{2\sigma}(p_0 - p_\infty) = 5$
$\frac{R_0}{2\sigma}(p_0 - p_\infty) = 2$

Fig. 3.1

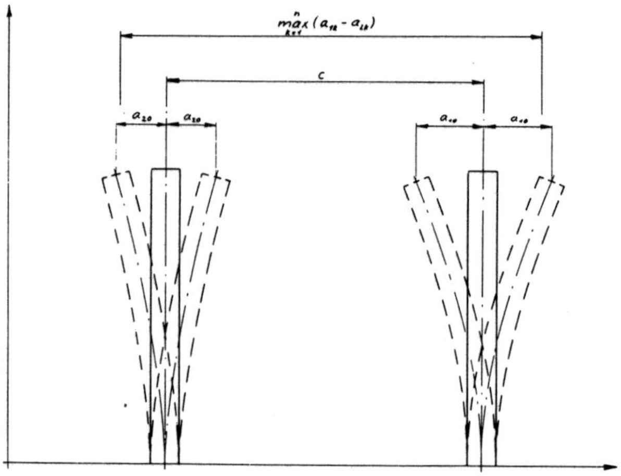
c

Fig. 4.1

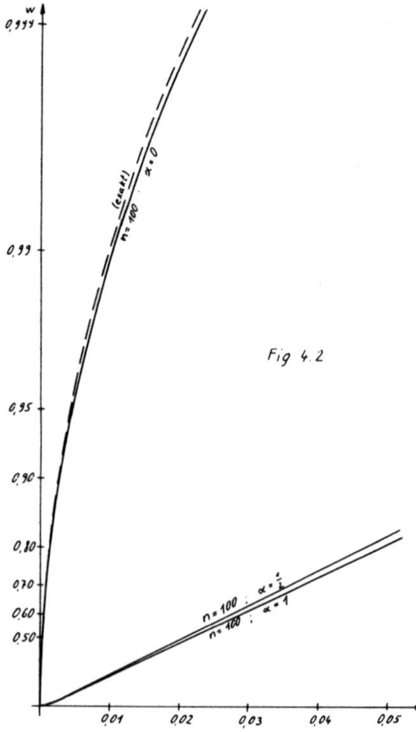
w
0,999
0,99
0,95
0,90
0,80
0,70
0,60
0,50
(exakt)
n = 100
α = 0
n = 100 ; α = 1/2
n = 100 ; α = 1
0,01
0,02
0,03
0,04
0,05
ε

Fig 4.2

On the integration of stiff differential equations

G. Wanner, Genève

1. Examples.

Let us try to integrate the differential equation of Van der Pol $y''-\varepsilon(1-y^2)y'+y=0$ with $\varepsilon=100$ by a standard integration routine, say, Fehlbergs method of order 7 with step size control. We write it in the form

$$\begin{aligned} y_1' &= y_2 && =f_1(x,y) \\ y_2' &= \varepsilon(1-y_1^2)y_2-y_1 && =f_2(x,y). \end{aligned}$$

The solution starts at $y_1=2$, $y_2=0$ and then follows very slowly the line $y_2=y_1/(100(1-y_1^2))$ where $f_2=0$. The solution there is very smooth and nobody, with the exception of those who already know the subject of this article, would ever expect numerical difficulties. Then suddenly, when x approaches 81, the solution shows the power that is contained in the differential equation by running down to $y_2=-134$ and coming up to $y_2=0$, $y_1=-2$ in a time interval of 0.04 only. See fig. 1.

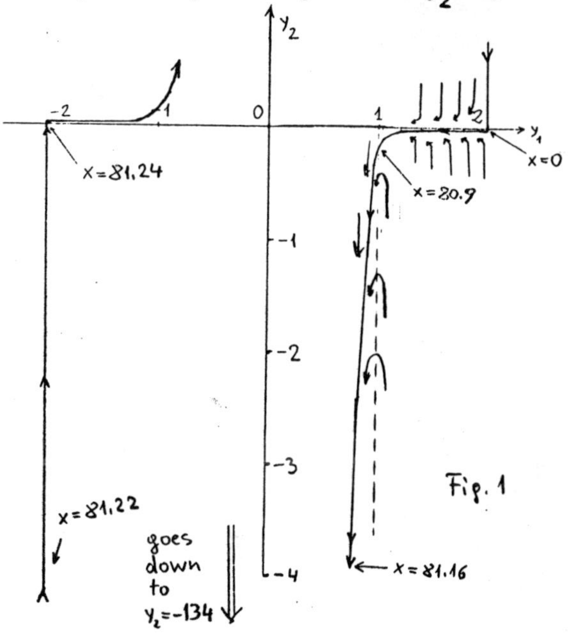

Fig. 1

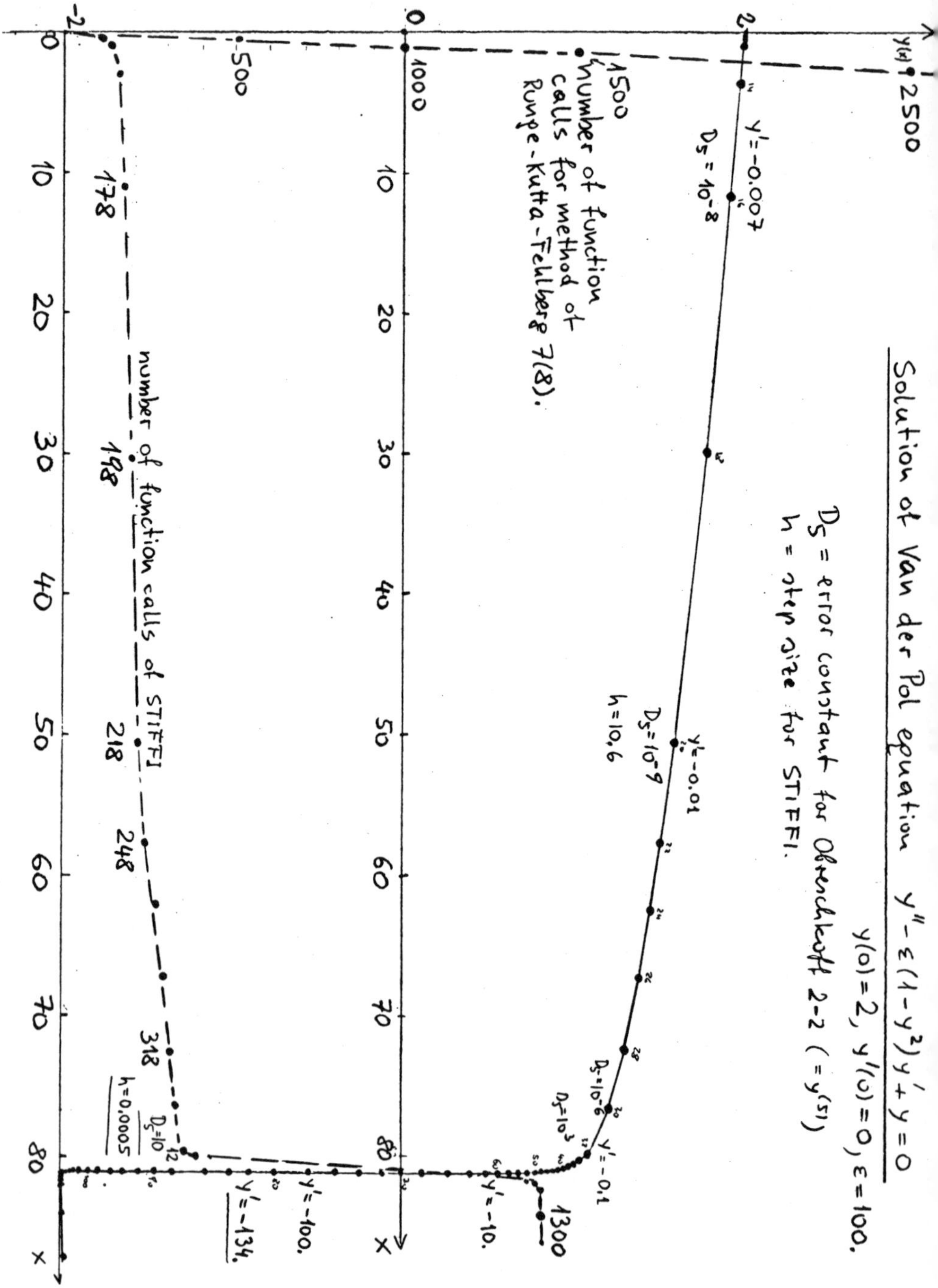
Solution of Van der Pol equation $y'' - \varepsilon(1-y^2)y' + y = 0$
$y(0) = 2,\ y'(0) = 0,\ \varepsilon = 100.$
D_5 = error constant for Obrechkoff 2-2 (= $y^{(5)}$)
h = step size for STIFFI.
y(x)
2500
2
$y' = -0.007$
$D_5 = 10^{-8}$
$y' = -0.01$
$D_5 = 10^{-9}$
h = 10,6
$D_5 = 10^{-6}$
$D_5 = 10^{3}$
$y' = -0.1$
1300
$y' = -10.$
$y' = -100.$
$y' = -134.$
1500
number of function calls for method of Runge-Kutta-Fehlberg 7(8).
1000
500
0
-2
178
198
218
248
318
number of function calls of STIFFI
$D_5 = 10$
h = 0.0005
10
20
30
40
50
60
70
80
x

As can be seen from figure 2, where the number of function calls necessary for Fehlbergs method has been plotted against x, this method was not at all a good choice for this equation. Up to x=5 some 5000 function evaluations were necessary when the computation was terminated by time-out. The following analysis will help us to understand why this method didn't work and why there exist methods that do the integration up to 80 in some 400 function evaluations and a half period in 1300 (see fig.2). For this we look at the point $y_{1o}=1.919$, $y_{2o}=-0.007153$ which lies on the solution. The value of f_2 there is very small $f_2(y_o)=-0.000164$, but the partial derivatives $\frac{\partial f_2}{\partial y_2}(y_o)=-268.26$, $\frac{\partial f_2}{\partial y_1}(y_o)=1.7453$ are quite important. Since the steps used with Fehlbergs program are very small $\Delta x=0.01$, leading to $\Delta y_1=0.00007$, $\Delta y_2=-0.000002$, we commit no big error when we replace, in the neighbourhood of this point, our original differential equation by its linear approximations

$$\begin{pmatrix} y_1' \\ y_2' \end{pmatrix} = \begin{pmatrix} 0 & 1 \\ 1.7453 & -268.26 \end{pmatrix} \begin{pmatrix} y_1-y_{1o} \\ y_2-y_{2o} \end{pmatrix} \quad \text{or} \quad y'=Ay.$$

If we now apply to this equation an expicit Runge-Kutta method, say for simplicity, modified Euler (Fig. 3)

$$k_1=y_o+\frac{h}{2}Ay_o$$

$$y_1=y_o+hAk_1$$

and if we transform the Matrix A to diagonal form

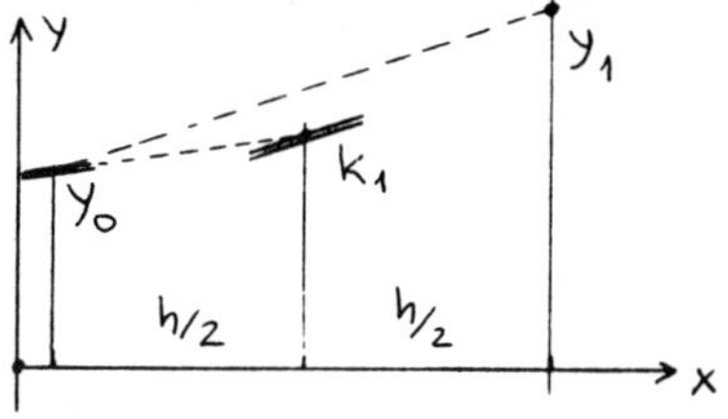

Fig. 3

$$T^{-1}AT = \begin{pmatrix} 0.0065 & \\ & -268.26 \end{pmatrix} = \begin{pmatrix} \lambda_1 & \\ & \lambda_2 \end{pmatrix}, \quad T^{-1}y=z, \quad T^{-1}k=g$$

we obtain $z_{1i}=z_{oi}(1+\lambda_i h+\lambda_i^2 h^2/2)$. Since the polynomial $1+x+x^2/2$ is smaller than 1 only if $-2<x<0$, the numerical solutions will become instable and blow up errors in later steps if h does not satisfy $0<h<-2/\lambda_1$, hence $0<h<0.0075$. Similar bounds are obtained with all other explicit methods too. We thus say

Definition. A differential equation problem is stiff, if some of the eigenvalues of $\frac{\partial f}{\partial y}$ have large negative real parts and if, at the same time, the interval of interest in the solution is relatively large. (The case when the eigenvalues have large imaginary parts but are close to the imaginary axis, the highly oszillatory problem, is not considered in this paper. Special methods are needed here).

Other origins of stiff equations:

Chemical reactions. The simultaneous presence of very fast and very slow reactions leads to stiff equations, for example the following equations which are treated in many papers on stiff equations

$$\begin{aligned} y_1' &= -0.04y_1 + 10^4 y_2 y_3 & y_1(0)&=1 \\ y_2' &= 0.04y_1 - 10^4 y_2 y_3 - 3.10^7 y_2^2 & y_2(0)&=0 \\ y_3' &= + 3.10^7 y_2^2 & y_3(0)&=0 \end{aligned}$$

where the eigenvalues descend to -4000.

Semi discretization of parabolic equations. If ever parabolic equations are discretized with respect to the space variables only, say by finite differences or by finite elements, the resulting ordinary system (linear or not) must necessarily contain eigenvalues of all sorts of largeness to be able to model the physical fact that rough initial functions change very rapidly into smooth functions but smooth functions then change only very slowly. For example the discretization of $\frac{\partial u}{\partial t} = \frac{\partial^2 u}{\partial x^2}$ by the standard three point rule leads to

$$\frac{du_i}{dt} = (u_{i+1} - 2u_i + u_{i-1})/h^2$$

where the eigenvalues range from zero to $-4/h^2$, so the equation is fairly stiff for small values of h.

Singular perturbation of differential equations.

Singular perturbations are small parameters in a differential equation, such that the order decreases when the parameters are set to zero. Typical examples occur in fluid dynamics, a general reference is the book of Wasow. Let us look at the trivial example $\varepsilon y''+\alpha y'+\beta y=5$, $y(0)=y(1)=0$, where α,β are positive constants and ε is small. The eigenvalues of this equation are for ε small close to $\lambda_1=-\alpha/\varepsilon$, $\lambda_2=-\beta/\alpha$. The solution corresponding to λ_1 is not negligible only in the neigbourhood of 0, where it forms a sharp peak (this is the boundary layer). Outside this boundary layer only the solution of the unperturbed equation ($\varepsilon=0$) is present. (See fig. 4).

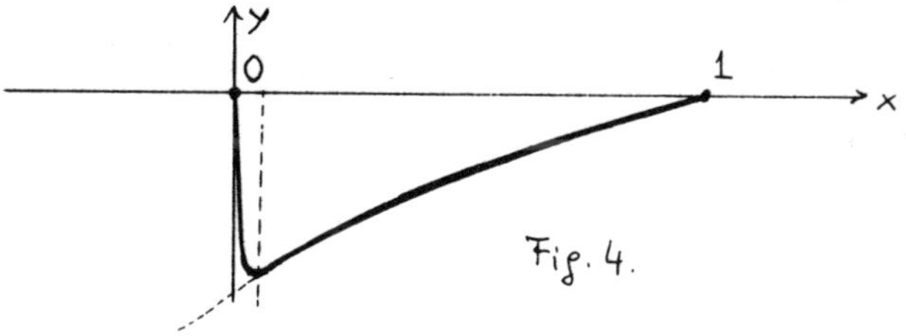

Fig. 4.

2. Collocation methods.

Among the methods applicable to stiff problems are the following:

a) Euler implicit

b) Trapezoidal rule, midpoint rule

c) Some multistep formulas (backward differences (Gear 1971), exponential fitted methods (Liniger Willoughby 1970))

d) implicit Runge-Kutta methods (Butcher 1964, Ehle 1969, Axelsson 1969, Butcher 1976)

e) Rosenbrock methods (Rosenbrock 1963, Nørsett 1975, Wolfbrandt 1976, Kaps 1976)

f) generalized Runge-Kutta methods (Runge-Kutta methods whose coefficients are rational functions of $\frac{\partial f}{\partial y}$, partly identical with Rosenbrock methods, Van der Houwen 1972 , Verwer 1973,74,75)

g) multiderivative methods, multistep-multiderivative methods

(Hermite, Obreschkoff, Liniger-Willoughby 1970,..)

h) multistep-multistage formulas, composite RK methods, RK methods with matricial coefficients, cyclic use of multistep formulas (Rubin-Bickart 1972, Lambert-Sigurdsson 1972,..)

i) multistage-multiderivative formulas (Kastlunger-Wanner-Fuchs 1972,75)

j) any of the above methods (usually trapez or midpoint) with Richardson extrapolation (Dahlquist-Lindberg 1971,72, Stetter)

k) direct use of exp(A) (Lawson 1967, Friedli 1976).

A great deal of these methods can be seen under the point of view of collocation methods.

Definition. Let a number m and reals $\alpha_1,..,\alpha_m$ (usually in $|0,1|$) be given. Then the corresponding collocation method consists in constructing a polynomial of degree m passing thru the initial values x_o,y_o that satisfies the differential equation in the points $x_o+\alpha_i h$ $(i=1,..,m)$ where h is the step size. If some of the α's coin ide, the condition is to be replaced by one in higher derivatives. More precisely

$$p(x)=y_o + \sum_{i=1}^{m} c_i(x-x_o)^i$$

so that

$$p'(x_o+\alpha_k h)=f(x_o+\alpha_k h,p(x_o+\alpha_k h)) \qquad k=1,..,m$$

or,for multiple α's

$$p''(x_o+\alpha_k h)=(\frac{\partial f}{\partial x} + \frac{\partial f}{\partial y}\cdot f)(x_o+\alpha_k h,p(x_o+\alpha_k h)) \qquad \text{etc.}$$

A particulary simple resultat is available in the case when the values of α are equal to 0 and 1 only:

Lemma: Let q(x) be a polynomial of degree m. Then for any y(x) n+1 times differentiable

$$\sum_{i=o}^{m}(-1)^i\left[q^{(m-i)}(1)y^{(i)}(1)-q^{(m-i)}(0)y^{(i)}(0)\right]=$$

$$= (-1)^m \int_0^1 q(x)y^{(m+1)}(x)dx.$$

The proof is by partial integration starting with

$$0 = \int_0^1 q^{(m+1)}(x)y(x)dx=0.$$

Thus, transforming this result to an arbitrary interval of legth h, we have that for any polynomial q(x) of degree m the formula

$$(1) \qquad \sum_{i=o}^{m} (-h)^i q^{(m-i)}(1)y_1^{(i)} = \sum_{i=o}^{m} (-h)^i q^{(m-i)}(0)y_o^{(i)}$$

defines a one-step multiderivative formula of order m with error term

$$(-h)^{m+1} \int_0^1 q(\xi)y^{(m+1)}(x_o+h\xi)d\xi \ .$$

As an example let $q(x)=1-\theta-x$ which leads to

$$(1') \qquad y_1+(\theta-1)y_1' = y_o+\theta y_o' \ , \ ^{*)}$$

the socalled θ-method which is used in parabolic equations (see Zlámal). It has order 1 and optimal error properties for real negative eigenvalues when $\theta=0.122$.

Formula (1) represents a collocation method, if we put $q(x)=x^k(x-1)^{\ell}/(k+\ell)!$, since in this case the lower derivatives of q at x=0 and x=1 vanish. So the formula does not involve higher derivatives of y than the collocation formula with $\alpha_1=..=\alpha_{\ell}=0,\alpha_{\ell+1}=..=\alpha_{\ell+k}=1$. Since the error term vanishes when y is a polynomial of degree m, the methods must coincide. A calculation of $q^{(m-i)}(1)$ and $q^{(m-i)}(0)$ leads to the formula

$$(2) \qquad \sum_{i=o}^{k} \frac{k!(\ell+k-i)!}{(k-i)!(k+\ell)!} \frac{(-h)^i y_1^{(i)}}{i!} = \sum_{i=o}^{\ell} \frac{\ell!(k+\ell-i)!}{(\ell-i)!(k+\ell)!} \frac{h^i y_o^{(i)}}{i!}$$

with error term

$$\frac{(-h)^{k+\ell+1}}{(k+\ell)!} \int_0^1 \xi^k(\xi-1)^{\ell} y^{(k+\ell+1)}(x_o+h\xi)d\xi =$$

$$= (-1)^{k+1} \frac{k! \ \ell!}{(k+\ell)!} \frac{h^{k+\ell+1}y^{(k+\ell+1)}(x_o+h\theta)}{(k+\ell+1)!}$$

Examples are given in the following table:

Survey on some collocation methods.

m	$\alpha_1,..,\alpha_m$	Method	
1	$\alpha_1=1$	$y_1=y_o+hf(x_o+h,y_1)$	Euler implicit
1	$\alpha_1=0$	$y_1=y_o+hf(x_o,y_o)$	Euler explicit
m	$\alpha_1=..=\alpha_m=0$	$y_1=y_o+hy_o'+hy_o''/2!+..$	Taylor
2	$\alpha_1=0,\alpha_2=1$	$y_1=y_o+\frac{h}{2}\, f(x_o,y_o)+f(x_o+h,y_1)$	Trapezoidal rule
1	$\alpha_1=1/2$	$k_1=y_o+\frac{h}{2}f(x_o+h/2,k_1)$, $y_1=y_o+hf(x_o+h/2,k_1)$	implicit midpointrule *)
3	$\alpha_1=0,\alpha_2=\alpha_3=1$	$y_1-\frac{2}{3}\,hy_1'+\frac{h^2}{3}\,\frac{y_1''}{2!}=y_o+\frac{h}{3}\,y_o'$	Obreschkoff 2-1
4	$\alpha_1=\alpha_2=0,\alpha_3=\alpha_4=1$	$y_1-\frac{h}{2}\,y_1'+\frac{h^2}{6}\,\frac{y_1''}{2!}=y_o+\frac{h}{2}\,y_o'+\frac{h^2}{6}\,\frac{y_o''}{2!}$	Obreschkoff 2-2
	$\alpha_1=..=\alpha_\ell=0,\alpha_{\ell+1}=..=\alpha_{\ell+k}=1$		Obreschkoff k-ℓ
m	$\alpha_1,..,\alpha_m$ nodes of Gaussian Quadr.form.		implicit Runge-Kutta methods of J. Butcher 1964.
m	$\alpha_1,..,\alpha_m$ nodes of Radau quadrature f.		implicit Runge-Kutta methods of Axelsson and Ehle (type IIA)

If ever one has decided to work with one of these methods, the problems are not yet all over, since these formulas give no computational algorithms, but just implicit equations determining the solution y_1. If the differential equation is linear, then these equations are linear too and can be solved relatively simple. For nonlinear equations, one usually applies, since Liniger-Willoughby, Newtons method. Let us carry out this for Euler implicit: We set

$$F(y_1)=y_1-y_o-hf(x_o+h,y_1),\quad F'(y)=I-hf'(x_o+h,y).$$

We take as initial approximation for example $y_1=y_o$ and obtain after one iteration $y_1=y_o-(I-hf'(x_o+h,y_o))^{-1}hf(x_o+h,y_o)$

or

(3) $\quad y_1=y_o+hk_1 \quad$ where $\quad (I-hf'(x_o+h,y_o))k_1=f(x_o+h,y_o)$.

Remark. The resulting implicit system when one uses implicit Runge-Kutta methods would have dimension m.n. Thus a straightforward application of this idea would be particularly unfavourable for differential systems of higher dimension. In order to avoid this, J.Butcher (1976) has recently published an algorithm that overcomes this disadvantage.

3. Rosenbrock methods (generalized R-K methods).

Nowbody will now expect a long speech for an accurate repetition of Newton's method in equation (3), since this consists in an expensive computation of a value which itself, as the result of a numerical method, is full of error. So formula (3) is just as good as the implicit Euler formula. Now the idea lies at hand to construct more general formulas of the type (3) by introducing auxiliary functions k_i and parameters à la Runge-Kutta, for example (in the case of an autonomous system)

$$(5)\qquad \begin{aligned} (I-ch\, \frac{\partial f}{\partial y}(y_o))k_i &= f(y_o+h \sum_{j=1}^{i-1} a_{ij}k_j) + h \sum_{j=1}^{i-1} c_{ij}\, \frac{\partial f}{\partial y}(y_o)k_j \qquad (i=1,..,s) \\ y_1 &= y_o+h \sum_{j=1}^{s} b_j k_j . \end{aligned}$$

Formula (5) consists, for $i=1,..,s$, in a sequence of linear equations for the computation of $k_1,..,k_s$ with allways the same matrix. So the LR decomposition of this matrix can be saved leading to advantageous algorithms. The parameters a_{ij},c_{ij},c,b_j are then adjusted to assure stability properties and to give the method a certain order. This is best done, for higher orders, using the theory as given in Hairer-Wanner (1974) and extended by Nørsett. The following set of parameters defines a method of order 4 and has been calculated by E.Hairer and P. Kaps:

$$s=3,\quad c=1.0685790213016288\ (=\text{largest zero of } c^3-\tfrac{3}{2}c^2+\tfrac{c}{2}-\tfrac{1}{24}=0)$$

$$a_1=0,\ a_2, a_3 \text{ free parameters},$$

$$a_{21}=a_2,\ b_2=(4a_3-3)/(12a_2^2(a_3-a_2)),\ b_3=(3-4a_2)/(12a_3^2(a_3-a_2)),$$

(6) $$b_1=1-b_2-b_3,\ d_1=(1/12-c/3)/(b_3a_2^2),\ d_2=(1/6-c+c^2)/(b_3d_1),$$

$$c_{21}=d_2-a_{21},\ a_{32}=(1/8-c/3)/(b_3a_3d_2),\ c_{32}=d_1-a_{32},\ a_{31}=a_3-a_{32},$$

$$c_{31}=(1/2-c-b_2d_2-b_3d_1)/b_3-a_{31}.$$

A good choice (d'après Kaps) for the free parameters is

$a_2=.7958110934$, $a_3=.75$

Kaps (1976) has computed methods of order 5 (with s=5) and order 6. Wolfbrandt (1976) gives methods of oder 3 and 4 with error estimation à la Fehlberg.

Following is the equivalent of formulas (5) written for a nonautonomous system of differential equations $y'=f(x,y)$

$$(I-ch\,\frac{\partial f}{\partial y}(x_0,y_0))k_i = f(x_0+ha_i, y_0+h\sum_{j=1}^{i-1}a_{ij}k_j) + hc_i\,\frac{\partial f}{\partial x}(x_0,y_0) +$$

(5') $$+\ h\,\frac{\partial f}{\partial y}(x_0,y_0)\sum_{j=1}^{i-1}c_{ij}k_j \qquad (i=1,..,s)$$

$$y_1 = y_0 + h\sum_{j=1}^{s}b_jk_j\ ,\quad a_i = \sum_{j=1}^{i-1}a_{ij},\ c_i = c + \sum_{j=1}^{i-1}c_{ij}.$$

There are many other possibilities of arranging parameters or functions. Special methods have been computed by Rosenbrock (1963),Callahan, Van der Houwen (1972), J.G.Verwer (1974-76) and others. Notice that in formula (5') $\frac{\partial f}{\partial y}$ is a matrix, f, $\frac{\partial f}{\partial x}$, k_i, y_0, and y_1 are vectors.

4. Stabitity Definitions.

As we have seen in our example at the beginning, it seems crucial that a methods "works well" at equations of the form $y'=\lambda y$ where $Re(\lambda)<<0$. We thus have

Definition (Dahlquist 1963). A method is called A-stable, if, when applied to $y'=\lambda y$ where $Re(\lambda)<0$, the numerical solutions $y_1, y_2, y_3, \ldots \to 0$.

Theorem (Dahlquist). A linear multistep formula

$$\sum_{j=0}^{k} \alpha_j y_{n-k+j} = h \sum_{j=0}^{k} \beta_j y'_{n-k+j}$$

can be A-stable only if the order is ≤ 2. Among the A-stable methods, the trapezoidal rule minimizes the error constant.

The proof of this theorem, originally very difficult, given in Genin (1974) is simple but, for non-specialists, not complete.

Theorem (Ehle, Axelsson 1969). The Obreschkoff formula (3) is A-stable if $k=\ell$, $k=\ell+1$, $k=\ell+2$ for all $\ell=1,2,3,\ldots$.

There is an amusing Conjecture of Ehle: All other Obreschkoff methods are not A-stable. This conjecture is trivial for $k<\ell$ $(\lambda\to\infty)$, true for $k=\ell+3$, $k=\ell+4$, $k=\ell+5$, $k=\ell+6$, $k=\ell+7$ (Ehle, Nørsett, Hairer), it can also be seen true for k,ℓ up to 30, but the general case is to my knowledge not yet proved though very probably.

The Obreschkoff methods with $k=\ell$ are thus A-stable multiderivative formulas of the type

$$\sum_{j=0}^{k} \alpha_j y_{n-k+j} = h \sum_{j=0}^{k} \beta_j y'_{n-k+j} + \ldots + h^{\ell} \sum_{j=0}^{k} \gamma_j y^{(\ell)}_{n-k+j} \tag{7}$$

of order 2ℓ which extend the trapezoidal rule. One could hope to raise their order if one consideres a formula of type (7) which ranges over several steps. No such formulas (A-stable) have yet been found (those given in Genin (1974) are not stable) and in analogy to the theorem of Dahlquist one has

Conjecture (Daniel-Moore 1969). A multistep-multiderivative formula (7) can be A-stable only if its order is $\leq 2\ell$. If you want, you can add: The Obreschkoff $k=\ell$ formula minimizes the error constant.

This conjecture is partly proved in R. Jentsch (1976).

More weak than A-stable.

For many problems, e.g. autoadjoint operators, the eigenvalues are known to be on the real axis or close to it. So the demand of complete A-stability is not necessary. The following concepts of stability have been introduced when one has stability in the case that λ is in the indicated region:

$A(\alpha)$-stable "stiffly" stable A_0-stable A_D-stable

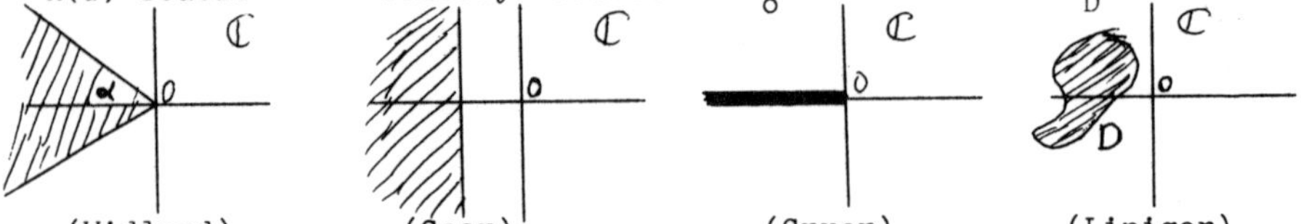

(Widlund) (Gear) (Cryer) (Liniger)

More strong than A-stable.

Strongly A-stable at infinity: When the above convergence to zero also holds for "$\lambda=\infty$". For example the Obreschkoff methods with $k=\ell$ (including trapezoidal rule) and the implicit Runge-Kutta methods based on Gauss points (including impl. midpoint rule) do not satisfy this condition. In contrary, Obrechkoff $k=\ell+1$ (including Euler implicit), $k=\ell+2$ and the implicit Runge-Kutta methods based on Radau points (again including Euler implicit) satisfy this stability condition.

S-stable: (Prothero-Robinson 1974). If one has convergence to the exact solution $g(x)$ when $n\to\infty$ for the differential equation

$$y'=g'(x)+\lambda(y-g(x)) \text{ for } g \text{ arbitrary (diff)}, \lambda \text{ with } \mathrm{Re}(\lambda)<A \text{ for all } h \text{ that satisfy } h<h_0(g,A).$$

This is largely equivalent to the strong A-stability at infinity.

R-stable: (van Veldhuizen 1973, Dahlquist..) Study of convergence at the model

$$y'=A(x,\varepsilon)y + Q(x,y,\varepsilon) + b(x,\varepsilon)$$

where

$$A(x,\varepsilon)=\begin{pmatrix} A_1(x)/\varepsilon & 0 \\ 0 & A_2(x) \end{pmatrix}$$

for $\varepsilon\to 0$ where $A_1(x), A_2(x), Q, b$ are "brave".

G-stable: (Dahlquist 1975). Using this stability concept, Dahlquist arrived for the first time to obtain strict error estimates for nonlinear problems that are independent of "λ", i.e., independent of the Lipschitz constant. Later on, a different kind of approach has been found by Dahlquist and Nevanlinna (and indepently by Odeh and Liniger) which needs only the A-stability of the methods.It is clear that these foundamental results diminish somewhat the interest in other stability concepts as G and S.

B-stable: (Butcher 1975). This was introduced in the sequence of Dahlquist's G-paper for one-step methods by J.Butcher. It is demanded that, for all differential equations satisfying $\langle u-v, f(x,u)-f(x,v)\rangle \leq 0$, one has $\|u_n - v_n\| \leq \|u_{n-1} - v_{n-1}\|$ where u and v are two different solutions.

Theorem (Butcher). The implicit Runge-Kutta methods based on Gauss and Radau points (and some others not mentioned here..) are B-stable.

It is, in my opinion, remarkable that this theorem posseses a very elementary proof (Wanner 1976).

5. Error estimation and step size control.

The necessity of error estimation has two reasons:

1. The numerical result of a computation is of no great use when it is not accompanied with a, strict or approximative, indication of the error of this result. It is, however, not easy to estimate all the errors, accumulated over many steps, which possibly have been blown up by instability properties of the differential equation. Progress in this direction has been made since the work of Zadunaisky.
2. Beside this it is simply necessary that an algorithm is able to change the step-size automatically during the computation.

Consider the example of the Van der Pol equation in section 1. There the error constant $y^{(5)}$ for Obreschkoff 2-2 varies between 10^{-9} and 10^{+12}. This causes the necessity of changing the step size between 10.6 and 0.0005. Now an algorithm using constant step-size throughout is forced to do all the computation with h=0.0005 and hence is of no more use than an explicit method. One step methods are more agreable for changing the step size than multistep formulas.
For an estimation of the size of the error per step three procedures are possible:

1. The construction of formulas containing two different methods of different orders so that the difference of the two results is taken as the error of the lower order method. Examples are given in Wolfbrandt (1976).

2. Extrapolation. Having computed two successive steps with the same method between the point y_{n-2}, y_{n-1}, y_n with step sizes h_1, h_2 respectively (Fig. aside), we recompute a long step with step size h_1+h_2 starting with y_{n-2} giving the numerical result y_n^*. Now from the fact that the error of the two-step computation is $C(h_1^{p+1}+h_2^{p+1})$ and that of the long step is $C(h_1+h_2)^{p+1}$, a still better result $\bar{y}_n$ can be extrapolated leading to the error estimation

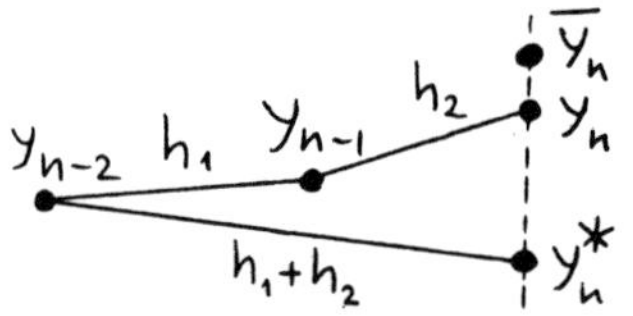

$$\text{error of } y_n = \bar{y}_n - y_n = \frac{(y_n - y_n^*)(h_1^{p+1}+h_2^{p+1})}{(h_1+h_2)^{p+1}-h_1^{p+1}-h_2^{p+1}} \; .$$

This method of estimation is particularly advantageous using Obreschkoff methods since, if all derivatives have been stored, no additional computations are necessary for the long step.

3. With Obreschkoff 2-2 method a direct evaluation of $y^{(5)}$ based on the values $y_{n-2}, y'_{n-2}, y_{n-1}, y'_{n-1}, y_n, y'_n$ using divided differences gave in numerical studies the most satisfying results.

6. Program STIFFI.

A FORTRAN Program has been written in order to study the numerical application of the Obreschkoff 2-2 formula of order 4. This formula has the following advantages:

1. it has, according to the Daniel-Moore conjecture, maximal order for two-derivative methods;
2. in spite of this it is one-step;
3. it allows, with no additional function evaluations error estimates with both the methods 2. and 3. as mentioned above;
4. it allows, likewise with no additional work, the computation of the derivatives of the solution with respect to the initial values and parameters. Thus it allows to handle boundary value problems and questions of parameter adjustments via least-square-Newton-Gauss (-Marquart) methods.

All the necessary derivative computations (the Jacobian and derivatives for the Newton method) are computed automatically using recursion formulas.

A detailed program description has been written as internal report and can be obtained on request. The program is written in double precision for the Univac 1108. Modifications are necessary at some places for other machines. These have been done for the CDC by Y. Depeursinge, Ecole Polytechnique de Lausanne, who also has detected several errors in the original version of the program.

Literature.

The following two articles describe experience with different numerical methods:

Byron L. Ehle, A comparison of numerical methods for solving certain stiff ordinary differnetial equations, Report 70, Dept. of Mathematics, University of Victoria, Victoria B.C., Canada, Nov 1972;

W.H.Enright, T.E.Hull,and B. Lindberg: Comparing numerical methods for stiff Systems of differential equations, Techn.Rep 69, Sept 1974 Department of Computr Science, Univ. of Toronto, Canada; also:BIT 15,1975.

Referenced Articles:

Gear 1971: Numerical initial value problems in ordinary differential equations, Prentice-Hall, Englewood Cliffs, n.j.

Liniger Willoughby 1970: Efficient integration methods for stiff systems of ODEs, SIAM j. Numer. Anal 7, 47-66.

Butcher 1964: Implicit Runge-Kutta processes, Math.Comp. 18, 50-64.

Ehle 1969: On Padé approximations to the exponential function and A-stable methods..., Res. Report CSRR 2010, Dep. of Appl. Analysis University of Waterloo, Ontario.

Axelsson 1969: A class of A-stable methods, BIT 9, 185-199.

Butcher 1976: On the implementation of implicit Runge-Kutta Methods BIT 16 (1976).

Rosenbrock 1963: Some general implicit processes for the numerical solution of DE, Comp.J.5, 329-330.

Nørsett 1975: Runge-Kutta methods with coefficients depending on the Jacobian, Rep No 1/75, Dep.of.num.Math.,NTH 7034 Trondheim, Norway.

Wolfbrandt 1976: Thesis, Department of Computer Sciences, Chalmers Univ. of Technology, FACK, S-40220 Göteborg, Sweden

Kaps 1976: Thesis, Institut f. Mathematik, A-6020 Innsbruck, Technikerstr.

Van der Houwen 1972: One-step methods with adaptive stability functions for the... Lecture Notes in Math 333, p 164-174.

Verwer 1975: Internal S-stability for generalized Runge-Kutta methods, Report NW 21/75, mathematisch Centrum, 2e boerhaavestraat 49, Amsterdam.

Zlámal 1975: Finite element multistep..parabolic ..,Math.Comp.29.

Lambert Sigurdsson 1972: A-stable multistep methods with variable matrix coefficients, SIAM J. Numer. Analysis.

Kastlunge-Wanner 1972: On Turan type implicit Runge-Kutta methods, Computing 9, 317-325

Fuchs 1976: A-stability of Runge-Kutta methods with single and multiple nodes, Computing 16, 39-48.

Lindberg 1972: A simple interpolation algorithm for improvement of the numrical sol.., SIAM J. Numer. anal, 9, 662-668.

Stetter 1973: Analysis of discretization methods, Springer Verlag Berlin, last chapter, last section, last page.

Lawson 1967: Generalized Runge-Kutta Processes for stable..., SIAM J. Numer. Anal, 4, 372-380.

Friedli 1976: Thesis, Seminar f angew. Math., Clausiusstr.55, 8000 Zürich

Hairer Wanner 1974: On the Butcher Group and general multivalue methods, Computing 1974.

Dahlquist 1963: A special stability criterion for linear multistep methods, BIT 3, 22-43.

Genin 1974: An algebraic approach to A-stable lin. multistep-multiderivative ... BIT 14, 382-406.

Jeltsch 1976: Note on A-stability of multistep multiderivative... BIT 16, 74-78.

Prothero Robinson 1974: On the Stability and Accuracy of one-step... Math. Comp 28, 145-162.

van Veldhuizen 1973: Convergence of one-step discretizations for stiff.. Thesis, Rijksuniversiteit te Utrecht, Holland.

Dahlquist 1975: Error analysis for a class ... for stiff nonlinear..., Numerical Analysis Dundee 1975, Lecture Notes in Mathematics 506.

Dahlquist Nevanlinna 1976: ℓ_2-estimates of the error in the ... of nonlinear differential systems, Royal Inst. of Technology,

S-10044 stockholm, Report TRITA-NA-7607.

Odeh Liniger 1975: Non-linear fixed-h stability of linear multistep methods, IBM Research Report RC 5717, Yorktown Heights.

Butcher 1975: A stability property of Runge-Kutta methods, BIT 15, 358-361.

Wanner 1976: A short proof on nonlinear A-stability, BIT 16.

Finally I want to mention the book

Stiff Differential Systems, Ed. by Ralph A. Willoughby, Plenum Press 1974.

Gerhard Wanner

Section de Mathématiques

2-4, rue du Lièvre

Case postale 124

1211 Genève 24

Switzerland

Foot notes:

---

*) Remark that the collocation method $m=1$, $\alpha_1=1-\theta$

$$k_1=y_o+(1-\theta)hf(x_o+(1-\theta)h,k_1)$$

$$y_1=y_o \qquad +hf(x_o+(1-\theta)h,k_1)$$

is another extension of the so-called θ-method to the nonlinear case. It is identical to (1') for the equation $y'=Ay$. In contrary, it has an interesting stability property: It is not only A-stable ($0\leq\theta\leq1/2$), S-stable ($0\leq\theta<1/2$), strongly A-stable at infinity, but also B-stable ($0\leq\theta\leq1/2$).

NUMERICAL SOLUTION OF SOME NONLINEAR PROBLEMS : APPLICATION TO PHYSICS AND TECHNIQUE.

Hubert Froidevaux

1. INTRODUCTION

We formulate a method to solve boundary-valued problems of the form :

1.1
$$\left|\begin{array}{l} -\sum_{i,j=1}^{n} \frac{\partial}{\partial x_j}\left[\frac{a_{ij}(x)}{a(x,p)}\frac{\partial u}{\partial x_i}\right] = f(x) \quad \text{in} \quad \Omega \subset \mathbb{R}^n \\ \text{nonlinear or linear boundary conditions} \end{array}\right.$$

with $a_{ij} \in C^1(\bar{\Omega})$ symetric and

1.2
$$\alpha \sum_{i=1}^{n} \xi_i^2 \leq \sum_{i,j=1}^{n} a_{ij}\xi_i\xi_j \leq \beta \sum_{i=1}^{n} \xi_i^2 \qquad \forall \xi_i \in \mathbb{R}$$

1.3
$$p(x) = \sum_{i,j=1}^{n} a_{ij}(x) \frac{\partial u}{\partial x_i} \frac{\partial u}{\partial x_j}$$

1.4 where the properties of the function $(x,p) \longrightarrow a(x,p)$ will be given later.

Example 1.1 : Mechanics of ideal compressible fluids.

Let us consider a irrotational plane flow in $\Omega \subset \mathbb{R}^2$. This flow can be characterized by the current function $\psi(x,y)$ solution of

$$\left|\begin{array}{l} \frac{\partial}{\partial x}\left[\frac{1}{\rho}\frac{\partial \psi}{\partial x}\right] + \frac{\partial}{\partial y}\left[\frac{1}{\rho}\frac{\partial \psi}{\partial y}\right] = 0 \quad \text{in} \quad \Omega \\ + \text{boundary conditions} \end{array}\right.$$

where ρ is the specific mass and

$$p = \left(\frac{\partial\psi}{\partial x}\right)^2 + \left(\frac{\partial\psi}{\partial y}\right)^2 .$$

One can notice that $\vec{w} = (\frac{1}{\rho}\psi,_x , -\frac{1}{\rho}\psi,_y)$ is the speed of the fluid and $|\vec{w}|^2 = p/\rho^2$.

The relation between ρ and p is given by the classical Bernoulli's equation.

Example 1.2 : Magnetostatics [1] .

For a problem in two dimensions the potential vector A is solution of

$$\left| \begin{array}{l} -\frac{\partial}{\partial x}\left[\frac{1}{\mu}\frac{\partial A}{\partial x}\right] - \frac{\partial}{\partial y}\left[\frac{1}{\mu}\frac{\partial A}{\partial y}\right] = J(x) \quad \text{in} \quad \Omega \subset \mathbb{R}^2 \\ + \text{ boundary conditions.} \end{array} \right.$$

where $\vec{B} = (\frac{\partial A}{\partial x} , \frac{\partial A}{\partial y} , 0)$ is magnetic induction

$p = (\frac{\partial A}{\partial x})^2 + (\frac{\partial A}{\partial y})^2$ and $\mu = \mu(x,p)$ is the permeability.

Example 1.3 : Electrochimestry (nonlinear polarization).

One of the problems of electrochimestry is to find a potential φ, such that

$$\Delta\varphi = 0 \quad \text{in} \quad \Omega \subset \mathbb{R}^3 \text{ or } \mathbb{R}^2$$

with Dirichlet's or Neumann's boundary conditions on a subset $\Gamma_1 \subset \partial\Omega$ and on $\Gamma_2 = \partial\Omega\setminus\Gamma_1$ we have

$$\varphi + h(\frac{d\varphi}{dn}) = K = \text{constante}$$

where h is a function of the normal outward derivative $\frac{d\varphi}{dn}$.

2. VARIATIONAL FORMULATION OF GENERAL BOUNDARY-VALUED PROBLEMS

2.a) Spaces and Notations [2],[4]

Let Ω be an open and bounded subset of $\mathbb{R}^n$. $\partial\Omega$ the boundary of Ω is supposed to be smooth enough. Let $\Gamma \subset \partial\Omega$ be an non-void subset of $\partial\Omega$ with meas $(\Gamma) \neq 0$.
$L^2(\Omega)$ denotes the space of square-integrable functions on Ω.
$(f,g) = \int fg dx$ the scalar product in $L^2(\Omega)$ and $\|\cdot\|$ the norm. (Ω) is the space of function C^∞ with compact support in Ω , H^1 the sobolev space of order 1.

$$H^1(\Omega) = \{f \in L^2(\Omega) : \frac{\partial f}{\partial x^i} \in L^2(\Omega) \ , \quad i = 1,2,\ldots n\}$$

where $\frac{\partial f}{\partial x^i}$ is the generalized derivative of f . H^1 is an Hilbert space for the scalar product defined by :

$$(f,g)_{H^1} = \int_\Omega fg dx + \sum_{i=1}^n \int_\Omega \frac{\partial f}{\partial x^i} \frac{\partial f}{\partial x^i} dx$$

and consequently the norm is given by $\|f\|^2_{H^1} = (f,f)_{H^1}$.
$f|_\Gamma$ is the trace of f on Γ . It is well known that if $f \in H^1(\Omega)$ then $f|_\Gamma \in L^2(\partial\Omega)$.

$H^1_0(\Omega) = \{f \in H^1(\Omega) \ ; \ f|_{\partial\Omega} = 0\}$

$H^1_0(\Omega)$ is an Hilbert space included in $H^1(\Omega)$. On $H^1_0(\Omega)$ there exists a norm noted $\|\cdot\|_{H^1_0}$ equivalent to the norm of H and which is associated with the scalar product

$$(f,g)_{H^1_0} = \sum_{i=1}^n \int_\Omega \frac{\partial f}{\partial x^i} \frac{\partial g}{\partial x^i} dx = \int_\Omega \vec{\nabla} f \cdot \vec{\nabla} g \ dx \quad .$$

Let us recall that 2 norms $\|\cdot\|_1$ and $\|\cdot\|_2$ are equivalent on H if there exists two positive constants C_1 and C_2 such that

$$C_1 \|f\|_1 \leqslant \|f\|_2 \leqslant C_2 \|f\| \qquad \forall f \in H$$

$H^1(\Gamma,\Omega) = \{f \in H^1(\Omega) \;;\; f|_\Gamma = 0\}$ is a subspace of $H^1(\Omega)$ and $(\cdot,\cdot)_{H^1}$, $(\cdot,\cdot)_{H^1_0}$ are scalar products on $H^1(\Gamma,\Omega)$. The two norms $\|\cdot\|_{H^1}$ and $\|\cdot\|_{H^1_0}$ are equivalent on $H^1(\Gamma,\Omega)$.

On $H^1(\Omega)$ equivalent norms to $\|\cdot\|_{H^1}$ can be defined in the following way :

$\Gamma \subset \partial\Omega$ is always a non empty set of measure different from zero.

$$(f,g)_{H^1(\Gamma)} = \int_\Gamma fg\,d\Gamma + (f,g)_{H^1_0}$$

is a scalar product on $H^1(\Gamma,\Omega)$ and the norm associated $\|\cdot\|^2_{H^1(\Gamma)} = (\cdot,\cdot)_{H^1(\Gamma)}$ is equivalent to the norm $\|\cdot\|_{H^1}$.

2.b) Variational formulation

Let Γ_D, Γ_N, Γ_P be a partition of $\partial\Omega$ and $\Gamma_D \neq 0$, meas $(\Gamma_D) \neq 0$. Γ_N and Γ_P are empty sets or sets of measure different from zero. Let g be a function defined on Γ_D and

2.1 $\quad W = \{u \in H^1(\Omega) \;,\; u|_{\Gamma_D} = g\}$

if $w \in W$ we have $W = w + H^1(\Gamma_D,\Omega)$.

Let $h(\xi)$ be a real valued function of a real variable and let us assume that its inverse exists. $a(x,p)$ is a real valued function defined on $\Omega \times \mathbb{R}^+$ such that the linear form

$$2.2 \quad \begin{cases} \eta \longmapsto G(\eta) = \sum_{i,j=1}^{n} \int_{\Omega} \frac{a_{ij}(x)}{a(x,p)} u,_j \eta,_i dx - \int_{\Gamma_P} h^{-1}(K-u)\eta \, d\Gamma \\ H^1(\Gamma_D,\Omega) \longmapsto \mathbb{R} \end{cases}$$

defined for all $u \in W$, $(p = \sum_{i,j=1}^{n} a_{ij} u,_i u,_j)$ is continuous on $H^1(\Gamma_D,\Omega)$. Then, from the Riesz representation theorem there exists a mapping T defined by

$$2.3 \quad \begin{cases} (T(u),\eta)_{H^1(\Gamma_D)} = G(\eta) \qquad \forall \eta \in H^1(\Gamma_D,\Omega), \ \forall u \in W \\ T : W \longrightarrow H^1(\Gamma_D,\Omega) \end{cases}$$

Let also k be a real valued function defined on Γ_N and $f \in L^2(\Omega)$. We consider the continuous linear form,

$$2.4 \quad \begin{cases} \eta \longmapsto F(\eta) = \int_{\Omega} f\eta dx + \int_{\Gamma} k\eta d\Gamma \\ H^1(\Gamma_D,\Omega) \longrightarrow \mathbb{R} \end{cases}$$

which can be rewritten

$$2.5 \quad (b,\eta)_{H^1(\Gamma_D)} = F(\eta) \qquad \forall \eta \in H^1(\Gamma_D,\Omega), \ b \in H^1(\Gamma_D,\Omega) .$$

Let us consider the following variational problem :

$$2.6 \quad \left| \begin{array}{l} \text{find } u \in W \text{ such that} \\ (T(u)-b,\eta)_{H^1(\Gamma_D)} = 0 \qquad \forall \eta \in H^1(\Gamma_D,\Omega) . \end{array} \right.$$

First we assume that there exists a unique solution $u \in C^2(\bar{\Omega})$ and let us study the properties of u.

$\mathcal{D}(\Omega)$ contained in $H^1(\Gamma_D,\Omega)$, let $\eta = \varphi \in \mathcal{D}(\Omega)$.

Then (2.6) can be written as

2.7 $$(T(u),\varphi)_{H^1(\Gamma_D)} = (b,\varphi)_{H^1(\Gamma_D)} \qquad \forall \varphi \in \mathcal{D}(\Omega)$$

which using (2.2) and (2.4) and properties of $\mathcal{D}(\Omega)$ can be rewritten as

2.8 $$\sum_{i,j=1}^{n} \int_\Omega \frac{a_{ij}}{a} u,_j \, \varphi,_i \, dx = \int_\Omega f\varphi dx \qquad \forall \varphi \in \mathcal{D}(\Omega)$$

Let us integrate by part the left part of the equality, then it is not difficult to see that u is solution of

2.9 $$-\sum_{i,j=1}^{n} \frac{\partial}{\partial x_j} \left[\frac{a_{ij}(x)}{a(x,p)} \frac{\partial u}{\partial x_i} \right] = f(x) \quad \text{in } \Omega$$

Now we can study the properties of u on $\partial\Omega$. $u \in W$ therefore $u\big|_{\Gamma_D} = g$.

Let us multiply 2.9 by $\eta \in H^1(\Gamma_D,\Omega)$ and integrate over Ω. Using the Green's formula we get

2.10 $$\sum_{i,j=1}^{n} \int_\Omega \frac{a_{ij}}{a} u,_j \, \eta,_i dx - \int_\Omega f\eta dx - \sum_{i,j=1}^{n} \oint_{\partial\Omega} \frac{a_{ij}}{a} u,_j \eta n_i d\Gamma = 0 \quad \forall \eta \in H^1(\Gamma_D,\Omega)$$

$n_1, n_2, \ldots n_n$ unit outward normal of $\partial\Omega$.

Thus 2.6 can be rewritten as

2.11 $$\sum_{i,j=1}^{n} \int_{\Omega} \frac{a_{ij}}{a} u_{,j} \eta_{,i} dx - \int_{\Omega} f\eta dx - \int_{\Gamma_P} h^{-1}(K-u)\eta d\Gamma - \int_{\Gamma_N} k\eta d\Gamma = 0$$

and, using 2.10 and 2.11 and the fact that $\eta \in H^1(\Gamma_D, \Omega)$ we get

2.12 $$\int_{\Gamma_P} \frac{du}{dn} \eta d\Gamma + \int_{\Gamma_N} \frac{du}{dn} \eta d\Gamma = \int_{\Gamma_P} h^{-1}(K-u)\eta d\Gamma + \int_{\Gamma_N} k\eta d\Gamma$$

$\forall \eta \in H^1(\Gamma_D, \Omega)$

with

2.13 $$\frac{du}{dn} = \sum_{i,j=1}^{n} \frac{a_{ij}(x)}{a(x,p)} u_{,j} n_i$$

We get :

2.14 $$\frac{du}{dn} = k \quad \text{on } \Gamma_N$$

2.15 $$\frac{du}{dn} = h^{-1}(K-u) \quad \text{on } \Gamma_P$$

Therefore, the solution of the problem 2.6, u, belongs to $C^2(\bar{\Omega})$ and is solution of

2.16 $$\left| \begin{array}{l} -\sum_{i,j=1}^{n} \frac{\partial}{\partial x_i} \left[\frac{a_{ij}(x)}{a(x,p)} \frac{\partial u}{\partial x_j} \right] = f(x) \quad \text{in } \Omega \\ u|_{\Gamma_D} = g \ ; \ \frac{du}{dn} = k(x) \text{ on } \Gamma_N \ ; \ h(\frac{du}{dn}) = K-u \quad \text{on } \Gamma_P \\ \cdot \text{ with } 2.13 \end{array} \right.$$

If the solution u of 2.6 is not in $C^2(\Omega)$ it is said that u is a generalized solution of 2.16. T defined by 2.3 is a mapping from W to $H^1(\Gamma_D,\Omega)$. And, if $u = v+w$ (2.1) the mapping

2.17
$$\left| \begin{array}{l} v \longmapsto T(v+w) = \tilde{T}(v) \\ H^1(\Gamma_D,\Omega) \longrightarrow H^1(\Gamma_D,\Omega) \end{array} \right.$$

is a mapping from an Hilbert space H into H . Therefore to find a solution of problem 2.6 can be reduced to problem of finding the solution of the problem

2.18
$$\left| \begin{array}{l} \text{find } u = v+w \text{ such that} \\ \tilde{T}(v) = b \qquad v,b \in H^1(\Gamma_D,\Omega) \end{array} \right.$$

3. EXISTENCE OF SOLUTION

3.a) A fixed-point theorem

Let us consider a mapping

3.1 $S : H \longrightarrow H$

from the Hilbert space H whose scalar product and norm are denoted by $(\cdot,\cdot)$ and $\|\cdot\|$, respectively. It is said that S is lipchitzian mapping in H if there exists $\mu>0$ such that

$$\|S(u) - S(v)\| \leq \mu \|u-v\| \qquad \forall u,v \in H$$

S is strongly monotone in H if there exists $\nu > 0$ such that

$$(S(u)-S(v),u-v) \geqslant \nu \|u-v\|^2 \qquad \forall u,v \in H$$

And S is strongly contracting in H if S is a lipchitzian mapping in H with $\mu < 1$. It is well known that in this case there exists a unique fixed point in H for S .

Theorem 3.1 [3]

Let S be mapping from H to H which is lipchitzian and strongly monotone in H . For any $\ell \in]0 , \frac{2\nu}{\mu^2}[$ and $f \in H$ the mapping

3.2 $$R : H \longrightarrow H$$
$$u \longmapsto R(u) = u-\ell[S(u)-f]$$

is strictly contracting in H i.e.

3.3 $$\|R(u)-R(v)\| \leqslant \kappa \|u-v\| \qquad 0<\kappa<1 \qquad \forall u,v \in H$$

with $\kappa^2 = \ell^2\mu^2 - 2k\nu+1$.

The optimal value of f is attained when κ^2 is minimum i.e. $\frac{\nu}{\mu^2} = \ell_0$ and $\kappa_0^2 = (1- \frac{\nu^2}{\mu^2})$. Therefore the fixed point of R is the solution of S(u) = f .

3.b) Existence and uniqueness of solution

In this section conditions on $a(x,p)$, $h(\frac{du}{dn})$ will be given in order that the mapping $\tilde{T}$ defined above is lipchitzian and strongly monotone in $H^1(\Gamma_D,\Omega)$.

Theorem 3.2

If

H^1: $p \longmapsto \frac{1}{a(x,p)}$ non-decreasing $\forall x \in \bar{\Omega}$

H^2: $\frac{1}{a(x,p)} \geq B > 0$ $\forall x \in \bar{\Omega}$

H^3: $\xi \longmapsto h^{-1}(\xi)$ negative, non-increasing, then $\tilde{T}$ is strongly monotone in $H^1(\Gamma_D,\Omega)$.

Proof

We use the algebric relation

$(ab-cd) = \frac{1}{2}(a-c)(b+d)+\frac{1}{2}(a+c)(b-d)$

to compute

$$(\tilde{T}(v_2) - \tilde{T}(v_1) , v_2-v_1)_{H^1(\Gamma_0)} =$$

$$\frac{1}{2} \sum_{i,j=1}^{2} \int_\Omega a_{ij}(x)\left[\frac{1}{a(x,p_2)} - \frac{1}{a(x,p_1)}\right]\left[u_{2,j}+u_{1,j}\right]\left[v_{2,i}-v_{1,i}\right] dy +$$

$$+ \sum_{i,j=1}^{n} \int_\Omega a_{ij}(x)\left[\frac{1}{a(x,p_2)} + \frac{1}{a(x,p_1)}\right]\left[v_{2,j}-v_{1,j}\right]\left[v_{2,i}-v_{1,i}\right] dx -$$

$$- \int_{\Gamma_P} \left[h^{-1}(K-u_2)-h^{-1}(K-u_1)\right] (v_2-v_1) d\Gamma$$

Using the symmetry property of a_{ij} and the definition of p and H1 it can be easily shown that the first integral is positive or null and, using the assumption H3 , it is immediate that the last integral is negative or null $(u_i = v_i + w)$. From the assumption H2 we have

$$(\tilde{T}(v_2)-\tilde{T}(v_1), v_2-v_1)_{H^1(\Gamma_D)} \geq \alpha B \| v_2 - v_1 \|^2_{H^1(\Gamma_D)}$$

where α is defined in (1.2).

Theorem 3.3

If we assume that H1 still holds and that :

H4 : $p \mapsto \frac{1}{a(x,p)} \leq A \qquad \forall x \in \bar{\Omega}$

H5 : $p \mapsto p \frac{\partial}{\partial p} \left[\frac{1}{a(x,p)} \right] \leq D \qquad \forall x \in \bar{\Omega}$

H6 : $\xi \rightarrow h^{-1}(\xi)$ is lipchitzian

then $\tilde{T}$ is lipchitzian in $H^1(\Gamma_D, \Omega)$.

Proof

Using the same algebric relation that above we get

$$(\tilde{T}(v_2)-\tilde{T}(v_1), \eta)_{H^1(\Gamma_D)} = I_1 + I_2 + I_3$$

$$I_1 = \frac{1}{2} \sum_{i,j=1}^{n} \int_{\Omega} a_{ij} \left[\frac{1}{a(x,p_2)} - \frac{1}{a(x,p_1)}\right] \left[u_{2,j}+u_{1,j}\right]\eta_{,i}\, dx$$

$$I_2 = \frac{1}{2} \sum_{i,j=1}^{n} \int_{\Omega} a_{ij} \left[\frac{1}{a(x,p_2)} + \frac{1}{a(x,p_1)}\right] \left[v_{2,j}-v_{1,j}\right]\eta_{,j}\, dx$$

$$I_3 = \int_{\Gamma_P} \left[h^{-1}(K-u_1)-(K-u_2)\right] \eta \, d\Gamma$$

for sake of simplification let $x \in \bar{\Omega}$, and u,v be two real valued functions and a_{ij} be definite positive and symmetric $((u,v)) = \sum_{i,j=1}^{n} a_{ij}(x)u_{,i}(x)v_{,j}(x)$ define a scalar product in $\mathbb{R}^n$ with $\|\cdot\|^2 = ((\cdot,\cdot))$ the associated norm. It can be noted that $\|u\|^2 = p$.

Using assumption H4 we have

3.3 $$I_2 \leqslant A \int_{\Omega} \|v_2-v_1\| \, \|\eta\| \, dx$$

To estimate I_1 we can multiply the function under the integral sign by

$$1 = \frac{p_2 - p_1}{p_2 \quad p_1} = \frac{\|u_2\|^2 - \|u_1\|^2}{p_2 - p_1}$$

and using H1 we get

3.4 $$I_1 \leqslant \frac{1}{2} \int_{\Omega} \left(\frac{1}{a(x,p_2)} - \frac{1}{a(x,p_1)}\right) \frac{\left|\|u_2\|^2 - \|u_1\|^2\right|}{p_2 \quad p_1} \cdot |((u_2+u_1,\eta))|\,dx$$

using a simple computation we can write :

$$3.5 \quad \left| \|u_2\|^2 - \|u_1\|^2 \right| \cdot |((u_2+u_1,\eta))| \leqslant 2(p_2+p_1)\|v_2-v_1\| \, \|\eta\|$$

and we get

$$3.6 \quad I_1 \leqslant \int_\Omega f(p_1,p_2) \, \|v_2-v_1\| \, \|\eta\| \, dx$$

with $f(p_1,p_2) = \frac{p_1+p_2}{p_1-p_2} \left[\frac{1}{a(x,p_1)} - \frac{1}{a(x,p_2)}\right]$

by the mean-value theorem and assumption H1, H2, H4, H5 we can get :

$$3.7 \quad f(p_1,p_2) \leqslant 2D+A-B$$

where

$$3.8 \quad I_1+I_2 \leqslant (2D+3A-B) \int_\Omega \|v_2-v_1\| \, \|\eta\| \, dx$$

using the definition of the norm $\|\cdot\|$ and the Schwartz inequality we get

$$3.9 \quad I_1+I_2 \leqslant \text{cste} \, \|v_2-v_1\|_{H^1(\Gamma_D)} \, \|\eta\|_{H^1(\Gamma_D)}$$

To estimate I_3 we shall use the hypothesis H6 and the equivalence of norms on $H^1(\Gamma,\Omega)$ (§2.a) we get

$$3.10 \quad I_3 \leqslant \text{cste} \, \|v_2-v_1\|_{H^1(\Gamma_D)} \, \|\eta\|_{H^1(\Gamma_D)}$$

where

$$3.11 \quad (\tilde{T}(v_2)-\tilde{T}(v_1),\eta)_{H^1(\Gamma_D)} \leqslant \text{cste} \, \|v_2-v_1\|_{H^1(\Gamma_D)} \|\eta\|_{H^1(\Gamma_D)}$$

and taking for value of η : $\eta = \tilde{T}(v_2)-\tilde{T}(v_1)$ the proof of the theorem is obtained.

3.c) Conclusion

The mapping $\tilde{T} : H^1(\Gamma_D,\Omega) \to H^1(\Gamma_D,\Omega)$ defined in the foregoing paragraph, with the hypothesis H1, H2, H3, H4, H5,H6 is strongly monotone and lipchitzian in $H^1(\Gamma_D,\Omega)$, thus the mapping $v \longmapsto R(v) = v - \ell\,[\tilde{T}(v)-b]$ for a suitable ℓ is strictly contracting in $H^1(\Gamma_D,\Omega)$ and its fixed point $\bar{v} = R(\bar{v})$ is the solution of the problem $\tilde{T}(\bar{v}) = b$. Thus, instead of looking for the solution of $\tilde{T}(v) = b$ we shall look for the fixed point of $R(v)$ and it is well known that for every $v_0 \in H^1(\Gamma_D,\Omega)$ the sequence

3.12 $$v_{i+1} = R(v_i) \qquad i = 0,1,2,\ldots.$$

converges strongly to $\bar{v}$ in $H^1(\Gamma_D,\Omega)$.

4. FINITE ELEMENT APPROXIMATION

Let H be a Hilbert space and S be a contracting mapping defined on H so that

4.1 $S : H \to H$,

$$\|S(u) - S(v)\| \leqslant \kappa \|u-v\| , \qquad \forall u,v \in H, \quad 0<\kappa<1 .$$

We want to find the fixed point of S ; i.e. to find

4.2 $\bar{u} \in H$ such that $\bar{u} = S(\bar{u})$.

Let H_n be subspaces of finite dimension n included in H. We say that the sequence $\{H_n\}$ is an approximation of H of finite element type if :

$$V = \bigcup_{n=1}^{\infty} H_n \quad \text{is dense in } H \ ;$$

i.e. $\forall u \in H$, $\exists u_n \in H_n$ such that $\lim_{n\to\infty} \|u-u_n\| = 0$.

We also have the following properties which are immediately shown.

<u>Property 4.1</u> Let $\{H_n\}$ be an approximation of finite element type of H. Then, $\forall u \in H$, $\forall \varepsilon > 0$, $\exists n_0 \in N^+$ such that $\forall n \geq n_0$, $\exists u_n \in H_n$ such that $\|u-u_n\| \leq \varepsilon$ holds.

<u>Property 4.2</u> Let $\{H_n\}$ be an approximation of finite element type of H. Let P_n be an orthogonal projection operator from H to H_n (according to the scalar product of H). Then $\forall u \in H$, $\lim_{n\to\infty} \|P_n u - u\| = 0$.

We can now formulate the problem (4.2) into a discretized form as :

$$\text{4.3} \qquad \left.\begin{array}{l} \text{find } \bar{u}_n \in H_n \text{ such that} \\ \bar{u}_n = P_n S(\bar{u}_n) = S_n(\bar{u}_n) \ . \end{array}\right\}$$

<u>Remark</u> : $S_n = P_n S$ is obviously a contracting mapping in H_n and the constant of contraction κ is the same as the κ for the problem in H.

Theorem 4.1

Let $\{H_n\}$ be an approximation of finite element type of H. Let $\bar{u}$ be the fixed point of S in H, and $\bar{u}_n$ the fixed point of S_n in H_n, then $\lim_{n\to\infty}\|\bar{u}_n-\bar{u}\| = 0$.

Proof

Consider

$$\begin{aligned}\|\bar{u}_n-\bar{u}\| &= \|P_nS(\bar{u}_n) - S(\bar{u})\| \\ &= \|P_nS(\bar{u}_n) - P_nS(\bar{u}) + P_nS(\bar{u}) - S(\bar{u})\| \\ &\leq \|S(\bar{u}_n) - S(u)\| + \|P_nS(\bar{u}) - S(u)\| \\ &\leq \kappa\,\|\bar{u}_n - \bar{u}\| + \|P_nS(\bar{u}) - S(\bar{u})\| .\end{aligned}$$

Therefore we have

$$\|\bar{u}_n - \bar{u}\| \leq \frac{1}{1-\kappa}\|P_nS(\bar{u})-S(\bar{u})\| = \frac{1}{1-\kappa}\|P_n\bar{u}-\bar{u}\|$$

and using Property 4.2, we have the result.

Estimation of the error

In practice H_n is given and $\bar{u}_n$ the fixed point of S_n is approximated by u_n^1, the solution obtained after ℓ iterations starting from the initial guess $u_n^0 \in H_n$. Let $\bar{u}$ be the fixed point of S. We want to find an estimate of $\|u_n^\ell-\bar{u}\|$. Using classical estimates for contracting operators, it is not difficult to show that

$$\|u_n^\ell - \bar{u}\| \leq \frac{3+\kappa^\ell}{1-\kappa}\|u_n^0 - S(u_n^0)\| .$$

5. NUMERICAL APPLICATION

Let Ω be the domain defined by fig (1). We look for the current function of a compressible subsonic flow which is irrotationnal in Ω i.e. we look for the solution of the following problem :

find ψ solution of

5.1 $$\frac{\partial}{\partial x}\left[\frac{\psi,_x}{\rho}\right] + \frac{\partial}{\partial y}\left[\frac{\psi,_y}{\rho}\right] = 0$$

$$\rho = \rho(p) \quad ; \quad p = \psi,_x^2 + \psi,_y^2$$

5.2 $\psi = 0$ on AFG ; $\psi = \phi_1$ on CEB ; $\psi = \phi_1$ on DH

ψ linear on DC, BA et GH

With $|\vec{w}^2| < c^2$; where c^2 is the local speed of the sound, $\rho = \rho(p)$ is given by the Bernoulli's equation

5.3 $$\frac{1}{2}\frac{p^2}{\rho^2} + \frac{\alpha\gamma}{\gamma-1}\left[\rho^{\gamma-1} \quad \rho_0^{\gamma-1}\right] = 0 \qquad \alpha,\gamma,\rho_0 \text{ given .}$$

The graph of 5.3 is given by fig(2). It can be noted that the relation $p \longrightarrow 1/\rho(p)$ does not satisfy the assumptions H3 and H6 (§3) . Since we are only looking for subsonic flows the relation $p \longrightarrow 1/\rho(p)$ can be modifed in the supersonic part in order that the hypothesis H3 and H6 be satisfied. Let $\frac{1}{a(p)}$ denote the new function (fig.2). Let w be a function in $H^1(\Omega)$ such that the boundary conditions 5.2 are satisfied, then the problém we must solve can be rewritten as

5.4
$$\left| \begin{array}{l} \text{find } v - H_0^1(\Omega) \text{ such that} \\ \frac{\partial}{\partial x}\left[\frac{v_{,x} + w_{,x}}{a(p)}\right] + \frac{\partial}{\partial y}\left[\frac{v_{,y} + w_{,y}}{a(p)}\right] = 0 \end{array}\right.$$

We use the methods developed in the paragraphs 3 and 4. Let $H_n \subset H_0^1(\Omega)$ be a space of the type "finite elements" formed by the parts of the planes which are defined on the triangles. Let S_n defined by 4.5 and $v_n^0 \in H_n$ the initial data. The algorithme is defined by

$$v_n^1 = S_n(v_n^0) \;; \quad \ldots\ldots\ldots \;; \; v_n^{i+1} = S_n(v_n^i) \;, \ldots$$

v_n^{i+1} which by definition can be written

$$v_n^{i+1} = P_n S\,(v_n^i) = P_n\,[v_n^i - \ell\, T(v_n^i)\,]$$
$$= v_n^i - \ell\, P_n T(v_n^i)$$

To compute $P_n T(v_n^i)$ we notice that from the definition of the projection P_n , $u^i = P_n T(v_n^i) \in H_n$ can be written as

$$(u^i,\eta)_{H_0^1} = (T(v_n^i),\eta) \qquad \forall\, \eta \in H_n$$

and with 2.2 and 5.4 we get :

5.5 $$(u^i,\eta)_{H_0^1} = \int_\Omega \frac{1}{a(p^i)}\left[\frac{\partial}{\partial x}(v_n^i+w)\,\frac{\partial \eta}{\partial x} + \frac{\partial}{\partial y}(v_n^i+w)\,\frac{\partial \eta}{\partial y}\right] dxdy \qquad \forall \eta \in H_n$$

and

5.6 $$v_n^{i+1} = v_n^i - \ell\, u^i$$

In a very classical way to find $u^i \in H_n$ we have to solve a linear system of equations. The iterations on i are stopped when a convergence test is satisfied. We have used the following test. Let at the ith iteration ε_i be the max on the finite elements of $\{|a(p^i)-a(p^{i-1})|\}$ where p^i is the function p computed at the ith step. p^i is a constant on each finite element. The procedure stops when $\varepsilon_i<k$ where k is given a priori.

The value of the constant ℓ (5.6) can be roughly estimated. In the example considered we have computed the relation beween ℓ and the number of iterations N in order that $\varepsilon^N \leqslant 10^{-10}$ (fig.3).

In fig. 4 we have given the relation between $\log\varepsilon^i$ and i for the optimal value of $\ell = \ell_{opt}$ given by fig. 3. It is immediate that if ℓ_{opt} is known the solution can be computed with very few iterations. ℓ_{opt} can be computed graphically using fig. 3 and 4 by looking for the minimum of the graph $(\log\varepsilon^i, \ell)$ for i fixed and say $i = 2$ or 3.

Fig. 1

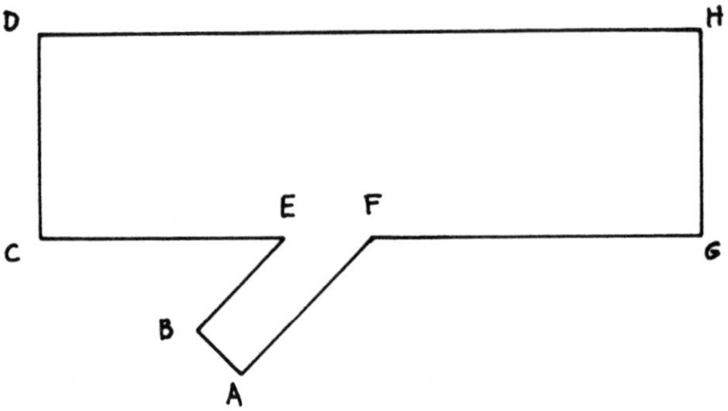

Fig. 2

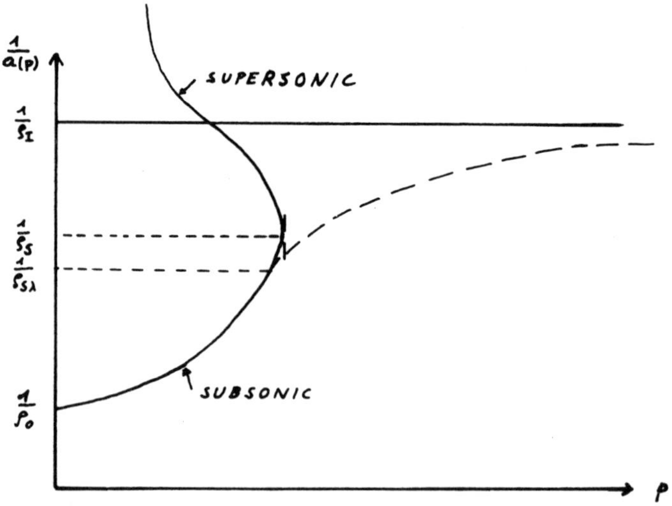

$$p(a) = 2a^2 \frac{\alpha\gamma}{\gamma-1} \left[\rho_0^{\gamma-1} - a^{\gamma-1}\right] \qquad a \in [\rho_{S\lambda}, \rho_0]$$

$$p(a) = -b \ln(a-\rho_I) + c \qquad a \in [\rho_I, \rho_{S\lambda}]$$

$$b = -2\rho_S \frac{\alpha\gamma}{\gamma-1} (\rho_{S\lambda}-\rho_I)\left[2\rho_0^{\gamma-1} - (\gamma+1)\rho_{S\lambda}^{\gamma-1}\right]$$

$$c = b \ln(\rho_{S\lambda}-\rho_I) + 2\rho_{S\lambda}^2 \frac{\alpha\gamma}{\gamma-1} (\rho_0^{\gamma-1} - \rho_{S\lambda})^{\gamma-1}$$

Fig. 3

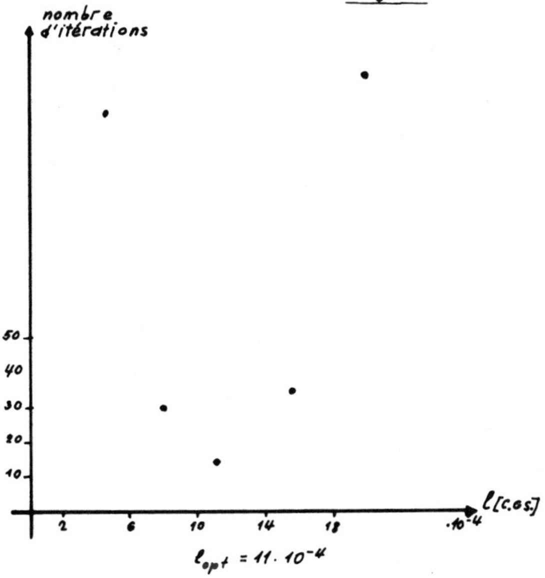
nombre d'itérations
50
40
30
20
10
2
6
10
14
18
.10^-4
l [C.G.S]
$l_{opt} = 11 \cdot 10^{-4}$

Fig. 4

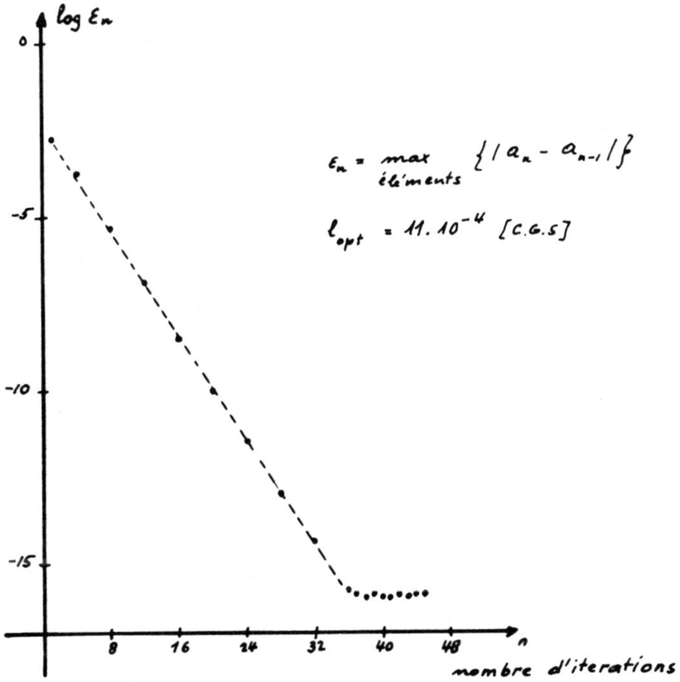
log ε_n
0
-5
-10
-15
8
16
24
32
40
48
n
nombre d'iterations
$\varepsilon_n = \max_{\text{éléments}} \{ | a_n - a_{n-1} | \}$
$l_{opt} = 11 . 10^{-4}$ [C.G.S]

REFERENCES

1. D.-L. DERRON
Intégration numérique des équations fondamentales des systèmes électromagnétiques.
Thèse EPF-Lausanne (1973)

2. J. NEČAS
Les méthodes directes en théorie des équations elliptiques.
Prague 1967

3. F.E. BROWDER
Problèmes non linéaires.
Presses de l'Université de Montréal 1966.

4. G. FICHERA
Linear elliptic differential systems and eigenvalue problems.
Lecutre notes in mathematics 8, Springer-Verlag, (1965)